DATE DUE

FE ~~02~~			
~~NO~~ ~~02~~			
NO 21'05			
NO 1 1'06			

DEMCO 38-296

COPING WITH LOSS

◇◆◇

The LEA Series in Personality and Clinical Psychology

Irving B. Weiner, Editor

Exner (Ed.) • Issues and Methods in Rorschach Research

Frederick/McNeal • Inner Strengths: Contemporary Psychotherapy and Hypnosis for Ego-Strengthening

Gacono/Meloy • The Rorschach Assessment of Aggressive and Psychopathic Personalities

Ganellen • Integrating the Rorschach and the MMPI-2 in Personality Assessment

Handler/Hilsenroth (Eds.) • Teaching and Learning Personality Assessment

Hy/Loevinger • Measuring Ego Development, Second Edition

Kelly • The Assessment of Object Relations Phenomena in Adolescents: TAT and Rorschach Measures

Kohnstamm/Halverson/Mervielde/Havill (Eds.) • Parental Descriptions of Child Personality: Developmental Antecedents of the Big Five?

Loevinger (Ed.) • Technical Foundations for Measuring Ego Development: The Washington University Sentence Completion Test

McCallum/Piper (Eds.) • Psychological Mindedness: A Contemporary Understanding

Meloy/Acklin/Gacono/Murray/Peterson (Eds.) • Contemporary Rorschach Interpretation

Nolen-Hoeksema/Larson • Coping With Loss

Sarason/Pierce/Sarason (Eds.) • Cognitive Interference: Theories, Methods, and Findings

Silverstein • Self Psychology and Diagnostic Assessment: Identifying Selfobject Functions Through Psychological Testing

Taylor (Ed.) • Anxiety Sensitivity: Theory, Research, and Treatment of the Fear of Anxiety

Tedeschi/Park/Calhoun (Eds.) • Posttraumatic Growth: Positive Changes in the Aftermath of Crisis

Van Hasselt/Hersen (Eds.) • Handbook of Psychological Treatment Protocols for Children and Adolescents

Weiner • Principles of Rorschach Interpretation

Wong/Fry (Eds.) • The Human Quest for Meaning: A Handbook of Psychological Research and Clinical Applications

Zillmer/Harrower/Ritzler/Archer • The Quest for the Nazi Personality: A Psychological Investigation of Nazi War Criminals

COPING WITH LOSS

Susan Nolen-Hoeksema
University of Michigan

Judith Larson
Stanford University

LEA LAWRENCE ERLBAUM ASSOCIATES, PUBLISHERS
1999 Mahwah, New Jersey   London

Lawrence Erlbaum Associates, Inc., Publishers
10 Industrial Avenue
Mahwah, New Jersey 07430-2262

Cover design by Kathryn Houghtaling Lacey

Library of Congress Cataloging-in-Publication Data

Nolen-Hoeksema, Susan, 1959–
        Coping with loss / Susan Nolen-Hoeksema, Judith Larson.
            p. cm. —(LEA series in personality and clinical
        psychology)
        Includes bibliographical references and index.
        ISBN 0-8058-2139-2 (hardcover : alk. paper).
        1. Loss (Psychology). 2. Grief. 3. Bereavement—Psycho-
    logical aspects. I. Larson, Judith. II. Title. III. Series.
    BF575.D35N65 1998
    155.9'37—dc21   98-35307
                                                                        CIP

Books published by Lawrence Erlbaum Associates are printed
on acid-free paper, and their bindings are chosen for strength
and durability

Printed in the United States of America
10 9 8 7 6 5 4 3 2 ´

Contents

Preface

This book is based on the Bereavement Coping Project, a long-term study of several hundred people who lost a loved one. The Bereavement Coping Project began as just another research study. It soon became an avenue for spending time with some of the most inspiring and interesting people we have ever met. Chief among these were the hospice people—the nurses, social workers, counselors, and volunteers—who have dedicated their lives to improving the last days of severely ill people and assisting families through grief. We consulted with these dedicated professionals and volunteers extensively in designing this study. The hospice staff then recruited family members into the study for us and gave us continual feedback through its end. We simply could not have done this study without them, and the information we gained would have been much less rich if not for the many questions and concerns hospice people suggested we address. We are deeply grateful to Maureen Medders, Carol Gray, Kitsy Schoen, Gayle Bigelow, Maxine Montgomery, Linda Appleton, Nancy Sabonya, Ruth Schlecta, Donna Bell, Barbara Noggle, Bonnie Kick, Barbara Weissman, Susan Poor, and all the other hospice people who allowed us to spend some time with them and the people they serve. Special thanks to Margaret Gainer for the many, many hours and great love she put into this project.

We are also deeply grateful to the family members who participated in this study. Many people were reluctant to participate, but did so in hope that the information they provided could be helpful to future bereaved people. Our goal in writing this book was to fulfill that hope—to serve as a conduit for their experiences and insights—so that bereaved people and those who serve bereaved people could be informed by these experiences and insights. We have tried to honor the great variety of ways that people grieve by allowing the people in our study to tell readers about their experiences in their own words as much as possible.

Finally, the Bereavement Coping Project was a labor of love because it brought the two of us together. One of us is more research oriented and one more clinically oriented, and our strengths have complemented each other wonderfully in conducting this study and in writing this book. We quickly became the best of friends and have learned tremendously from each other. In writing this book, we have tried to weave together, as seamlessly as possible, the basic research findings from this study, our clinical reflections on people's experiences, and the voices of the families participating in the study. We hope that this serves to inform a broad range of laypeople and professionals who interact with bereaved people, or are themselves bereaved.

ACKNOWLEDGMENTS

This study was supported by U.S. Public Health Grant 1 R01 43760. We thank the following hospices and home health care agencies for recruiting participants into this study: Hospice of Contra Costa, Hospice Caring Project of Santa Cruz County, Hospice of Marin, Hospice of the Valley, Lifesource of Larkspur and Mountain View, Mills-Peninsula Hospital, Mission Hospice, Vesper Hospice, Visiting Nurse Association of San Jose, and Visiting Nurses and Hospice of San Francisco. We also thank Dr. Louise Parker for her contributions to the early phases of this study, Dr. Sarah Erickson, Dr. Peter Goldblum, and Dr. Claire Costello for their contributions to the AIDS-related interviews, Leslie Smithline, Lenore Diaz, and Michael Bishop for their tireless administrative work on this project, and the many wonderful interviewers who made participants feel comfortable in sharing their experiences.

—*Susan Nolen-Hoeksema*
—*Judith Larson*

1

Perspectives on Loss

When my son died, I worried that I was going crazy. I'd go to the store to get milk and bread, and I'd stand there like a fool, and not know why the hell I was in the store. I found out that was normal—the stress and the grieving caused me to be forgetful. And once I found out that it was normal for me to be forgetful, then it was okay. I think it's important for people to know that they are going to do a lot of stupid things, and not know why. And time does heal you. (Jean, 54, whose 35-year-old son died of a brain tumor)[1]

There's no rules. There's no right way or wrong way to feel. You have to take care of yourself. You really have to take care of yourself. I used to think that you get to a certain point and you're not grieving anymore. What I tell people now is you finally realize you're in a place where you can contain it so that it's manageable. You kind of integrate it into what you're doing every day. But it never really goes away. You don't "get over" a loss. No, you just learn to live with it, but you have to also accept the fact that you're changed as a result of it. You're never going to be able to go back to the way you were before it. That's what I see people having the hardest times with, that inability to accept that change. (Phyllis, 35, whose 70-year-old mother died of pancreatic cancer)

---

[1]Names and some other identifying characteristics have been changed to protect the confidentiality of the people quoted.

It's going to get worse before it gets better. All one can do as it progresses is just hang on to whatever it is that helps them getting through each day. It might vary from day to day. It can be anything, from the slightest little thing—a program on TV, a radio station, or just a picture, or a word. Whatever it is to get you through that day, do it. People don't think about those things until you go through it. You don't think about it because we get so preoccupied and so busy. It's natural, we're all human, but you don't become aware of it until you're in that situation. (Marla, 42, whose 65-year-old father died of lung cancer)

I know you go through anger, and the stages. But everybody's different. I was never angry. I think that they're trying to pinpoint it too much and categorize too much. I think that each person is an individual and has different feelings. You can say that they might go through these things. I've read books, people gave me books, poems. I didn't get anything out of those kind of things. I didn't get anything out of them. It's individual. Each person has to cope in their own way. And if they don't cope, then they got a problem. (George, 59, whose 58-year-old wife died of ovarian cancer)

At some time in their lives, most people experience the death of someone close to them. Although most people who lose a loved one experience some degree of emotional and physical distress, there are tremendous differences in how severe this distress is and how long it lasts. This book explores the personal and contextual factors that lead to differences in how people respond to loss.

Our intent in this book is to review the empirical literature on bereavement— scientifically sound studies that have tested predictions about who will have more or less difficulty adjusting to a loss—in a user-friendly manner. In this chapter, we review traditional and more contemporary theories of bereavement, and note the factors these theories predict will affect people's recovery following loss. Then we test these predictions by examining the studies that have tracked bereaved people over time to determine who fares well and who fares poorly. Although we present some specific results from certain studies, we summarize primarily the main research findings and provide information as to where the reader can find more details on each study.

We also use our own research to illustrate key points and findings. This research goes under the title of the Bereavement Coping Project. The details of this research is presented in the appendix. Briefly, we interviewed more than 300 people within 1 month of losing a loved one to a terminal illness, then reinterviewed these people 6 months, 13 months, and 18 months after their loss. Our interviews were comprehensive, covering a wide range of emotional and physical symptoms, questions about the loss, and assessments of the bereaved people's social environments and personalities. The people we interviewed had all lost a loved one to a terminal illness, so their experiences may not match those of people who lose a loved one to homicide, accidents, natural disasters, or other means. Because the majority of people who die in the United States and Europe die after a prolonged illness, the experiences of the participants in our research apply to a large percentage of bereaved people. To provide a comprehensive picture of coping with loss, we discuss also the existing studies on how people cope with unexpected losses and violent deaths. Before we examine the theories of grief to determine what factors affect people's adjustment to loss, we need to define *grief*—the response to bereavement.

WHAT IS GRIEF?

One of the most difficult aspects of studying grief is defining it, and in particular, defining what "normal" grief and "abnormal" grief are. What emotional, cognitive, and physiological symptoms make up the grief syndrome? Which of these symptoms do most bereaved people show? Which ones should they show? How intense are they? How long do they last? Perhaps surprisingly, there are no definitive answers to these questions.

Stage models of the grief process have been very popular in clinical writings on grief (Bowlby, 1980; Glick, Weiss, & Parkes, 1974; Horowitz, 1976; Kubler-Ross, 1969; Pollock, 1987; Shuchter & Zisook, 1993). Although they differ in their details, most of these models have postulated at least three phases in the grief process (see Table 1.1). The first is an initial period of shock, disbelief, and denial, which may last from hours to weeks. Bereaved people feel numb and paralyzed, and may not believe that the death is real. They may actively search for the dead loved one, may imagine hearing or seeing the

TABLE 1.1

Symptoms and Experiences at Various Phases of Grief

Cognitive	Affective	Behavioral	Somatic
EARLY PHASE			
Slowed thinking	Psychic numbness	Crying	Physical numbness
Disorganized thinking	Blunting	Weeping, sobbing	Feeling of unreality
Suicidal ideation	Euphoria	Outbursts	Feeling outside body
Disbelief	Hysteria	Talkativeness	Dizziness
Appears unaffected	Appears unaffected	Hyperactivity	General physical distress
		Unaware of others	
		Passivity	
		Sighing	
		Appears unaffected	

(Continues)

TABLE 1.1 (Continued)

Cognitive	Affective	Behavioral	Somatic
MIDDLE PHASE			
Preoccupation with thoughts of deceased	Sadness	All of the above +	General physical distress
Idealizing the deceased	Yearning	Restlessness	Muscle weakness
Searching	Anxiety	Accident proneness	Muscle aches
Ruminating	Fear	Psychomotor retardation	Headaches
Dreams of deceased	Anger	Withdrawal	Stomachaches
Impaired concentration	Irritability	Support seeking	Chest pains
Impaired memory	Guilt	Dependence	Tightness in chest
Meaninglessness	Depression	Avoidance	Heartbeat irregularity
Loss of interest	Loneliness	Lack of initiative	Shortness of breath
Lowered self-esteem	Apathy		Sleep disturbance
Worry	Anguish		Change in appetite
"I'm going crazy"	Relief		Vulnerability to illness
Hears voice of deceased			Nausea
"Sees" deceased			Low energy
RESOLUTION			
Realistic memory of deceased	Return to normal range of emotions	Return to normal functioning	Return to normal functioning
Pleasure in remembering		New or renewed social relationships	
New meaning in life		New or renewed activities	

Note. People can experience any combination of symptoms and experiences, they can move in and out of various experiences, and not everyone experiences everything. People often have periods of feeling quite well, thinking "I'm over it." Then there is a sudden recurrence of grief or symptoms. This can be scary. They think, "I'm back to square one." Or they won't connect the symptoms (e.g., irritability or memory impairment) with grief and begin to feel like something is wrong with them. Often, there is a fear of disclosure.

Common metaphors are roller coasters and ocean waves. Peaks and valleys (or size of waves) vary in size and intensity. Gradually, over time, they come less frequently and are of shorter duration.

deceased, or may simply yearn and pine for the loved one. As some participants in our study described:

> It's an emotional rollercoaster. I've been told that's normal and I've certainly experienced the whole gamut of feelings. It helps to know what to expect and that no matter what you feel it's probably normal. I've had a lot of spaciness; putting things somewhere and then not remembering where I put them. I was so terrified that I'd lose his ashes, that I made his daughters observe where I put them, and I said, "I don't move them unless I notify

you." I'll forget where I put my car, can't find my keys, there's a special letter or card that someone's written that I want to share with someone and then I can't find it. The first couple of weeks I had a very strong sense that he was present. If someone asked me a question and I didn't know the answer I would turn around and ask John and realize he wasn't here. Some days I'm numb, some days I think, "God, you really are a bitch, you don't feel anything." (Nell, 57, whose 60-year-old husband died of lung cancer 1 month previously)

My dad still exists because I still feel him and see him in my dreams ... I can actually hear his voice. So, my dad has not left me. My dad will not leave me until I leave. (Rosa, 42, whose 70-year-old father died of prostate cancer 1 month previously)

It doesn't feel real. It feels like a dream. And yet I know it's not a dream, I know it's real, but I want it to be a dream. And I want to wake up, and have all this wisdom that I have attained. And I want to look at my husband and say, "That was a good dream. I'm going to learn from it." I think this would be one heck of a dream to wake up from. So, yeah, there's times when it doesn't seem real. I expect him to come home. I think I hear him coming down the hall. (Jenny, 50, whose 55-year-old husband died of cancer 1 month previously)

This is so morbid. I know that she's just not here but I have visions of [her] body deteriorating, like rotting away. It disturbs me. I don't dwell on it, but once in a while I've had this thought of my mother in a box in the ground. My dad died 22 years ago, I never had these thoughts about my dad. My mother's death was different from my dad's. (Dorothy, 42, whose 65-year-old mother died of bone cancer 1 month previously)

I feel like I'm—somebody's standing off watching me. It's not me, really—this is happening to someone else. It doesn't seem like it really happened to me. And yet I know of course it did. So it's kind of like denial. Something that makes me feel that way, too, is, it's because I've coped so well. If somebody had told me this was going to happen to me, 5 years ago, I would have thought I would have been a basket case, and it surprises me that I am doing so well. (Lara, 61, whose 67-year-old husband died 6 months previously)

I still feel like I'm going through things that I haven't really experienced quite yet. I'm starting to feel more. Even a month ago, I would have thought, "Hey I got through this like a piece of cake." All of a sudden, now, things are coming to the surface that weren't there. (Carol, 36, whose 45-year-old sister died of lung cancer 6 months previously)

The second phase begins when the death is acknowledged cognitively and emotionally. This phase of acute mourning includes intense feelings of sadness, despair, loneliness, anxiety, and anger. The full syndrome of depression may occur, with loss of interest in life, disruptions in sleep and appetite, inability to concentrate or make decisions, a sense of hopelessness and helplessness, and even suicidal wishes. Bereaved people may withdraw from others and be preoccupied with their loss. Even when they try to engage in everyday living, they may have intrusive, painful thoughts about their loss. They may have a variety of somatic symptoms, including symptoms that mimic symptoms the deceased had just before the death. This acute mourning phase may last for several months. It is during the acute mourning phase that bereaved people often seek help or support. People often feel that they are suddenly doing worse than they had just after the loss, and do not understand why:

> At the time I was so numb and tired, that some days I think I coped better right at first than I do now. (Ellen, 70, whose 73-year-old husband died of prostate cancer 6 months previously)

> I'm really denying. I even sometimes think I'm hearing him. I know it's not him. I know it's just a thought. … I realize now it's going to be a very slow process. I still see him in bed, I see him in his last 2 weeks. I don't want to forget, but I don't want to have those kinds of thoughts in my mind. (Mary, 57, whose 61-year-old husband died of cancer 6 months previously)

Eventually, in most people, the acute mourning phase is replaced by a restitution phase in which the bereaved return to a feeling of well-being and an ability to go on living. They may come to some understanding or acceptance of the loss, and most of the time they are able to be engaged in everyday life in a positive way. Yet, grief can reappear from time to time for years, or throughout one's lifetime (Bornstein, Clayton, Halikas, Maurice, & Robbins, 1973; Lehman, Wortman, & William, 1987; Parkes, 1971; Zisook, Shuchter, & Lyons, 1987). Said one man in our study, who had lost his mother to cancer 1 year previously:

> When I stop and feel myself, it's like a piece missing. There's a physical gap. There's an emotional gap.

Another participant, 1 year after losing mother, said:

> I still doesn't seem real. I think it's hitting me more now than before. I think I was numb for a long time. I was so strong for her, I held everything inside, and now, it' just hitting me.

And another participant, an elderly woman who lost her husband to cancer said what many people say, that the grief actually gets harder with time rather than easier:

> It's getting harder. It's beginning to be more and more real.

Grief is often triggered by a holiday, an anniversary, a special occasion. New griefs can trigger old griefs. For example, if a man's father died when he was

20, and a co-worker in his office died when he was 32, he might reexperience intense grief regarding his father again, even if the coworker's death is not traumatic. And, many people will suddenly find themselves with intense grief pangs that are not brought on by an identifiable stimulus.

Although these stage models have been useful in bringing the literature on grief to the public, many clinicians prefer to conceptualize grief as a process, not a set of stages or a state (Parkes, 1971; Worden, 1982). Moreover, clinicians emphasize the individual differences among people in the types and duration of symptoms they experience. Indeed, the variety of symptoms people experience—from classic symptoms of depression, to symptoms of posttraumatic stress (hypervigilance, numbness, flashbacks, intrusive memories), to symptoms of physical pain and illness—are what has made characterizing grief so difficult.

Many different theorists have described abnormal grief, otherwise called pathological, complicated, morbid, unresolved, or atypical (see Middleton, Raphael, Martinek, & Misso, 1993). Often, the definition of abnormal grief is grief that lasts longer than expected, referred to as *chronic* or *prolonged* grief (Parkes, 1965). Yet, there is little agreement as to how long we should expect grief to last. The current psychiatric diagnostic criteria in the *Diagnostic and Statistical Manual* (*DSM-IV*; APA, 1994) specify that a diagnosis of major depression should not be given when the depression is in reaction to the death of a loved one unless the symptoms are still present 2 months after the loss. As noted earlier, however, many people experience symptoms of grief for much longer than 2 months after their loss.

One of the most consistent assertions in the literature on grief is that the absence of acute grief symptoms shortly after a loss is abnormal. The assumption is that grief is a normal and healthy response to a loss, so people who do not experience grief symptoms are not experiencing the normal reaction to loss (Deutsch, 1937; Lindemann, 1944; Parkes, 1965). Another form of abnormal grief described by theorists is *delayed grief* (Parkes, 1965), in which the symptoms of grief are initially absent, but appear with intensity weeks or months after the loss. One woman we knew lost two husbands, both naval pilots, who were killed when the woman was in her 20s. She did not consciously experience grief until her 50s, when something triggered the grief she had never experienced. About the time between the loss and her experience of the grief, she said, "I had children to raise, things to do."

One 65-year-old woman in our study, Abby, lost her husband Fred to prostate cancer when he was 67. Abby's son Joe is disabled from juvenile-onset diabetes, is blind, requires dialysis, and is angry and depressed. At her interview 18 months after the loss, Abby said,

> I don't think I ever really got to grieve for him, because Joe has been here since he died. His condition has just steadily deteriorated since his Dad died.

I keep thinking it can't get any worse, and it does. I have never been alone in this house since Fred died. Sometimes at night when I dream about Fred, which I do a lot, it's just really really hard. I think what I want to do is just sit down and cry for him and not cry for all this other stuff. I just want to cry for my grief. Sometimes I think I'd like to cry for a whole day, just for him and not for anything else, not any of the other awful stuff that's around. And I can't do that—just go away someplace all by myself and just think about him and make myself know that he really is not with me anymore. Then maybe I'd do better if I could do that.

There has been less consensus as to whether certain symptoms are seen in abnormal grief but not in normal grief. Surveying the bereavement literature and experts on bereavement, Middleton, Raphael, Martinek, and Misso (1993) argued that the following symptoms indicate a pathological grief reaction: low self-esteem, hopelessness, suicidal ruminations, fantasies of reunion with the lost person, severe psychomotor retardation, severe restlessness, hypervigilance and arousal, preoccupying guilt, profound depressed mood, traumatic and intrusive images of the death, and frequent reexperiencing of the death. Mild forms of these symptoms may be seen in the acute phases of normal grief, but when these symptoms are intense or prolonged, many experts view them as signs of pathology. The *DSM-IV* (APA, 1994, pp. 684–685) asserts that the presence of the following symptoms are not part of normal grief and may help distinguish grief from major depression:

1. Guilt about things other than actions taken or not taken by the survivor at the time of the death.
2. Thought of death other than the survivor feeling that he or she would be better off dead or should have died with the deceased person.
3. Morbid preoccupation with worthlessness.
4. Marked psychomotor retardation.
5. Prolonged and marked functional impairment.
6. Hallucinatory experience other than thinking that he or she hears the voice of, or transiently sees the image of, the deceased person.

Measurement of Grief Symptoms

Given that there is little consensus on what constitutes normal and abnormal grief, it is not surprising that there is not a uniform way of measuring grief in empirical studies. A few measures of grief have been developed (see Hansson, Carpenter, & Fairchild, 1993). Two of these, the Grief Experience Inventory (Sanders, Mauger, & Strong, 1979), and the Texas Revised Inventory of Grief (Faschingbauer, Zisook, & DeVaul, 1987) are instruments that assess bereaved people's functioning across multiple dimensions. Another measure frequently used in studies of grief is the Impact of Events Scale (Horowitz, Wilner, &

Alvarez, 1979), which assesses intrusion of thoughts, images, and feelings about the trauma, and attempts to avoid such feelings and cognitions.

Many researchers have used measures of depression to assess grief-related symptoms, with the assumption that the depressive syndrome closely mirrors the grief syndrome. Some commonly used measures include the Center for Epidemiological Studies Depression Scale (CESD; Radloff, 1977) and the Beck Depression Inventory (BDI; Beck & Beck, 1972). The CESD was designed for nonclinical populations, whereas the BDI was designed to track symptoms in clinically depressed populations. In our work, we used the Inventory to Diagnose Depression (IDD; Zimmerman & Coryell, 1987). This instrument provides both a continuous measure of depression, and information to determine whether participants qualify for a diagnosis of depression. We also included measures of anxiety and posttraumatic stress symptoms (numbness, hypervigilance, jitteriness, flashbacks or intrusive memories, nightmares; see the appendix for details). In some of our analyses, we combined all these emotional symptom measures into one general distress measure, in line with arguments that we must look at a wide range of emotional symptoms among the bereaved, rather than just at symptoms of depression.

GRIEF ACROSS CULTURES

What we have just described is grief as it has been observed in contemporary Western society, which has been influenced powerfully by Judeo-Christian values. There is good evidence, mostly from anthropological studies, that grief takes many different forms across cultures in line with cultural norms for how people should feel and behave after a loss.

Contemporary Western cultures specify that people should experience pain and longing after an important loss, but that the intensity and duration of these symptoms should be contained to some extent. Models of successful recovery emphasize the importance of the bereaved breaking bonds with the deceased or moving on to new relationships or activities (Stroebe, Gergen, Gergen, & Stroebe, 1992). Once this occurs, the bereaved is expected to be engaged fully in daily life and not to be preoccupied with thoughts or feelings about the deceased.

Other cultures, however, emphasize the importance of remaining connected to the deceased (Rosenblatt, Walsh, & Jackson, 1976; Stroebe et al., 1992). For example, Shinto and Buddhist religions in Japan emphasize the importance of maintaining contact with the deceased (Yamamoto, Okonoji, Iwasaki, & Yoshimura, 1969). Altars to the deceased are built, food or gifts are offered, and the bereaved talk with their dead relatives. These practices would be considered signs of abnormal grief in Euro-American cultures, but are normal in Japanese culture.

Still other cultures have norms for grieving that differ from both Euro-American and Japanese practices. Among the Hopi of Arizona, the bereaved may experience the pain of their loss, but they are expected not to overtly mourn (Mandelbaum, 1959). Instead, the deceased is to be forgotten and life is to be resumed as soon as possible. These practices reflect cultural beliefs that contact with death brings pollution, and that supernatural spirits are not Hopi and do not have the characteristics of dead relatives or friends.

Even cultures sharing a religious orientation can have very different grief practices. Consider the norms in two Muslim societies, one in Bali and one in Egypt (Wikan, 1991). In Egypt, the bereaved are allowed to dwell at length on their loss, surrounded by friends and family who recount stories about the deceased and mutually express deep sorrow in emotional displays. In Bali, the bereaved are expected to contain their sorrow, and are judged harshly if they openly mourn or pine after the deceased. Thus, grief practices are often tied to religious beliefs about death and the afterlife, but they also can be tied to traditions that have their roots in other aspects of the cultural history of a region.

Within the United States, different cultures of people with different ethnic backgrounds can clash. We observed this in our study, when we talked with people who were not of European-American descent, about their experiences with the medical community and hospices. Rachel, a 58-year-old African-American woman whose husband Cal, 69, died of cancer said:

> In Black culture, "death" and "dying" are unspoken words. Hospice just wanted to come in and talk about funeral arrangements and everything. It's just not done in our culture.

Very little research has been done on the cross-cultural appropriateness of standardized measures of grief (Hansson et al., 1993). These measures seldom take into account cultural norms for certain symptoms among the bereaved. And even if we want to apply Euro-American models of grief to people from other cultures, it is not clear that assessment measures are appropriate for people not part of the dominant Euro-American culture.

One of the most pervasive cultural differences in the presentation of symptoms is the tendency to report psychological distress in emotional symptoms or in somatic (physical) symptoms. Following a psychologically distressing events such as loss, Euro-Americans tend to report feeling anxious or sad, but members of many other cultures report having physical aches and maladies (Kleinman & Kleinman, 1985). To conduct an accurate assessment, clinicians must know about cultural differences in the manifestation of disorders and in the presentation of symptoms, and use this information in interpreting the symptoms that their clients report to them. This is further complicated by the fact that not every member of a culture conforms to what is known about that culture. That is, within every culture, people differ in their acceptance of cultural norms for behavior.

Summing Up Definitions of Grief

Descriptions of the grief process provided by Euro-American theorists and clinicians specify three phases of grief: shock, denial, and numbness; intense yearning for the deceased, depressive-like symptoms, anxiety, and protest over the loss; and acceptance of the loss and reengagement in everyday life. It is clear, however, that within Euro-American cultures and across other cultures, people vary greatly in the specific symptoms and the duration of these symptoms following a loss.

We turn now to theories of bereavement, focusing on how these theories explain why some people show long and intense symptoms of grief and others do not. These theories are rooted in Euro-American psychology, and thus do not have much to say about the cross-cultural differences in the grief process. But they form the background for most of the empirical literature on bereavement that is the focus of the remainder of this book.

THEORIES OF BEREAVEMENT AND INDIVIDUAL DIFFERENCES

Two different types of theories of bereavement can be identified from the literature (Stroebe, Stroebe, & Hansson, 1993). The earlier group of theories derive from psychoanalytic and attachment theories (Bowlby, 1980; Freud, 1917/1957; Lindemann, 1994). These theories focus on the importance of close relationships in the self-concepts of individuals, and attribute the symptoms seen in bereavement to the individual's adjustment to the loss of an important relationship. Although these theories remain highly influential in clinical practice, certain assertions of these theories have not been supported empirically. The more recent group of theories derives from stress and coping theories (Epstein, 1993; Parkes, 1993; Stroebe & Stroebe, 1987). These theories view bereavement in the larger context of stressful events, and focus on how different ways of thinking about and coping with the loss can affect the symptoms seen in bereavement.

Psychoanalytic Theory

One of Freud's (1917/1957) most famous and enduring theories was his theory of mourning. Freud argued that all important relationships are imbued with a psychological energy, or *cathexis*. When a relationship is lost, the bereaved must withdraw the energy invested in that relationship, and reinvest the withdrawn energy in other relationships. The process of withdrawal and reinvestment is a painful one, however, and not done without protest. During this process, the bereaved are preoccupied with thoughts of the deceased, lose interest in the outside world, and experience sadness and anxiety at giving up the relationship.

The fatigue and somatic symptoms of grief are said to result from energy being used as the bereaved detaches from the image of the deceased. Eventually, however, most bereaved people are able to detach and reinvest in new relationships.

Complicated bereavement, or what Freud called *melancholia*, occurs when the bereaved cannot relinquish the old relationship, although the person is gone. Instead, their anger at the deceased is turned inward on the image of the deceased that is part of their own self-image, and they engage in self-punishment. Melancholia is most likely to occur in people who had ambivalent relationships with the deceased. These people have a great deal of anger toward the deceased, but also a great attachment to the deceased, which creates conflict over the anger they feel. Ambivalence and melancholia frequently arise in people whose self-images are made up largely of the images of important others in their lives—people dependent on their relationships with others for their own self-concept. Their attachment to others is very strong, but they harbor resentment at the others for their own dependency. Their conflict over these dual feelings makes it difficult for them to let go of the lost loved one, and simultaneously they remain very angry at the loved one for abandoning them. Thus, Freud suggested that everyone experiences some distressing grief symptoms following a loss, but people who had ambivalence over the lost relationship and who are dependent on others for their self-concepts are likely to have protracted, complicated, grief responses.

Attachment Theory

A second traditional, and highly influential, theory of mourning is the attachment theory of Bowlby (1969, 1980), which draws on both psychoanalytic theory and ethology (the study of animal behavior). Bowlby noted that a fundamental part of development in both humans and animals is forming attachments to important others. Children form attachments to their primary caregivers, even if the caregivers are neglectful or abusive because caregivers provide the main source of security and nurturance. Adults form attachments to other adults, most notably those with whom they choose to mate. Adults also form strong attachments to their own children. Bowlby (1980) argued that these attachments are instinctive and biologically driven. They foster survival by ensuring that children remain close to caregivers who will provide for them, that adults bond and mate with others to produce offspring, and that adults care for their vulnerable offspring.

These attachment relationships are so strong that when a relationship is threatened, people (and many animals) will engage in behaviors designed to maintain the relationship, such as clinging, crying, and protesting angrily. These behaviors are seen most obviously when children are unwilling to separate from a parent—children will hold onto their parents with all their might, cry uncontrollably, and if separated, may throw a tantrum. When an important attachment relationship is severed through loss, Bowlby argued that survivors go through four stages or phases of mourning or grief. (Bowlby's work inspired the descriptions of phases of mourning described earlier.)

The first phase is *shock*—a complete numbness or stunned feeling. Bereaved people will walk around in a daze and not take care of themselves. They may not believe that their loved one (whom Bowlby called the "attachment figure") is gone. The second phase is *protest*, and involves attempts to undo the loss, even if the survivor acknowledges this is impossible. The bereaved may physically search for the loved one, or may simply feel he or she "sees" the loved one often on the street or hears him or her in another room of the house. Bereaved people may be irritable and restless, angry that they cannot find the loved one or that the loved one does not return. Over time, these behaviors designed to restore the attachment bond decrease, and people move into the third phase of mourning, *despair*, in which they give up attempts to recover the deceased. It is during this period that the bereaved is most likely to show the signs of depression, which Bowlby attributed to a sense of helplessness and hopelessness at restoring the attachment bond.

In the last phase of mourning, *adaptation*, Bowlby argued that people begin to break down their attachment to the loved one and to establish new attachments to others. In contrast to Freud, Bowlby suggested that new attachments could never fully replace lost attachments because each attachment is unique and forms an important component of the individual's self-concept. Thus, the final phase of mourning does not involve a recovery of the same level of emotional tone and sense of identity one had before the loss occurred. Instead, it involves a reorganization of one's identity and emotional investments.

Drawing on Bowlby's model, Weiss (1988) argued that three processes are involved in this final phase of adaptation. *Cognitive acceptance* involves developing a satisfactory account of the causes of the loss. The bereaved must find a way of explaining why the loss occurred, even if that explanation is not true. This explanation may come from philosophical or religious beliefs ("It was God's will." "Death is a part of life."). But if it does not come, the individual remains anxious, ruminating about the meaning or purpose of their loss.

Emotional acceptance involves neutralizing memories and associations with the deceased so that recalling these memories and associations does not cause severe pain. This requires that the bereaved confront these memories and associations one by one, essentially habituating to them. This also requires the bereaved to put aside counterfactual thinking—those "if only" thoughts about things that might have prevented the loss. This work of emotional acceptance is what is often referred to as *grief work*. Finally, bereaved individuals must go through a process of *identity change*, in which their relationship with the attachment figure is accepted as a part of their past, and they move onto new relationships. Often the cognitive work and the emotional work of grief are out of sync with one another. Bereaved people often say how their heart and their head are not at the same place.

There are a number of factors that can impede the process of adaptation and recovery (Bowlby, 1980; Weiss, 1988). First, losses that are harder to explain and imbue with meaning make adaptation difficult. For example, losses that occur without forewarning, such as through a car accident or a homicide, seem to be more difficult to explain than losing a loved one after a long illness. Similarly, an untimely death such as the death of a child may be more difficult for most people to understand than the loss of an older adult, and thus may be more difficult to recover from (Lehman, Wortman, & Williams, 1987; Weiss, 1987).

Second, ambivalence toward the attachment figure creates confusion about one's emotional reaction to the loss, and perhaps self-blame or guilt, and thus may make it more difficult to accept the loss emotionally and to accept the relationship as part of one's past. Third, people who were too dependent on the attachment relationship may be panicked at the loss and unable to form a new identity that does not include the attachment figure (Bowlby, 1980). Fourth, people whose feelings of responsibility to the attachment figure were extremely strong may feel they are being disloyal if they recover, and thus may actively work against recovery (Bowlby, 1980).

Horowitz's Trauma Model

In an attempt to integrate psychoanalytic and cognitive models of reactions to trauma, Horowitz and associates (Horowitz, 1976, 1985) argue that immediately after a loss, people appear stunned and unable to process its meaning. They may deny that the loss actually occurred while feeling numbed and dazed. Painful thoughts regarding the loss intrude on consciousness, however. People oscillate between denial and intrusive thoughts, remaining with the intrusive thoughts as they work through the loss, but when these thoughts are too overwhelming and painful, they retreat into denial. More recently, Horowitz has argued that the process of working through involves assimilating the loss into one's understanding of the world and oneself. As this process of *assimilation* takes place, the intrusive thoughts become less painful, and the cycling between intrusions and denial becomes less intense (Shontz, 1975). This recovery process is delayed, however, in people who will not confront their intrusive thoughts, and desperately cling to denial and the suppression of their thoughts and emotions about the deceased.

Challenges to the Traditional Models

In the past 20 years, researchers have begun to challenge some of the fundamental assumptions common to the traditional models of bereavement (see Osterweis, Solomon, & Green, 1984; Silver & Wortman, 1980; Wortman &

Silver, 1987, 1989). These include the assumptions that (a) bereaved people go through predictable stages of grief; (b) depression following loss is inevitable, and people who do not experience severe distress over the loss will eventually show some psychopathology, and (c) working through the loss is essential to recovery. We review each of these assumptions and the evidence concerning them in turn.

Although stage models have been extremely popular among health care professionals and the public, supporters of these stage models have offered primarily clinical and anecdotal evidence for the notion that most bereaved people go through the same stages of phases of grief in a certain order and at a certain pace (Bowlby, 1961; Kubler-Ross, 1969). In contrast, the few empirical studies that have tested the stage models do not tend to support these models (Osterweis et al., 1984; Silver & Wortman, 1980). Many, perhaps most bereaved people do report the symptoms that stage theories describe—shock, denial, anger, despair, yearning, intrusive thoughts, and eventually a sense of recovery. But there is tremendous variability between people in the order in which these symptoms are experienced, and the duration of specific symptoms.

The failure of studies to support stage models is important given the influence of these models on interventions with bereaved people. These models form the backbone of education about bereavement for many physicians, nurses, therapists, social workers, members of the clergy, patients, and their families (Silver & Wortman, 1980; Wortman & Silver, 1987). Health care professionals may use models as a yardstick to assess the progress of bereaved people they are serving. Thus, people who are not following these stages might be labeled as pathological and may be intervened with unnecessarily or inappropriately. People who read about the stages of bereavement might also label themselves as abnormal because they are not experiencing bereavement as the books say they should.

Another pervasive assumption of the traditional models is that high levels of depression and distress are inevitable and healthy following a loss, and that failure to experience this distress is pathological (Bowlby, 1980; Freud, 1917/1957). Many studies have reported that feelings of sadness or depressed mood are very common among bereaved people (Bornstein, Clayton, Halikas, Maurice, & Robins, 1973; Faletti, Gibbs, Clark, Pruchno, & Berman, 1989; Thompson, Gallagher, Cover, Gilewski, & Peterson, 1989; Van Zandt, Mou, & Abbott, 1989). For example, a study of widows in the first year after their loss found that 88% reported experiencing depressed mood (Glick, Weiss, & Parkes, 1974). One month after the loss of their husbands, 70% of widows in another study scored above a criterion for psychiatric distress (Vachon et al., 1982). In a more recent study of gay men who lost their partners to acquired immunodeficiency syndrome (AIDS), about 80% scored above a cut-off for moderate depression 1 month following their loss (Folkman, Chesney, Collette, Boccellari, & Cooke, 1996).

Are those people who do not experience significant depression shortly after a loss destined to experience depression eventually, or to experience other pathology in place of depression? Several studies have found that people who are not highly distressed following a loss usually do not go on to experience severe distress in the future; instead, people who are highly distressed right after a loss are the ones most likely to be severely distressed in the future. One of the first studies to show this was a longitudinal study of 109 widows and widowers by Clayton and colleagues (1973). Seventy-one of these bereaved persons were not seriously depressed 1 month following their loss. Of these 71 respondents, only 4 became depressed over the next year, leading the researchers to conclude that delayed grief was rare. Similarly, in a study of 99 widows by Vachon and colleagues (1982), 32 women were classified as having little distress one month following the loss. Of these 32 women, 94% continued to show little distress over the next 2 years. Only 2 women with low distress scores 1 month following the loss had high distress scores at a follow-up interview 2 years after the loss.

This pattern of results does not hold only for spousal loss. A study of 124 parents who had lost an infant to sudden infant death syndrome (SIDS) found that only a small percentage of the parents with low distress scores 3 weeks after their loss developed high distress over the ensuing 18 months (Wortman & Silver, 1987). In our own study, we found no evidence that spouses, parents, adult children, or adult siblings of the deceased who had low levels of distress in the first month after their loss went on to develop high levels of distress in the following 18 months.[2]

A third assumption of the traditional theories is that working through the loss is essential to recovery (Bowlby, 1980; Freud, 1917/1957; Parkes, 1986; Raphael & Nunn, 1988). Working through generally means reviewing all aspects of one's relationship to the deceased, coming to terms with anger at the deceased, questioning meaning of the loss, assimilating the loss into the view of the self, and accepting the loss as permanent. While engaging in this work, bereaved people are likely to show high levels of distress, but this working through will eventually lead to low levels of distress. In contrast, people who do not work through their loss should, over time, be more distressed than those who do work through their loss.

The few studies with data that can begin to test this assumption have not supported it. In a ground-breaking study, Parkes and Weiss (1983) followed bereaved people for 2 to 4 years following the death of their spouse. The

---

[2]Correlations between levels of distess 1-month postloss and levels of distress at subsequent interviews were all high and significant at $p < .01$ for self-reported depression, interviewer-rated depression, and self-report measures of physical health, posttraumatic stress symptoms, and anxiety, suggesting that those people with low levels of these symptoms at 1-month postloss continued to have low levels through the 18-month interview. Separate analyses of people who scored one standard deviation below the mean on measures of distress 1-month postloss found that only a handful became acutely distressed later in the study, usually in response to some new stressor they had experienced.

bereaved were assessed for how much they were yearning or pining for their deceased spouse 3 weeks after their loss, and were divided into a high-yearning group, composed of respondents who appeared to yearn or pine constantly, frequently, or whenever inactive; and a low yearning group, who yearned never, seldom, or only when reminded of the loss. Contrary to predictions from the traditional grief theories, people in the high-yearning group had worse mental and physical health 13 months following their loss than people in the low-yearning group. The high-yearning group continued to fare worse over the 2 to 4 years following their loss.

Similarly, in the study of parents who lost a child to SIDS, working through was associated with a poorer recovery from loss (Wortman & Silver, 1987). Working through was operationalized in this study as active attempts by the parent to make sense of and process the death, including searching for an answer for why the baby had died, thinking of ways the death could have been avoided, and being preoccupied with thoughts about the loss. The more parents were engaging in this working through 3 weeks after their loss, the more distressed they were 18 months later.

In a more recent study, Stroebe and Stroebe (1991) tried to disentangle grief work from yearning or pining for the loved one. They operationalized grief work as the tendency not to use suppression or distraction to avoid thoughts of the deceased. In a longitudinal study of 60 widows and widowers, they found that men who had higher scores on their grief work measure showed less depression over time, whereas grief work was unrelated to depression in the women.

In our study, we looked separately at the process of searching for meaning in the loss and ruminating about the loss. These two activities were mildly correlated with each other—people who were searching for meaning also tended to be ruminating more about the loss and their symptoms of grief. More importantly, continuing to search for meaning (but not finding it), and ruminating were both related to more distress at all our interviews through 18 months following the loss.[3] This suggests that people whose grief work was not completed remained distressed over time, which is what the traditional models of grief would predict. Yet, contrary to predictions from the traditional grief theories, we found that people who did not ruminate about their loss, and who found meaning in their loss very shortly after the loss were the least likely to remain distressed over time.[4]

---

[3]The correlations between making sense and ruminating were all .20 or lower, p's < .05. The cross-sectinal correlations between making sense and self-reported depression or general distress, and rumination and self-reported depression or general distress, were significant at all interviews at $p < .05$.

[4]Correlations between making sense and rumination at 1-month postloss or 6-months postloss and self-reported depression at all subsequent interviews were significant at $p < .05$.

A final assumption of many grief models that seems not to be supported in empirical studies is that most people reach a stage of recovery or adaptation, characterized by low levels of depression or distress, and high levels of functioning (Bowlby, 1980; Klinger, 1977; Kubler- Ross, 1969; Raphael, 1983). Most theories do not specify how long it should take for this recovery to occur. But several studies following bereaved people for years after their loss find that a substantial portion still have not fully recovered. For example, Parkes and Weiss (1983) found that more than 40% of the widows in their sample still had significant symptoms of anxiety and depression, and problems in everyday functioning 2 to 4 years after their loss. Similarly, Vachon et al. 1982) found that 38% of widows still were experiencing a high level of distress 1 year after their loss, and 26% were experiencing high distress 2 years after their loss. Zisook and Shuchter (1986) found that, even 4 years after a loss, at least 20 % of widows and widowers assessed their own adjustment as "fair or poor," whereas only 44% assessed it as excellent. Finally, Lehman, Wortman, and Williams (1987) found that people who had lost a spouse or child in a motor vehicle accident showed higher levels of distress and lower levels of functioning than a control group 4 to 7 years after the loss.

In our own study, there were several participants who said that they do not feel they will ever recover from their loss:

> I'll never get over my son's death. And I'll never forget, you don't forget. (Bonnie, 48-year-old mother who lost her 28-year-old son to cancer)

> The last comment I want to make is that I don't think it's a process that once you get it, it's done. I think it's like an onion, and it gets deeper and deeper. And as you get to the core of the onion, there's nothing to peel, but that center of the onion is like a circle of emptiness, where there's nothing inside, and yet it's full and yet it's empty. (Phillip, 40-year-old man who lost his 79-year-old mother to pancreatic cancer)

Summing Up Challenges

Common assumptions in traditional grief models are that bereaved people go through predictable stages of grief; depression following loss is inevitable, and people who do not experience significant distress over the loss will eventually show some psychopathology—working through the loss is essential to recovery. Empirical studies of bereavement generally have not supported these assumptions.

Although many of the assertions of the traditional grief models about the structure of the grief process have not been supported, some of the predictions from these models may still hold true. These models suggest that factors putting people at risk for maladaptive reactions to loss include having had an ambivalent relationship with the deceased, a tendency to be dependent on others for one's self-concept, an excessive sense of responsibility for the loss, and a tendency to deny one's emotions and avoid thinking about the loss. In addition, attachment theories suggest that some types of loss, such as the loss of a child, may be more difficult to accept and thus create more difficulty in adjustment. As seen later, several of these factors are also identified as risks for poor recovery from loss by modern stress and coping models of bereavement.

Stress and Coping Models

The stress and coping models view bereavement in the larger context of stressful life events, or as Parkes (1971, 1993) called them, *psychosocial transitions*. Stressful events like bereavement require people to undertake a major revision of their assumptions and their ways of being in the world, and have long-lasting rather than transient implications. For example, the loss of a spouse may also mean the loss of a sexual partner, the loss of protection from danger, loss of companionship, loss of income, loss of a recreational and social partner, loss of a home, loss of a parent for one's children, and loss of the focus of one's self-definition. Thus, bereavement is a psychosocial transition that requires readjustments ranging from trivial everyday practices (e.g., setting one place at the table instead of two), to major life changes (e.g., finding a job to support oneself) and a redefinition of one's self (e.g., considering oneself as someone other than the husband/wife of ...).

Like other traumas, loss can challenge certain closely held assumptions people have (Epstein, 1985; Janoff-Bulman, 1989; Janoff-Bulman & Frieze, 1983; Parkes, 1988; Wortman, Silver, & Kessler, 1993). The first is the assumption of personal invulnerability. Most people believe that bad things happen to other people, and that they are relatively invulnerable to traumas such as losing a child in an automobile accident. When such an event does happen, the individual loses his or her illusion of invulnerability. Now chronically feeling vulnerable, the individual is hypervigilant for signs of new traumas, and may show signs of chronic anxiety.

The second basic assumption is the assumption that the world is meaningful and just and that things happen for a good reason (Lerner, 1980). This assumption can be shattered by events that seem senseless, unjust, perhaps evil, such as the terrorist bombing of a children's day-care center. The third assumption is the assumption that you are a good person, and if you just "play by the rules," bad things will not happen to you. Bereaved persons will often search for something they should have done to prevent their loved one's death, in part because they want to know how to prevent bad things from happening again in the future, and in part because their sense of themselves as good people is shattered by the fact of their loss (Janoff-Bulman & Frieze, 1983).

Certain types of losses may be more difficult to recover from because they violate more greatly these assumptions or because they require more psychosocial transitions (Parkes, 1993). First, when the deceased dies suddenly, survivors have no chance to prepare for their loss practically or emotionally, for example by making sure that wills are in order and that survivors will have sufficient funds to live on after the death, or by saying good-byes to the loved one who is going to die. Second, violent deaths, due to homicide, accidents, or suicides, are more likely to shatter basic assumptions about the goodness of life and the world and may require more adjustment. Third, the death of a child or young adult seems more likely to shatter these same assumptions, and is viewed widely as more difficult to adjust to than the death of an older person. Fourth, when a death occurs at a time when an individual is undergoing many other transitions (such as when a young person loses a parent during puberty or a man loses his wife at the same time he is retiring), or when a death is just one of several traumatic events that happen to an individual in a short period of time, then the individual must undergo massive, multiple changes simultaneously, making successful adjustment more difficult.

The stress and coping models also identify characteristics of the social environment that can help an individual adjust to a loss. The most important of these is the quantity and quality of social support available to the individual (Parkes, 1990; Vachon & Stylianos, 1988). People who have friends and family members who can help them adapt to all the changes the loss requires should, according to these models, adjust more easily and quickly to their loss than people who do not have this type of social support. Friends and family members may help the bereaved to come to terms with the loss by providing a philosophical or religious perspective on the loss, and restoring a sense that the world is benevolent and controllable, and that they are a good person. Friends and family members can also provide practical support following the loss, in the form of financial help, assistance in settling an estate, finding a new home or a job, or finding caretakers for surviving children.

Finally, there are a number of personality characteristics that can facilitate or impede adjustment to a loss, according to the stress and coping models. The coping skills or strategies of the bereaved person have been examined in many studies. Similar to the psychoanalytic theories, the stress and coping theories suggest that people who deny or avoid thinking about the loss will adjust more poorly because it takes a certain amount of thinking about the loss to incorporate it into one's worldview. The stress and coping theories also note that by not thinking about the loss, the individual will not habituate to the painful feelings associated with the loss. In addition, in order to shut off thoughts about the loss, the individual may engage in dangerous avoidant behaviors, such as heavy drinking, which carry their own maladaptive consequences. Thus, the stress and coping theories suggest that people who cope with their loss by denying it and avoiding thoughts about it will have poorer recoveries than people who do not have this coping style.

We have investigated a coping strategy that is the polar opposite of avoidance and denial (Nolen-Hoeksema, Parker, & Larson, 1994). We call this coping strategy *rumination*, and it involves focusing chronically and passively on one's distress without doing anything to overcome the distress. Thus, people who ruminate after a loss will spend much time thinking about the loss and their grief-related symptoms of sadness, emptiness, and loneliness. But they remain stuck in ruminative cycles of focusing on their negative symptoms rather than moving forward toward some acceptance of the loss and reengagement in life.

Other theorists have focused on differences between bereaved people in their appraisals of the meaning of the loss for their lives (Epstein, 1993). For one widow, the loss of her husband may mean the loss of her self-definition and her status in the community. For another widow, the loss of her husband may mean release from a tyrant and the freedom to pursue her own desires. Obviously these two meanings may lead to very different levels of distress following the loss.

A bereaved person's appraisal of his or her loss may be affected by a number of personality characteristics (Epstein, 1993; Sanders, 1993; Stroebe & Stroebe, 1993; Vachon et al., 1982). For example, people who are dependent on others for their self-definition and self-esteem will find losses more difficult to adjust to because they require a greater reorganization of self-concept and everyday life. People who are generally pessimistic, who believe they have little control over their lives, or who are emotionally unstable or neurotic, should recover less quickly and fully from loss than others because they appraise the loss as more threatening and are less able to regulate their emotions in adaptive ways.

Summing Up Stress and Coping Models

The stress and coping models of bereavement suggest that loss is a psychosocial transition or trauma that challenges people's basic assumptions about the world and requires massive reorganization of daily life and self-concept. To recover from a loss, people must adjust their working theories of the world to accommodate their loss. This is more difficult when the circumstances around the loss challenge people's basic assumptions about the goodness of the world and themselves. It is also more difficult for people who have little social support. People who have avoidant or overly ruminative coping styles may have more difficulty in regulating their grief-related emotions. And finally, people whose personalities are characterized by dependency, pessimism, lack of control and emotional instability will have more trouble adjusting to the loss.

ORGANIZATION OF THE BOOK

In the remainder of this volume, we review empirical studies that have tested predictions about which people will have difficulty in adjusting to a loss from either traditional models of bereavement or the stress and coping models. In chapter 2, we focus on the circumstances of the loss, and demographic characteristics of bereaved people in predicting adjustment to loss. We are interested in whether certain types of losses—anticipated versus sudden, loss of a child versus loss of an adult, loss due to violent death versus loss due to natural causes—generally affect people's ability to adjust.

In chapter 3, we test the claims that the ways people cope with their grief-related symptoms, and their global personality traits influence their recovery following loss. In chapter 4, we examine the impact of the social context of the bereaved person on his or her ability to adjust to a loss. Here we investigate the role of social support, religion, and support groups in bereaved people's recovery over time.

Chapter 5 focuses on the special case of children who lose a loved one. Although there is much less empirical research on bereaved children than on bereaved adults, it is critical that we understand the similarities and differences in children's and adults' bereavement experiences. In chapter 6, we shift our focus from people who adjust poorly to a loss to people who seem to adjust remarkably well following a loss, and perhaps even find new strengths and personal growth in the loss experience.

Finally, in chapter 7, we discuss the types of interventions that seem to help bereaved people who are having difficulty adjusting to their loss. We put special attention on what health care professionals in the medical and hospice system may be able to do to improve the adjustment of bereaved people with whom they interact.

At the end of each chapter, we have a section we call Voices. This section honors the differences in the ways the people in our study experienced and expressed their loss by providing them with the space to make those expressions, with a minimum of commentary from us.

Voices

The respondents described a wide range of emotional and cognitive responses to their loss. Some of these emotions were especially strong in the first month after the loss, but for some respondents, strong emotions remained for several months after.

> Right now, I can't see too far into the future, and I can't seem to deal real well with the past. It's sort of like I'm in limbo right now. See, I haven't cried once since my husband died. I cried a lot before he died. Just, even though you expect someone is going to die, it's shocking. And probably I did a lot of my grieving then, as I saw him wasting away. That first year was terrible—I cried a lot. And then I cried in the middle. But it seems like I didn't have tears. (60-year-old woman who lost her husband 1 month previously)

I believe the death more than before. Which is so natural. When something happens to your neighbors, your relatives which are not very close to you, you always believe (that you know the reason—because they were bad, and that) it can't happen to you. That's human nature. But when somebody is really close to you … you say, "Oh, no. There is such a thing." And you will believe it. No matter you want it or you don't, you have to believe it. (39-year-old woman who lost a parent 1 month previously)

Just so I feel happy again—I don't feel happy at all. I miss her a lot. When she first died that Saturday, it happened that I got a surge of energy, until the day we buried her. Then, boom, collapse. (55-year-old woman who lost a parent 1 month previously)

See, there's that Limbo part. I know it's real, but sometimes it feels unreal. And I think the reason is it's fairly recent. Because I know that the grief just 1 week after—I think the Good Lord intended it that way so that you could draw away from it. But it was so REAL that I could almost feel him. I could almost feel like if he was here I could hug him, and just be a little nicer. That's how real it was. It's a dimension that really escapes you at times. It can be hard to take, and at the same time you have to face it. It's part of life. … And everybody has their own process. (69-year-old woman who lost her spouse 1 month previously)

The first week or two, a little bit of a numbness. I did focus on the positive aspects of his death, on the fact that there was no more discomfort for him, tiredness. I think what got me through was that I knew that he had a strong sense of dying, that he wasn't afraid, and it was a beautiful thing. So that's what got me through the first couple weeks. Then after that, just remembering the wonderful times we had. Now I can also think more about how much I miss him and the emptiness I feel. I think before it was a protective mechanism to help me through some painful days. Then I got through that, and I'm more thinking about the loss. When he first died, I really felt like he was still around. I felt his presence for almost a month. I knew he was with me. Then about 3 weeks afterward, I knew he was gone. (47-year-old woman who lost a parent 6 months previously)

When she finally goes, you're out of jail. For a little while, you're re-leased—you can go up to the hills for a few days if you want, not have to call home to see how things are. So you're almost in a euphoria for a few weeks. Then it gets to sink in. Actually, you have a bit of a high—it's not really a high—and then you start coping with all the things you have to cope with. I guess after, 3 or 4 months out, things are worse than you expected that they would be 3 or 4 months out. (74-year-old man who lost his wife 6 months previously)

I'm depressed sometimes. Everybody says, "Well give it a year and a half or two and you'll start feeling better about it." But somehow I haven't noticed that I feel any better about it now. At the time I was so numb, and tired, that some days I think I coped better right at the first than I do now. I very much need something worthwhile to do, and I just don't know where to start. If I thought I was being useful or doing something useful, that'd be different, but all I'm doing is making myself go from day to day now. Some mornings I just think, "Why do I have to get up?" but you always do. Once I get going and get out and around, then I'm all right. It seems like he's been gone a lot longer than 6 months now. (70-year-old woman who lost her husband 6 months previously)

I realized that I'm not as strong as I think I am. You think you're strong, but something happens and you find you're not. If anybody had told me that my mother dying was going to wipe out my life, I'd have said—you know—In fact, I found out I'm a lot more sensitive to those kinds of things. (36-year-old woman who lost a parent 6 months previously)

You see, all the things that I thought were going to happen didn't, so it came as a big surprise. I wasn't prepared. I thought I would be scrubbing pots and shining up my house. And these are things I'm finding very uninterest-ing—I'm not doing it. The things I thought were going to keep me busy, and be like therapy for me, that's not happening. That is surprise me. (71-year-old woman who lost her husband 6 months previously)

The pain has eased off. It's not as bad as it was. You know, this pain—no one understands if they haven't been through it. There are no words. It's not pain like you cut your arm. It's a terrible pain—no one knows. You have to feel it yourself to know. It's here [hand on heart]. (65-year-old man who lost his wife 13 months previously)

I'm still learning to deal with the guilt that I felt, because I was pregnant and I wanted attention being pregnant, even though he was sick. I don't know how to describe it. I was feeling like "put him out of his misery." I was feeling really selfish at that time and I'm still dealing with the guilt of "how could I have felt that way?" when my only brother was dying and I was feeling that way. So I'm still trying to learn that. There's nothing positive though. I don't see anything positive. I know—I wanted all the attention and all the glory of this new little baby that was growing inside me. Yes, I was concerned and loved my brother and was devastated by what was hap-pening, but it was almost like I didn't want it to drag on and on and on and on. I wanted it to end. I didn't want him to die, but I wanted him to not suffer anymore. But I felt guilty for having those feelings. (27-year-old woman who lost her brother 18 months previously)

Sometimes when I used to go to the doctor, I wouldn't answer questions that they asked. But now, if I'm the least bit suspicious or worried about anything concerning me and my children, I feel free to talk with the doctor. I don't keep anything hidden from him. When I go to the doctor, I guess I worry them to death. I'm always wanting to know how would I know if my circulation was poor, different things. I'd insist that she take my blood to see if my potassium is at a level that's safe. So I found that since his death, I'm a lot concerned about my feelings and the children's feelings and encouraging them to at least go and see.... I just feel that there is hope and there's a chance that anything can be corrected if it's caught in time. So I freely talk with my doctors about things that I want to know more about. (60-year-old woman who lost her husband 18 months previously)

It's very dim, has no real impact. Sometimes I even think she's still alive. I've actually thought about picking up the phone to call her. Isn't that strange—I haven't accepted. I think of how she'd react to something. I want to tell her something good. I think about finality of death. My uncle had the last words with her. They were angry and he has a lot of guilt. He wants his words back. When they go, they're gone forever. (51-year-old man who lost his sister 18 months previously)

I've accepted it more. Now the things I think about when I think about my mother are the good things, before she had developed senile dementia, the fun things that we used to have. So I remember the fun things. If I really analyzed it, I could remember the down side of her illness, like in the middle of the night when the phone rang. That was horrible, I try to block it out. Now when I think about her, I think about the good times we had and the fun things we did, the traveling we did together. If I really stop and think, I can go to the negative, but I try not to. That was too horrible to even think about. (46-year-old woman who lost a parent 18 months previously)

The death of somebody you love, or maybe just seeing death, I'm not sure—it's amazing to me how much that psychic trauma can affect every-thing about your physical life. It still manifests physical behaviors even 2 years later, maybe even 5 years later, I'm not sure. But I know that I'm still part of some kind of process that my brain and body are going through. It has nothing to do with my will. I might will myself free of it, but my brain and my body still go through it. (43-year-old woman who lost her husband 18 months previously)

I guess I can see a pattern and I think I've improved since—. I feel better, and time does heal. After a year and a half it's been easier for me, even though there are times when I still get emotional and teary-eyed over just thinking about her; that hasn't gone and probably won't, ever. But you have to realize that life goes on. I had a conversation with my oldest son. He said that Christmas was difficult for him because he missed his mother and all the things she used to do at Christmas time. He said it was a little strange. So I said I was glad that he told me that because I felt the same way—that I missed her also and just wanted to let him know that he's not alone, that we all still feel that way. I was glad to hear he felt that way because sometimes the younger ones don't say too much about their mother. They seem to be very, very happy. It's probably true that the older ones are more attached; of course they lived longer with her and they have that bond. They younger ones—Kerry was only 9 when she died—. It makes a difference when you're a little bit older. You have all those things to look back on. (44-year-old man who lost his wife 18 months previously)

I haven't gone into any of the places we used to go, like for breakfast Friday mornings. I haven't gone into any of those, since. That kind of helps things along. I don't know. We used to go back East every year to visit family. Last year I went back for the first time by myself and it was a little rough. I went back this year and it was a little bit easier. I suppose it'll get easier still as it goes along. But, can't change it. You learn to live with it. (73-year-old woman who lost her husband 18 months previously)

I was a very angry person for 6 months; not only that, very sad for 6 months. In fact I've had several people comment on my job in the last 4 months that I'm back to the old me. I'm not the kind of person who smiles just for the sake of smiling or putting on airs, and if I was sad, they knew I was sad; I told them, so they would give me space, so it was easier for me to work—I didn't have to pretend. And if people said, "How are you doing?" I didn't lie; I said, "I'm not doing good today. It's not a good day." So I didn't have to put out all that energy. (47-year-old woman who lost her son 18 months previously)

I guess it's even more frustrating when you see other people that are so unappreciative of life, senior citizens especially. Everybody's retired in our neighborhood, and a lot of widows. What my Mom would have given to have their problems and still be alive! That's real frustrating. You feel like shaking these people and saying, "Don't you realize what you've got? Don't you realize how fortunate you are just to be alive and have your family and your friends?" They just don't realize what they have. (31-year-old woman who lost her parent 18 months previously)

In each interview, we asked the respondents if they felt the death was "real." They provided a range of answers that illustrate the ways the mind deals with the mysteries of death. Some excerpts from the first interview, conducted 1 month after the loved one's death:

I thought that he was there this morning. I mean, we were very close, and. … I know, practically, he's not there, but, you know, he's been around so long, and I can see him in front of my eyes, you know. (37-year-old man who lost a sibling)

I don't know if I think she's dead, I don't know. I think she lives in me. I think as long as I live, my mother will live in me. Whenever the weather changes, I remember her. I told my brother "don't feel sad about thinking about her. Think about her like when she was still alive—it's not a sin to think about her. It's real. She lives with you. She's a part of you." (47-year-old woman who lost a mother)

(At the funeral) I could feel my Dad there (not the remains, that wasn't him) … I felt him for 2 weeks. I could drive along the freeway and it would be a beautiful day, and I would know that Dad was there. It might be because he decided that I was ok, maybe he worried about me more, I don't know, but I feel like he has gone on, and that's the way it should be…. What is so heartwarming is that I feel that he cuddled us, each our own way. (48-year-old woman who lost a father)

I have mixed feelings. I know he's dead, but sometimes I don't feel like he is. And sometimes I feel like he is. But I feel like he's trying to contact me. If not him, something. Before he died, I asked him, if it was at all possible, to come back and tell me he was ok; we did that for about a year (brought it up occasionally). (Described hearing knocks, hearing him call her, a tobacco smell that comes and goes—a friend mentioned the smell in her car, on sweater.) I feel like he's been here, on and off. I know that it's not going to last 'cause he has to get on his own way and complete his journey. But I feel like he came back to let me know that he was ok. I thought it was unique, but then I read a book, and it's real common. (60-year-old woman who lost her husband)

Over the course of the remaining interviews, done 6, 13, and 18 months after the loss, more respondents indicated that they felt the death was real, but some respondents said that they still did not feel the loss was real, at least not emotionally. They also described the changes in their emotions and attitudes toward the loss that had occurred since the loss.

I feel as though it's almost schizophrenic. Intellectually I know—I was here. Part of me thinks I'd find him in bedroom, or he'll come back. It's not a conscious thought, just a want. It started in last month. Grieving takes a tremendous amount of energy. (56-year-old woman who lost her spouse, 6 months postloss)

It's very real. It's very real because I experienced it from the beginning to the end. I know that it was not a fantasy, or I don't know how to explain it—I was in touch with the process of it. I was totally aware of what was going on every step of the way, which was very helpful. I found that it wasn't frightening. (55-year-old woman who lost a parent, 6 months postloss)

It doesn't feel real. For a long time, I felt like she was on vacation and she was just going to call me up or show up. The woman who I cared for during the year wasn't really my mother, and so it's like my mother just went away. I don't know if it's going to get more real. Sometimes I think that I'll never really feel like it happened. (33-year-old woman who lost a parent, 6 months postloss)

At this point, it's pretty real. For about a month afterwards, it was numb. And then gradually it became depression. Now it's sort of become a reality in its own perspective. (41-year-old woman who lost a parent, 6 months postloss)

I think I'm beginning to realize that he's gone. I just think it's taking me a long time to realize it. It just seems like I know he's gone, but sometimes I find myself leaving notes … on the refrigerator. I've done that a couple of times. But I think that it's getting a little easier than it was. (56-year-old woman who lost her spouse, 6 months postloss)

I still find myself—my kneejerk reaction is, "I have to tell Mom" and then I realize (that she's gone) and then I feel sad. So in that sense it hasn't all the way permeated. Lots of times it's real, but the realness has with it a real sadness. Someday it will just be a fact of life, like the fact that I have green eyes. When I see mothers and grown daughters together, I just get angry, especially when they are being really awful to one another. Like in the mall, I see families together, and I feel cheated and angry and sad, real sorry she's gone. I was also profoundly aware of the next generation—that the generation ahead of me is gone now, and we're the next one. So my own aging is very evident. (40-year-old woman who lost a parent, 13 months postloss)

When you're dead, you're dead, deadsville, croaked, gone. You're not coming back, period. (27-year-old man who lost a parent, 18 months postloss)

Oh, it's definitely real. For a long time it was very, very hard. I knew the death was real, I saw him, but it was just really hard to fathom that. The reality of death, how real—it's permanent, it's forever here on earth, never again, it's definite—you don't realize the impact of that until you're in that place. It's awesome, incredibly awesome! (42-year-old woman who lost a parent, 18 months postloss)

It's very real. He's not here anymore. But sometimes I think I just can't believe it. I can't believe that happened to our family, if that makes any sense at all. It's very real, but I just can't believe it happened. I can't believe I can't pick up the phone and call, or that he can't come see his new little nephew. It's senseless and it should not have happened. He should not have gotten cancer and died. The only thing I can make sense out of is that this is what God wanted—to relieve him from his pain. I don't know if my parents would have lasted if he would have continued for another year. (27-year-old woman who lost a sibling, 18 months postloss)

It's amazing, can't put a finger on it. I know it's happened, that I'm supposed to accept it, but—. It's like walking through a mirror, no return. I feel he's a part of me, so he's not completely gone because I think of him often and have lots of tangible things from him—haven't given [them] up. That's how it made it ok for him to exit. I use his personal things—makes me feel better. (45-year-old woman who lost a sibling, 18 months postloss)

It doesn't feel real. I still feel like she should be here. I still in my mind am talking to her. On the other hand, there's so many thousands of people that die from cancer that why would it exclude our family? They say time heals, but I'm still waiting. (30-year-old woman who lost a parent, 18 months postloss)

It's very real. When he died, I saw him dead and I saw them come in and take him out, and that kept going through my mind over and over. It was like a replay. I could not get that out of my mind. I think it was my brain's way of telling me it really happened because death is such a hard thing to really grasp. But it wasn't haunting—it was like it was just constantly there—you really saw him dead and he is really gone. … Every time we go by my Dad's apartment, I think of him sitting in there in that chair, even though I know he's not; but it's kind of a nice thought, of him sitting there. Sometimes I even say, "Hi, Dad!" But it's very real. (40-year-old woman who lost a parent, 18 months postloss)

I'd say it's very real. I don't let things get to me where I get real emotional and get real upset about things. I think I'm true to form with her death. I think there's a period where your just kind of numb, and you're just on automatic pilot. I was. It's very real to me. I think subconsciously I try not to think a lot about it, just to stay away from the pain and the discomfort of it. I don't blame anybody. I don't dwell on it. I guess I used to think about it more often than I am right now, with another relationship happening. I think my mind's on that more often, which is good. I just don't want to forget. I don't want the children to forget. I think getting more active in the church was to try to help—I guess I'm not getting everything I wanted to out of that. I want to know why it happened. I really don't know, I haven't got an answer. I haven't gotten peace within myself as to why or what it means. I wish I could get there. Maybe as time goes on I will. Just the cliche—it doesn't seem fair. But it's definitely real. I don't have an answer, but I've asked myself that. That religion thing—I feel kind of guilty that I'm not more at peace with it. I feel that as a Christian and somebody that's going to church I should have more peace with this being something that is God's will and that there is a good reason for it. I haven't come to that. That bothers me. I wish I felt more at peace with it, understood it more. (45-year-old man who lost his wife, 18 months postloss)

It's like I forget. Sometimes it doesn't feel real at all, and sometimes it feels very real. I notice there are a couple things that I've really been avoiding doing. One has been going anywhere close to where he used to live—it's just real uncomfortable for me. And another is, there was a group of about 10 of us who cared for him before he died. We were able to keep him from being hospitalized. I feel guilty because I feel I did the least of any of them. We tried to be with him in shifts. It was an amazing experience. It was an incredible experience. We became like a family. We had meetings with each other, just to talk about our emotional state, to plan mechanics of food, social worker contacts, visiting nurse contacts, his parents. I'm sure I'll never have another experience like that again with a group of people. And they're wonderful people and we all said we'd keep in touch, and we would maintain the relationship, and I noticed that I haven't done that. I've spoken with a few of the a couple of times, but not at all what I thought I would do. What was the question? I guess I kind of got off track. Sometimes it seems very real and I miss him very much. And sometimes I forget that he's gone. (48-year-old man who lost a close friend, 18 months postloss)

It's less real now than it was when it happened because it's less painful now. In a sense it's more real now, it's more normal now. The fact that my Mom's dead and she's not around is very much like she's in LA and I'm up here. That's the way it seems now. It's real and it's not real, it's surreal. It's been hard. It's all those things at once. Death is a bizarre state. (36-year-old man who lost a parent, 18 months postloss)

It's 100% real. I've gone through all the denial, shock, all of that. One of the things that came to me is that acceptance is freedom. Once I reached full acceptance of his death, which was about 6 months ago, it gave me a sense of freedom. He wasn't coming back, no matter how much I cried. So I don't think about his death; I think about how much I miss him. (47-year-old woman who lost her son, 18 months postloss)

Right afterward it didn't feel real. Now it feels real, but in a funny way. It's pretty hard to grasp that someone's not there. You know intellectually they're not. I guess it's harder for me because I never saw her that much. I didn't live there. My sister saw her a lot. I think it's been a lot easier for her to adjust to it. For me, my mother is—I think about her a lot. I know she's dead, but it's real hard to grasp. I'm surprised that I still think about her so much. I've had a lot of dreams about her too. It's funny, because we weren't really very close. It's real hard to accept it. I feel like I've accepted it, but death is a difficult thing. There isn't any way to prepare people for it either. (45-year-old woman who lost a parent, 18 months postloss)

It doesn't seem real. I lost both my mother and my father. It was his birthday last Friday and I went to the cemetery, and it was completely unreal to me. (Interviewer: Your father's death?) Both of them. It's not real. I really feel that they're with me, and it's just my spiritual belief. I just feel that they're not there in that ground. My life feels very unreal. (Interviewer: So it's not just their death?) No. It's everything that's happening and that's going and ongoing. I feel like I'm in limbo right now. (50-year-old woman who lost a parent, 18 months postloss)

We asked the respondents if they had ever asked themselves, "why me?" Many said they had never asked the question. Those who did ask the question sometimes found an answer in religion or their personal philosophy. Often, when people asked the question, they didn't ask "why me?" but "why my loved one?"

Why my husband. Prayer and therapy helped. I just questioned why someone who was basically a good human being would be forced to go through so much pain. But then he set a good example for others, so that's how God wished it to be. You have to accept what you're given. It takes a while sometimes to put it all in perspective. (You have to learn to) accept it—or live with it, not accept it. (48-year-old woman who lost her husband)

It's God's will. It's God's choice. God has a purpose for everything. Actually I have a belief in a mixture of straight Catholicism, but at some level I believe in reincarnation. So I believe that he and I had some contract to live this life together, and we did it. Now, whatever is in store for me, we'll have to wait and see what it is. Only once, when my brother was diagnosed—he was dying of cancer 2 months ago. I said, "Why me? I've had it. This load is too heavy." Then I realized that if you believe in God you have the strength to survive anything—to meet it and deal with it. (Interviewer: So you feel it's God's will?) Everything is God's will in the long shot. I can't figure out, there *is* no figuring out the reason, why he died of AIDS as opposed to a heart attack, but that's not for me to know, I guess. (60-year-old woman who lost her husband)

Everyone asks it, but no one can answer it. I don't think it should be asked. If not me, then someone else, and I wouldn't wish that on anyone. The suffering B. went through—no one should have to suffer like that. (53-year-old man who lost his son)

Sometimes when I see other people I wonder, "Why Max and not you, you asshole?" But it's rhetoric, I mean—what's not fair? (48-year-old woman who lost her husband)

Yes, why my mother. It's so hard to answer. She was such a good person it's hard to understand why God would choose to take her. I lost a brother in 1974 at age 26—there's still that left over. A drunk driver hit him. My son was born on his birthday. (38-year-old woman who lost a parent)

It doesn't make any sense. Rationally it makes a lot of sense ... disease.... But in a spiritual way, maybe it does make sense—maybe.... There's lessons from all of this. (49-year-old woman who lost her husband)

There's never sense out of death. Somebody so young, too young, too much ahead of him, kids too young, shouldn't have to grow up without a father. Not fair, life isn't fair. (40-year-old woman who lost her husband)

I've always planned that I was going to go first. I smoked too much and I was too fat. I had all the finances and everything all set up, educated my eldest son how to take care of things after I was gone, and it didn't work out. It went the other way. Why did it happen? I don't know. (63-year-old man who lost his wife)

Many of the respondents who had been caregivers to their loved ones before they died expressed deep appreciation for having had the experience.

I think being with him when he died, and seeing ... death being a very natural process. I think it was tremendous. I think it was just a fantastic experience. The last breaths, being there. Although he had cancer he died a kind of natural death because he just kept kind of winding down. (Described physical death)—a natural progression. I think it's wonderful to experience that. And to have someone be allowed to die the way he wants without being (subjected to intervention), just to accept what's happening and have faith in the future. One of my daughters was here. She said she had no idea death was so beautiful. Her fears of death were just gone because it was so natural. (54-year-old woman who lost a parent)

Finally, many respondents expressed a personal philosophy about death and loss.

I think that my father's illness was meant to be, and that was God's plan. He lived a really long life, and everybody has their way to go out from this world, and that was his way. (55-year-old woman who lost a parent)

We had so many happy times. It's just life, that's all. We're never given somebody to last forever. I think I appreciate everybody a lot more. Everytime you lose somebody you think, "Oh gosh!" and then you appreciate the ones you still have. (61-year-old woman who lost an adult child)

My mother has passed through an open door from this life into the next and I shall someday be there with her. Her life is changed, and I'm not ready for my change yet. It's very real, but it won't be forever. There it is, a matter of faith. (56-year-old woman who lost a parent)

I'm a Christian and I believe in the hereafter. She's with God and I think she's probably happier. When she died, somebody said, "You know, I'll betcha God's got a big garden up there for her." I said, "I hope so." (Interviewer: Ever ask, "Why me?") Other than go back to what the Bible, which says don't challenge God. Did you create the world? Then who are you to challenge God? (56-year-old woman who lost her sibling)

One can never make sense of a death unless they've given up to God—that's what I've heard. People can make sense of things that are unpleasant as long as they don't take responsibility for it and put the responsibility someplace else. It's easy for religious people, because you need something to grab onto to help you through. Fortunately or unfortunately, I don't know. I haven't been able to say, "God knows best." I haven't been able to get to that point yet. I have talked myself into what I want to believe. (Summary: Talked about heaven and hell with her son. He asked her permission to die. She said,) "Go ahead, die. I'll see you in heaven." So in my mind I will see him again. And wherever he is, his spirit or whatever is ok. That's my way of making some sense of it. It works for me, because I'm a logical person. Things have to make sense to me. I'm not very good at the unknown The other thing is I don't allow other people to tell me how I should feel. It's not my personality. I don't allow you to tell me how I should think. I have to accept the fact that I will always have a void, for the rest of my life. (47-year-old woman who lost her child)

2

The Special Challenges
of Different Types
# of Losses

I think you never really come to terms with the death of a young person. (Ellen, 45, whose 20-year-old son died of AIDS)

I can't accept the way my son died. He was a police officer and I always knew he could be killed. But the way it happened was so senseless. (David, 62, whose 40-year-old son died of cancer)

I had 6½ years to prepare for her death while she was ill. That should have made it easier. But it didn't. (Harriet, 50, who lost her 70-year-old mother to cancer)

As these quotes illustrate, all types of losses can be experienced as extremely difficult. This chapter explores the special difficulties of several different types of losses. A theme emerging from our analysis of the literature and of our own data is that each type of loss carries its own meanings and set of stresses with which survivors must cope. There are few broad generalizations that can be made about what type of loss is most difficult to bear. Instead, the circumstances of different types of losses may require different strategies for coping and different types of support from family members and friends.

LOSS OF A CHILD

One of the strongest bonds of attachment in human experience is that between a parent and child (Bowlby, 1969). Children represent their parents' greatest hopes, their "immortality project" (Yalom, 1989). The death of a child violates the natural order: Parents are supposed to die before their children (Videka-Sherman, 1982). Said one participant in our bereavement study who lost his 31-year-old son,

> Children are not supposed to predecease you. It's not the law of the land, so to speak. When they do it just throws everything just a little bit off center. Children are supposed to be around to love you in your old age, to take care of you, come over to see how you're doing, and when they go before you, it's just this great big huge void in your life that's never going to be filled. I don't know. It's just a strange, strange feeling.

The death of a child can also challenge people's most strongly held assumptions about goodness and evil. Thus, even people who are not related to a child who dies often feel strongly moved by a child's death:

> When I heard that David's daughter was killed in a car accident, I just cried and cried. I never really knew the girl—I only met her once. But just the idea that a person could lose his child hit me very hard. I knew David would be devastated and I cried for him, too.

Thus, it is not surprising that several studies find bereaved parents experience more intense and longer lasting grief symptoms than any other group of bereaved people (Littlefield & Rushton, 1986; although see McHorney & Mor, 1988; Murphy, 1988; Rando, 1986). For example, Sanders (1979) found that parents who had lost a child 2 months earlier showed greater depression, anger, guilt, and despair than people who had lost a spouse or parent. Similarly, a study focusing on bereaved women found that bereaved mothers were more depressed than both widows or bereaved daughters when questioned about 10 months after their loss (Leahy, 1992). Indeed, more than 60% of the bereaved mothers scored in the moderate-to-severe range of the depression inventory used.

In our bereavement study, we also found higher levels of depression in the parents of adult children who died than any other bereaved group (see Fig. 2.1).[1] Parents were also less likely than any other family group to say they could make

---

[1]Repeated measures analysis of variance of depression scores at 1, 6, 13, and 18 months revealed significant main effects of time, $F(3, 213) = 7.90, p < .001$; relationship to the deceased $F(3,214) = 3.39$, $p < .05$; and a marginally significant interaction between relationship to the deceased and gender $F(3, 214 = 2.29, p = .079$. The main effects of gender and all other interaction terms were nonsignificant. Repeated measures analyses of variance on (PTSD), anxiety, health, and general distress scores showed no significant differences by relationship to the deceased or gender interactions.

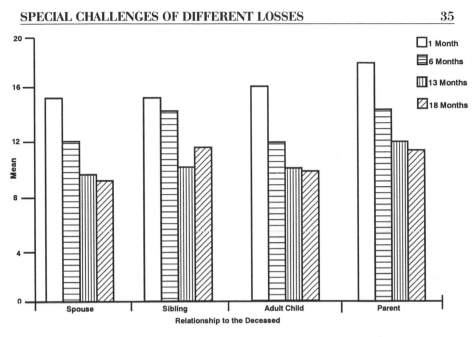

FIG. 2.1. Self-reported depression from 1 to 18 months in different family group members.

sense of the loss of their child (Fig. 2.2).[2] As these parents, all of whom lost adult children to terminal illnesses, said:

I just think he was robbed and cheated of life. He could have been anything. He was deprived.

I just think it was a senseless waste. There's no redeeming factor.

It just seems too unfair. She hadn't started her life. She hadn't done any of the things she had planned on doing.

I feel I never will [make sense of his death]. I quote the Serenity Prayer quite often and I will never make sense of this. Perhaps that's because I'm not a deeply religious person and I'm not one to say that God did it for a reason and a purpose, so I don't fall back on that. So, since I don't fall back on that, I will never find sense in it. I will just accept it. I accept it because I have no choice, not because I want to.

We might expect mothers of deceased children to be even more depressed than the fathers, both because in the general population women typically have higher levels of depression than men (Nolen-Hoeksema, 1995) and because the

---

[2]Chi-square tests showed significant differences at $p < .05$ between family groups in whether they answered "yes" or "no" to the question "Do you feel you have been able to make sense of the death?" at each of the 1-, 6-, 13-, and 18-month interviews.

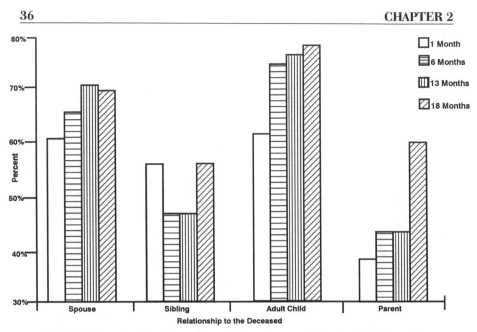

FIG. 2.2. Percent of family members able to make sense of death at 1 to 18 months.

mothers' level of attachment might be expected to be stronger than the fathers' attachment. Some previous studies primarily focusing on parents who lost a newborn or infant have found bereaved mothers to have higher levels of distress than fathers (Bohannon, 1990; Cornwall, Nurcombe, & Stevens, 1977; Dyregrov & Matthiesen, 1987; Fish, 1986; Helmrath & Steinitz, 1978; Smith & Borgers, 1988; yet see Defrain, Taylor, & Ernst, 1982; Hunfield, Mourik, Passchier, & Tibboel, 1996). In the case of very young children, mothers are likely to have had much more opportunity than fathers to develop strong attachments to the child, both during the pregnancy, and in the intense days of caring for the child as a newborn and infant.

Many fathers develop strong attachments to their children, however, particularly as the children grow older. Some studies of parents who have lost an adult child find little or no difference in the grief reactions of fathers and mothers—both parents suffer greatly (Florian, 1989; Lieberman, 1989). Parents who lose an adult child to illness, accidents, or in war, often have heightened levels of anxiety, depression, and physical illness years after their loss (de Vries, Davis, Wortman, & Lehman, 1997; Levav, Friedlander, Kark, & Peritz, 1988; Rubin, 1993; Shanfield & Swain, 1984). In our study, all the children who died were adult children, and we found that fathers and mothers were both highly distressed, and there was a slight trend for men to show greater distress than women over the course of the study (see Fig. 2.3).

Parents who lose a child are often tormented by thoughts of what they might have done to prevent the child's death. One young father whose 18-month-old son died from burns he received in a kitchen accident said:

> I haven't slept much since it happened [almost a year ago]. I just lay awake every night kicking myself for not watching Alex more closely, thinking that I could have prevented him from getting burnt. I go over and over what happened that night, how I turned to watch the news on the TV, and all of a sudden I heard Alex screaming. I think about how it could have been different, what I should have done.

These "undoing" or counterfactual thoughts are common anytime a traumatic event occurs, particularly if the event is one that parents believe could have been prevented, such as the accident the young father describes. Undoing thoughts may be especially common among bereaved parents because parents feel and are responsible for their children's safety and well-being (Klass & Marwit, 1988). At times, these undoing thoughts are highly irrational—the action the parent thinks could have saved the child truly had nothing to do with the child's death. Here are some "if only" thoughts by parents who lost a child in a traffic accident (Davis & Lehman, personal communication):

> If I'd told him to come on home and not stay for basketball, he'd still be alive.

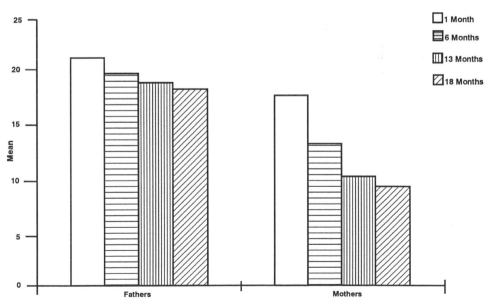

FIG.2.3. Self-reported depression from 1 to 18 months for fathers
and mothers of deceased children.

If I hadn't fixed her bike, it wouldn't have happened.

If I'd bowled better, I would have stayed later in hopes of collecting a jack pot (then we wouldn't have been on the road at the time the accident happened).

Even if the death of their child was completely unavoidable, parents may feel that there must be *something* they could have done to prevent it. When researchers interviewed parents whose infants had died of SIDS, they found that 76% were engaging in undoing thoughts 3 weeks after the infant's death, and 42% were still engaging in undoing thoughts 18 months after the death (Davis, Lehman, Wortman, Silver, & Thompson, 1995). Most of these parents described something that they did or did not do, around the time of the infant's death that they thought might have made a difference. For example, one parent said, "I thought about maybe if I'd stayed awake, or woke up more frequently (to) check on the baby. I keep thinking of different ways" (p. 118). Another parent said, "I've thought about a lot of those things, like if I'd never set him down; if I'd never gone to school that morning; if I had never been going to school, leaving him in the mornings. I thought about it, checking him every 5 to 10 minutes instead of every 15–20 minutes. I thought about all these things I could have done but didn't do" (pp. 118–119).

Even when a child does not die suddenly, but after an extended illness, parents report frequent thoughts about what they should have done to protect their child. In our study, more than 60% of parents who lost their child to cancer thought something could have been done to prevent the illness or death:

I have some guilt—had I done something different—some minute thing—that maybe his life would have been different. I could've been a better mother, things might've been different. (Francis, 52, whose 32-year-old son died of AIDS)

Parents who have lost a child also report being preoccupied with thoughts about their child. A study of parents who lost sons in Israeli wars 4 to 13 years previously found that 87% said they thought about their sons very frequently, with almost all of them thinking about their sons a great deal during family events, on holidays, or on the anniversaries of the death (Rubin, 1993). Some of these parents had pleasant thoughts about their sons, but half of them denied any pleasant feelings associated with the memories, and reported only a sense of sadness and yearning (see also Florian, 1989).

Not surprisingly, the death of a child can also disrupt parents' relationships with each other. Several studies have found that bereaved parents have high rates of separation and divorce following the loss of their child (Kaplan, Smith, Grobstein, & Fischman, 1973; Nixon & Pearn, 1977). For example, a study of 39 couples whose children died in a motor vehicle accident found that 25% of the couples separated or divorced in the 4 to 7 years after their loss, compared to less than 10% of couples in a matched control group of 39 nonbereaved parents (Lehman, Lang, Wortman, & Sorenson, 1989).

Even parents who remain together can experience significant tension in their relationships. Parents may blame one another for the child's death, justifiably or not. They may also grieve differently, one needing to openly express the grief and the other needing to suppress expression of grief (Carroll & Schaefer, 1993; Dyregrov & Matthiesen, 1987). One small study of parents who had lost a newborn infant described the conflicts in patterns of grieving that arose between the husbands and wives in this study, who apparently had highly traditional gender roles:

> The man's frustration grew out of his inability to aid his wife in resolving her feelings of sadness and acute grief, and in finding little support from his wife for his own feelings. Coming home each day after work to a crying, grieving wife proved to be a tremendous problem for each of the men. The women, home alone and without anyone to share their feelings, unloaded their anguish on the only one they felt understood and would listen to them. The found it difficult to understand why their husbands were not feeling the grief as intensely as they themselves. (Helmrath & Steinitz, 1978, p. 789)

Parents' relationships with their surviving children can also be disrupted by the loss. Some parents may idealize the deceased child and hold the surviving child to this idealized standard they have created (Rubin, 1993). Others may be so preoccupied with thoughts of the deceased child that they simply neglect the surviving children. And still others may become overprotective of the surviving children. "I have a underlying sense of impending doom. I worry that something is going to happen to the kids. Not that I carry it all the time, but I just think things are going to happen and that makes me more controlling which is not healthy for the kids" (Martinson, McClowry, Davies, & Kuhlenkamp, 1994, p. 21).

Sometimes, however, the loss of a child can bring parents and families together. In the study of parents whose children died in car accidents, although 21% said their marriage had become worse following the loss, 29% said it had become better:

> Her death has brought us closer together. My husband is more compassionate and listens to me more. More in tune to my feelings than before" and "the pain and harshness of the type of death has strengthened the marriage. We've been able to communicate so much better than before. I've come to appreciate my son and my husband a lot more. (Lehman et al., 1989, pp. 355–356)

In our study of bereavement, more than 60% of bereaved parents interviewed just 1 month after their loss said they had gained something positive in their loss and nearly all interviewed 6 and 13 months after their loss reported finding something positive (for additional discussion of this see chap. 6). They often reported an increase in closeness in their relationships with their spouse and other children.

In summary, the loss of a child can be devastating for many people. It violates the natural order and can cause parents to feel guilt and shame. Some people, however, may be able to achieve new closeness and levels of communication in their relationships with their partners and others as they work together to cope with their loss.

LOSS OF A SPOUSE

The vast majority of bereavement literature has focused on spousal loss. Several studies have found that the surviving spouse often suffers an intense grief reaction in the few months after the loss. Some studies find that by 6 months postloss, many widows and widowers report that their grief symptoms are less intense than just after the loss (Bornstein, Clayton, Halikas, Maurice, & Robins, 1973; Lieberman & Videka-Sherman, 1986; Zisook & Schuchter, 1986).

In our own study, we found levels of depression in bereaved spouses to be highly similar to levels in bereaved adult children and siblings (see Fig. 2.1). Bereaved spouses were also as likely as bereaved adult children and siblings to make sense of their loss (see Fig. 2.2).

Although studies of nonbereaved samples typically find that women report higher levels of depression and distress than men, several studies of widows and widowers have found that men report higher levels of distress than women (Cramer, 1993; Radloff, 1977; Siegel & Kuykendall, 1990; Stroebe & Stroebe, 1983; Umberson, Wortman, & Kessler, 1992). Men also suffer more physical illness and death than women following the loss of a spouse (Cramer, 1993; Gallagher, Thompson, & Peterson, 1981; Jacobs & Ostfeld, 1977; Stroebe, Stroebe, & Schut, 1997)

Men may have a greater propensity than women to depression and physical health problems following loss of a spouse because men are less likely than women to have strong social support networks of people to whom they feel emotionally close (Stroebe & Stroebe, 1983). Roy, whose wife Charlotte, died of a brain tumor 6 months previously said:

> The way I look at things, I think a lady would be able to cope so much easier in my situation than me myself. I think if (my wife) would be here, she had a lot of lady friends ... I'm sure she would keep on going. Me, I'm sitting here in a big empty house. Like today, you're the person that's here talking to me; sometimes it goes for a week (with no one to talk to). The phone doesn't even ring any more.

As seen in chapter 4, having a strong, emotionally supportive social network appears to help people greatly in recovery from loss. Men may also not make use of the social supports they have as much as women do because they are less comfortable openly grieving and taking comfort from others (Stroebe, Stroebe, & Schut, 1997).

Others have argued that widowhood may be more difficult for men than for women because men have more difficulty going on with the tasks of daily living following the death of their spouse. Men usually rely on their wives to do all the cooking, housekeeping, and other daily chores of life. When their wives die, men may literally not know how to care for themselves and the household. Furthermore, if a man is retired, he may be isolated at home, amidst constant reminders of his dead wife and his own inabilities. Umberson, Kessler, and Wortman (1992) found that the daily strains of caring for oneself contributed to depression in men, but not in women. In our study a 45-year-old man whose 38-year-old wife died, leaving him with young children, said:

> It's really hard for me—I'm just not a Mr. Mom guy. I'm lucky to have had [my mother-in-law] around here. It's just overwhelming for me to think about trying to raise a couple young children.

And 65-year-old widowed man said:

> It would have been much better if it had been me. Women cope much better than men with these things. It's been hard learning to do things—laundry, shopping.

Yet not all bereavement studies find that men suffer more following loss than women. Several studies have found higher levels of distress in widows than in widowers (Carey, 1977; Gilbar & Dugan, 1995; Jacobs, Kasl, Ostfield, Berkman, & Charpentier, 1986; Lund, Caserta, & Dimond, 1986; Sanders, 1979; Zisook, Shuchter, & Lyons, 1987). In our own study, widows reported higher levels of depression and physical health problems than the widowers.[3]

Stroebe and Stroebe (1989) argued, however, that interview studies may not paint an accurate picture of the gender differences in depression because different groups of widows and widowers are attracted to interview studies. They suggest that women are more likely than men to find talking about their loss comforting and helpful. Thus, highly distressed widows will be attracted to studies that involve face-to-face interviews because these interviews give them an opportunity to talk about their loss (when family and friends may not wish to hear about the loss) and to receive some social support. In contrast, widowers may find face-to-face interviews distressing because these interviews force them to discuss painful feelings that the widowers are trying to overcome or suppress.

---

[3]Repeated measures analyses of variance on depression scores among bereaved spouses showed a main effect of gender $F(1, 237) = 15.21, p < .001$.

Most of the studies cited earlier showing men to suffer more from widow-hood than women included comparison groups of nonwidowed people. These studies often found that the absolute levels of depression among the widowed were equal or higher in the women than the men. But whereas widowed women often are not more depressed than nonwidowed women, widowed men usually appear significantly more depressed than nonwidowed men. It is this compari-son of widowed women and men to nonwidowed people that has led researchers to conclude that men suffer more from widowhood than women.

The ethnicity of the participants in studies of bereavement may also impact the apparent gender differences in depression among the widowed. A study comparing White and African-American bereaved spouses found no overall differences in levels of depression, but differences between the two groups in the impact of loss on women versus men (Williams, Takeuchi, & Adair, 1992). Among the Whites, the men were consistently more distressed than the women, whereas among the African Americans, the women were consistently more distressed than the men.

The age at which an individual loses a spouse is important to the meaning of the loss and the stresses the survivor must face (Lund, Caserta, & Dimond, 1993). Many people expect to lose their spouse when they are elderly, but they do not expect to lose their spouse in early or middle adulthood. Losing a spouse long before one expects to can shatter those basic assumptions about order and purpose in life. People who lose their spouses in early or middle adulthood report feeling cheated of decades of time they expected to have with their spouse. They also report feeling abandoned. They are often left with young children to raise alone, large mortgages, only a moderate amount of savings, and at best, one income instead of two.

Some studies find more depression and physical health problems in young widows and widowers than in older widows and widowers (Carey, 1977; Jacobs & Ostfeld, 1977; Maddison & Viola, 1967; Parkes, 1964; Vachon et al., 1982; Zisook, Shuchter, & Lyons, 1987). In many of these studies, the young people who lost a spouse lost him or her unexpectedly following an accident or a brief illness, whereas the older bereaved spouses lost their spouse after a more protracted illness. As is discussed later, unexpected losses may be more difficult to adjust to than expected losses. This may be another reason why younger bereaved spouses are sometimes more distressed than older bereaved spouses.

Yet, losing a spouse in old age, after a decades-long relationship, carries its own meanings and burdens. The spouses' lives were intricately intertwined and much of their self-concepts may have been bound up in this relationship. The surviving spouses must completely restructure their lives to live again as a single person, without the companion they have had most of their adult life. Said Agnes, 60, whose 64-year-old husband died of lung cancer:

> When you've been married a long time, that person is the person you confide in, you tell things to, and you know you're communicating, and you just don't have that anymore. And at my age, you don't have time to set it up again.

And Paula, 65, whose husband George, 67, died of prostate cancer:

> I think when you live with someone for a long time, that when they go, you should be able to go, too. I think people should be able to go together. I think it's useless for one person of a pair to stick around. I just think that it should be a natural order of things that if you're together with somebody a long time, you should just go with them when they go. It doesn't make any sense ... we grew up together, really. All those years and all the things we did. I don't want to do anything by myself. I don't want to be alone. It was great with him. It's sure a big zero without him.

Thus, spousal loss can be highly distressing at any age because the loss of a spouse has different meanings for people of different ages.

Finally, some spousal relationships clearly are stronger and more positive than others, and the quality of the spousal relationship can affect the surviving spouse's grief reactions. A widow whose relationship with her husband was warm and supportive, with equity and mutual admiration, may feel a greater sense of loss than a widow whose husband was abusive or distant. Indeed, some spouses may feel primarily relief when they are released from highly negative relationships by the loss. Said Nora, 57, whose husband died of lung cancer:

> For the first time in my life, I don't have to answer to anyone. I'm free to do whatever I want. I don't have to worry about what time I come home, or what I buy, or how I use the money, or how I use the boning knife. ... It's the first time in my life I'm not under someone's wing. I'm accountable to no one. It's nice to be able to test that and see how good it feels. For the first time in my life I don't have to nurture anyone, I don't have to be a caregiver. I get to be the person that I thought I was going to be before I started taking care of people.

On the other hand, psychodynamically oriented theorists have suggested that spouses who were ambivalent or conflictual in their relationship to their deceased spouse will have more difficulty in adjusting to the loss. In support of this claim, a study of 189 widows and widowers found that those who reported having had a difficult, tense relationship with their spouse were more likely to be anxious 2 months following the spouse's death, but were not more depressed, than those who had had a supportive and positive relationship (Zisook, Shuchter, & Lyons, 1987; see also Parkes & Weiss, 1983; Shanfield, 1983).

We asked the bereaved spouses in our study whether they would characterize their relationship with their deceased spouse as having been "consistently close and loving," "close but conflictual," "some affection but conflictual," or "only obligatory." We found no significant differences in depression at any of our interviews between spouses with different types of relationships to their deceased spouse. Thus, it seems that the loss of a close and loving relationship and the loss of a conflictual relationship require different types, but equal levels, of adjustment for spouses.[4]

LOSS OF A PARENT

The meaning of parental loss depends greatly on the child's age. Losing a parent when one is a young child can mean the loss of one's caregiver and primary attachment figure. It can also mean disruption of every aspect of one's daily life—changing all the daily routines, perhaps moving in with other relatives or acquiring a step-parent and step-siblings. We consider children's reactions to the loss of a parent in detail in chapter 5.

Losing a parent as an adult can still have a great impact on an individual. Bowlby (1980) argued that one's primary cargivers remain one's primary attachment figures throughout life. Thus, the loss of a parent still severs the critical attachment bond, even if that loss occurs when one is 50. Said Joanne, 58, who lost her mother:

No matter how old you are you always expect your mother to be there. In a way, you feel like an orphan, especially if you've lost both parents.

Parents clearly represent much that is good or bad about one's life. We hold them responsible for many of our successes and failures. Many of us still seek our parents' approval or advice on what we do in our careers or our families, although we may live thousands of miles away.

In the bereavement literature, there has been relatively little attention paid to the impact of loss of a parent on adults. Leahy (1992) found levels of distress in adult daughters who lost their parents to be lower than either women who had lost a spouse or a child. Similarly, Sanders (1979) found that women and men who had lost a parent scored lower on most measures of distress than those who had lost a spouse or a child (see also Fulton, Gottesman, & Owen, 1982; Owen, Fulton, & Markusen, 1982). In our study, bereaved adults who lost a parent had levels of depression quite similar to those who had lost spouses or

---

[4]Neither repeated measures analyses of variance on depression, nor one-way analyses of variance (ANOVA) on depression scores at individual interviews for spouses showed any significant effects of quality of relationship to deceased.

siblings (see Fig. 2.1). Bereaved daughters were more depressed than bereaved sons. Other studies have found similar results (Pruchno, Moss, Burant, & Schinfeld, 1995; Scharlach, 1991; Umberson & Chen, 1994). Daughters may be more distressed than sons after their parents die because daughters generally spend more time with their parents and report greater emotional closeness with them than do sons (Rossi & Rossi, 1990; Umberson, 1992).

Just as with spousal relationships, some relationships between adult children and parents are closer and more positive than others. Yet, in our study, there was no significant relationship between the bereaved adult children's level of distress and how close or conflictual their relationship with their deceased parent had been. Similarly, a larger study of bereaved adult children found no relationship between the closeness of the relationship with the deceased parent and the intensity of grief reactions (Umberson & Chen, 1994).

In our study, the bereaved who lost a parent were somewhat more likely to say they could make sense of their loss over time than people who had lost a child, spouse, or sibling (Fig. 2.2). It may be easier to accept and understand the loss of a parent, who was usually elderly and had been ill for some time, as part of the natural order of things. Thus, the loss of a parent can be associated with significant stresses and distress, but many adults may be able to accept their loss more easily than other types of losses because they expect such losses as part of the natural order.

LOSING A SIBLING

The loss of a sibling can hold many meanings. Few other types of losses confront us with our own mortality as much as the loss of a sibling because siblings are typically close to our own age. Siblings are also lifelong partners of a kind. They shared our parents, our home, our growing-up years. Often a sibling is the only one who understands what it was like to live the life we lived as a child.

Sibling relationships may also be the most likely to be characterized by ambivalence or conflict of all the relationships we have discussed thus far. Jealousies and resentments can simmer for decades between siblings, covered by silences and separation. When a sibling dies, the surviving sibling is left to resolve these conflicts alone.

Unfortunately, although many people will experience the death of a sibling at some time in their adult life, the impact of sibling loss has been generally ignored in the adult bereavement literature. In our study, the bereaved siblings were as depressed as the bereaved spouses and adult children (see Fig. 2.1). Moreover, bereaved siblings were less likely than bereaved spouses or adult children to be able to make sense of their sibling's death (Fig. 2.2). The women who lost a sibling were more depressed than the men who lost a sibling. There was no relationship between how close and loving the siblings felt their relationship had been with the deceased and their levels of depression after the loss, however.

COMPARING THE LOSS OF A CHILD, SPOUSE, PARENT, OR SIBLING

Consistent with several other previous studies, we found that the bereaved parents in our study were more depressed than members of other bereaved groups. As we noted earlier, the loss of a child of any age can violate the most fundamental expectations for justice and goodness in the world. It also interrupts the strongest attachment bond that most people will ever form—a bond with their children. It is not surprising then, that this loss is so devastating.

We found no differences, however, in levels of depression among bereaved spouses, siblings, and adults who lost a parent. Survivors in all of these groups may need the attention of health professionals around the time of their loss. In talking with hospice professionals, social workers, and others serving bereaved people, we found that their attention tended to be directed primarily toward the parents or spouses of the deceased. In our interviews with other family members, however, we were struck by comments from the adult children and siblings of the deceased that they were being forgotten or overlooked. Many of these folks felt they had to support everyone else in the family, and had to take care of the funeral arrangements and settlement of the deceased's belongings, as if they were not also grieving their loss. Said one 37-year-old woman whose sister died:

> They always want to know how the widow or widower, or the mother, but nobody ever wants to know what the brother or sister is like, what you're going through.

Several of the adult children and siblings in our study had not even told their employers or fellow employees that they had suffered a loss, and even if they had, they felt they were getting only a modicum of sympathy and support from their workplace. Yet, as our data show, they were suffering as much distress as other family members.

We found interesting variations in the gender differences in depression across the family groups. Among the bereaved parents, the fathers had high levels of depression throughout the study whereas the mothers' depression decreased to a level similar to those in the other family groups over time. Men who lost a sibling clearly had the lower levels of depression than men who lost a parent or a spouse. Among the women, however, those who lost siblings, spouses, and parents had similar levels of depression.

EXPECTED VERSUS UNEXPECTED DEATHS

Expected deaths are thought to be easier to adjust to than unexpected deaths (Rando, 1986; Rees & Lutkins, 1967). Expected deaths allow the survivors to search for understanding of the death, to resolve conflicts with the dying person, to say good-bye to the dying person, and to do things for the dying person to make his or her last days easier. All of this is often referred to as *anticipatory grieving*—finding meaning in the loss and assimilating the loss into one's understanding of the world and oneself before the loved one dies. In contrast, unexpected deaths do not allow for anticipatory grieving. A 52-year-old woman whose 29-year-old child died after a long illness said:

> A lot of people ask if I'm alright. I think I surprised people by not being very distraught, hysterical, really down. Think it's because I was prepared for what happened. And surprised myself by feeling how I feel. I try to analyze this. From November he was so ill, went downhill quickly. I think I disassociated myself from that segment of his illness. I remember before when he was active, able. Up until November, he was here. After that, he really wasn't. He was a different person. He had the same mental state, still talked a lot, exchanged feelings. At the time I didn't think of him as different person. But looking back on it, I think I lost him in November and not February. That's why I could accept it. He was in so much pain at the end, and (after) seeing him suffer, I prefer remembering before that happened. But think of him after November, also.

Unexpected deaths may also be difficult to adjust to because their causes are often harder to accept and understand. Many unexpected deaths are violent deaths due to accidents, suicide, or homicide. Accidental deaths and suicides leave much room for blame and anger toward the deceased (e.g., "Why did he always have to drive so fast?" "How could he be so selfish as to kill himself?") and for self-blame (e.g., "I shouldn't have let him leave the house drunk." "I should have been able to see that he was suicidal"; Demi, 1984; Dunn & Morrish-Vidners, 1987). Family members of people who commit suicide also sometimes feel stigmatized and blamed by others for not preventing the suicide (Calhoun & Allen, 1991; van der Wal, 1989–1990).

Almost half of all homicides involve a family member being killed by another family member or someone close to the family (Federal Bureau of Investigation, 1996). The surviving family members thus have both grief over the dead family member and rage at the killing family member with which to contend (Rynearson, 1984). People who lose a loved one to homicide can feel rage toward the killer and toward the legal system if the killer is not found, or is not convicted and sentenced as the survivors believe justice requires (Rynearson, 1984). Even if the killer receives a punishment the family sees as just, months and years of trials and appeals can mean constant reopening of the wounds of the loss for the family (Sanders, 1982–1983).

Although in general, expected deaths may be somewhat easier to adjust to than unexpected ones, expected deaths often follow long-term illnesses, and the burdens of these illnesses on the surviving family members can be great. Caregiving for the dying person may put great strains on individual family members. The medical costs of protracted illnesses can wipe out family savings. And the emotional toll of watching a loved family member suffer greatly for weeks, months, even years, can be excruciating. Surviving family members may feel tremendous guilt for wishing the ill person would die so that the suffering and burden will end, and the survivors can get on with their lives. They lose touch with other friends and family members, becoming socially isolated:

> You get to a point where you're tired, worn out, not as patient as you could be, not quite as loving as you might want to be, so it's very difficult. (Carol, 62, whose 68-year-old husband died of prostate cancer)

And another person said:

> His death was a giant relief to me. He was really badly ill for about a year. He was so ill that if it had been me I would have taken my life; if it had been an animal I would have had him put to sleep. He was in misery for a year. He was ill for about 3 years. Very, very hard to watch a bright, talented person just disappear under your eyes. It was horrible. (Elizabeth, 42, whose 70-year-old father died of leukemia)

Some studies find that people who experience sudden loss fare worse than those whose loss occurs after a long illness (Carey, 1977; Glick, Weiss, & Parkes, 1974; Lundin, 1984b; Vachon et al., 1982; Zisook, Shuchter, & Lyons, 1987). One longitudinal study done in Sweden found that people who experienced a sudden loss had significantly more psychiatric problems following the loss than did people who lost a loved one after a protracted illness (Lundin, 1984b). The increase in psychiatric problems was especially large for relatives of people killed in accidents.

Other studies have found no significant differences in long-term adjustment between people who experience sudden loss and those who experience loss after a chronic illness (Bornstein, Clayton, Halikas, Maurice, & Robins, 1973; Breckenridge, Gallagher, Thompson, & Peterson, 1986; Maddison & Walker, 1967; Miles, 1985). For example, Sanders (1982–1983) found no differences in levels of overall distress between people whose loved ones died suddenly (within 7 days of the onset of an illness or accident) and those whose loved ones died after short-term illnesses (less than 6 months) or after longer illnesses, both at interviews done 2 months and 18 months after the loss. The three groups did differ on specific types of symptoms and concerns, however. Survivors of a sudden death loss had more anger, guilt, and a sense of helplessness, shock, confusion, and somatic complaints. Survivors of a loss due to long-term chronic illness showed more social isolation, loss of emotional control and vigor, and rumination. It was as if the physical and emotional strain of prolonged caregiving had sapped their resources and caused them to turn in on themselves. Finally, survivors of a loss due to short-term illness had higher levels of death anxiety compared to the other groups. They also had higher levels of ego strength, however, suggesting their emotional resources were more intact than the other groups.

The impact of long-term illness on adjustment may be influenced by the survivors' social and economic resources. In a group of low income widows, Ide, Tobias, Kay, and de Zapien (1992) found that the longer widows' husbands had been ill, the more destitute the women were following the death and the greater their symptoms were. Several other studies have found that widows of a low socioeconomic status (SES) are more depressed than of a higher SES (Atchley, 1975; Glick, Weiss, & Parkes, 1974; Lopata, 1973, 1979; Parkes & Weiss, 1983; Zisook, Shuchter, & Lyons, 1987).

In summary, there is some support for the common assumption that unexpected deaths are very hard to adjust to because they do not allow for anticipatory grieving and may be due to causes that are hard to understand and accept. Expected deaths, especially after a protracted illness, carry their own burdens, however, especially for caregivers who have given their all to the dying patient.

AIDS-RELATED LOSSES

The AIDS epidemic has created a large new group of bereaved people. The circumstances surrounding many AIDS-related deaths may make adjustments for survivors especially difficult. First, the people dying from AIDS-related causes are typically young adults, thus their deaths shatter those basic assumptions about a natural order to life and death. Second, death from AIDS-related causes is usually long, painful, and horrible, requiring family members to provide caregiving for extended periods (Folkman, Chesney, Cooke, Boccellari, & Collette, 1994). The opportunistic infections and diseases that occur during advanced human immuneodeficiency virus (HIV) infection create chronic and severe diarrhea, wasting, severe musculoskeletal pain, blindness, and dementia. Third, regardless of how it was contracted, AIDS is still a stigmatized illness. Thus, family members and friends may not receive the social support they need from others and may not feel comfortable openly grieving. Fourth, homosexual transmission accounts for more than 50% of AIDS cases in the United States (Centers for Disease Control and Prevention, 1995). If the surviving family members have not accepted their loved one's homosexuality or perhaps did not know about it before the AIDS diagnosis was made, they have another major adjustment to contend with in addition to their loss.

The few existing studies of people who lost a loved one to AIDS clearly show that survivors experience acute distress following their loss (Folkman et al., 1996; Martin, 1988). These studies have focused on gay men who lost a partner or very close friend to AIDS. They also did not directly compare AIDS-related losses to losses due to non-AIDS illnesses.

In our study, 68 persons lost a loved one to AIDS. We supplemented this subsample by interviewing another 74 people who lost someone to AIDS, as part of another study (Erickson, 1995). This gave us a sample of 142; 58 gay men lost their male partners, 6 women lost their husbands, 36 people lost siblings, 29 parents lost children, 1 person lost a parent, and 12 people lost a very close friend or cousin.

We wanted to compare experiences of people who lose a loved one to AIDS and people who lose a loved one to cancer or another non-AIDS-related disease. But among those people who lose a loved one to AIDS, some have traditional family relationships to the deceased—they are parents, siblings, heterosexual spouses—whereas gay partners have nontraditional, although completely committed and often longer lasting, relationships to the deceased. We wondered if the extra burdens on gay men—the discrimination against them, the possibility that they were also HIV positive, the likelihood that they had experienced multiple losses due to AIDS—would result in even greater symptoms of distress following their loss compared to the other groups. Thus, we divided our participants into three groups: family members who lost a loved one to a non-AIDS-related disease, traditional family members who lost a loved one to AIDS, and gay men who lost a partner to AIDS.

There were no consistent differences among the three groups on levels of depression in the 18 months following their loss, but there were significant differences on symptoms of posttraumatic stress through the first year after the loss. The gay partners reported the highest levels of posttraumatic stress, followed by the traditional family members who lost someone to AIDS, followed by the family members who lost someone to a non-AIDS-related disease.[5]

People who lost a loved one to AIDS were significantly more likely than those who lost a loved one to cancer to say they could not make sense of their loss.[6]

> I certainly don't make sense of a hideous disease that takes a young and vibrant life and just destroys it in such a horrible way. No, it doesn't seem to make sense to me. (62-year-old woman whose 32-year-old son died from AIDS)

---

[5]Separate ANOVAs were conducted on PTSD scores at each of the interviews because there was too much missing data on the subsample of gay partners to conduct repeated measures of analyses of variance. These ANOVAs showed significant differences across groups in PTSD scores at $p < .05$ at 1 and 6 months, and significant differences at $p = .08$ at 13 months. There were no significant differences $p < .20$ at 18 months. Among the traditional family members who lost a loved one to AIDS, there were no significant differences between people with various relationships to the deceased (siblings, parents, etc.) in levels of depression or PTSD symptoms.

[6]Chi-square tests showed significant differences at 1, 6, 13, and 18 months, $p < .05$.

I mean, my mother's death I can make sense of, my father's death I can make sense of. But a young man dying of a disease that they can't seem to do anything about—no, I can't make sense of that. (48-year-old woman who cared for a close friend who died from AIDS)

SUMMARY

Every type of loss carries its own meanings and challenges. The loss of a child means the breaking of the most important bonds of human attachment and is a violation of people's sense of a natural order. The loss of a spouse or partner means the end of a relationship that was often decades-long, sometimes deeply supportive and enriching, sometimes not. At the least it means tremendous changes in the everyday life of the surviving spouse. The loss of a parent often means the loss of a stable support system on which the individual relies even as an adult. People can feel alone and abandoned. They also can feel challenged to move on as the newly senior generation in the family. The loss of a sibling raises issues of one's own mortality and may mean the loss of a confidant and lifelong friend. Unexpected losses can be experienced as shocks; expected losses can be anticipated but can also bring long-term caregiving burdens to survivors. And AIDS-related losses carry stigma and confusion.

Within each type of loss, most people find some way of coping and adjusting. The voices of our participants tell us more about the special challenges of the particular type of loss they faced. In the following chapters, we explore the ways people cope with and adjust to their losses.

Voices

The comments of our participants give further testimony to the different types of challenges that different types of losses present to people.

Parents Who Lost a Child

Sometimes there's a part of the intellect that just doesn't comprehend that there was the loss of a child. There are other feelings that you have—the horrible pain at the very beginning that you no longer have—there's a numbness that eventually comes. I think sometimes you just want to feel that pain again to make it feel real, but you don't. (55-year-old woman who lost a son)

I assured her of my love all the time. Sometimes it wasn't very convenient to get up at 11 p.m. after you've worked all day and talk because she wanted to talk, and you're so tired you're ready to drop. I've slept in her bed with her when she was frightened. I've just climbed in bed with her when I couldn't get her warm. Because that was one thing I regretted in my son's life—that I had not done that. And I was able to do it in A's life, just lay there and hold her. (73-year-old woman who lost two adult children)

I think if I was to become a parent again I would be a very good one because I would be very tolerant. Before I had this idea—I was working all the time, nothing-could-stop-me kind of thing, my-kid's-going- to-be-the-most-intelligent kind of attitude. If you're like that, you don't let the kid be a kid. So I want the opportunity again. So I don't like what happened, but I've got to take the best out of it. (59-year-old man who lost a daughter)

People Who Lost Spouses or Partners

Women who lost their husbands sometimes felt they lost the rock on which they stood, and other times expressed a sense of freedom.

'Cause my husband was always one who was trying to build me up. I have no one to build me up anymore. I have to do it to myself. I guess now that I put it out in the open like that—I guess that's one of the things that bothers me more than anything, that's the hardest for me, that there isn't someone to build me up. (76-year-old woman)

It panics me at times that he is gone. We were never apart for our married life. We saw each other every day for 27 years. I can't make sense of it. There is no sense as far as I'm concerned. He was 60, worked hard since high school, with hands and back, and got two jobs so I didn't have to and could be with the kids. He thought of us first. He was a good person with ordinary faults. There is no sense to it. It still irritates and hurts me. This should be our time together. (49-year-old woman)

I was very angry at him for leaving me alone. I should have not called the paramedics. They brought him back to life. He begged me not to call, and let him die in peace, but I couldn't help it. It was selfish of me. I couldn't let him go. (74-year-old woman)

I don't think "Why me" or "Why him" but sometimes I see people in the supermarket that are more or less his age, and I see them looking so comfortable, so nice, and I say, "Why can't my husband be the way that man is now?" I realize that's a selfish feeling, but you can't help it. (40-year-old woman)

I never found out about his investments until he took morphine. When I had to do taxes, I didn't know if he'd made or lost money. I didn't know how to get an answer. Once he was on morphine I couldn't ask him. (65-year-old woman)

My advice to any woman would be she's got to have a roof over her head. Get a trust so that she doesn't have to put herself through a lot of probate and grief. And not to let anybody else handle her investments. I've heard some terrible and sad stories. If she could get all that stuff done, if she's got some time, get it all done in advance, 'cause the less she has to do when the time comes, the better off she'll be. (49-year-old woman)

I'm not lonely, but I'm lonesome for him, especially making decisions. I think that'll always be difficult. (64-year-old woman)

Sometimes I feel that he's going to come back from work. There are times when I think he is coming back. His things are still here. It's like he hasn't left. I still have a lot of anger—a lot of unfairness. I feel we were cheated out of what was coming up. We thought when the kids were gone we would be together. (49-year-old woman)

Women need to get involved in their lives. I see so many people so devastated after they lose a loved one. That's because we don't know how to do nothing, mostly. I was totally independent. When he didn't work, I worked, and I made good money working. I wasn't dependent on his money at all. I miss his companionship. Most of the time I see widows devastated because they don't know nothing. They don't know how to tend to business, they don't know nothing. Go to your husband, "I need a new dress." Bullshit, go buy you a new dress. Like a kid. I miss the guy so much, especially when you meet some jackass. Here you are got to start all over again, knowing this character. That's when I really miss him, because I didn't have to know what he was going to do because I knew exactly what he was going to do. Now I got to study—is this guy going to rip me off? I've been lucky, but you still have this hanging in the back of your mind—is he going to try to use me or something? (58-year-old woman)

My self-confidence has gone up. I find there's a lot more I can do that I just never did before. I depended on my husband. I think just knowing that I can manage fairly well makes me feel better. (54-year-old woman)

There's a sense of freedom that I have without him that I've never experienced before—maybe the ability to be assertive. I was never assertive. I had a very authoritarian husband who was a very kind, sweet person, really, but he was authoritarian and he never let me do, not that I wanted to do anything spectacular—I never wanted to climb up a flagpole naked, though I threatened to once. I was able to be a business woman, but I never felt free. And I have felt so free and able to say that I can cope, I can do this. (56-year-old woman)

People have said to me that I've coped so well and that I carried on like nothing happened. This is what they tell me. I just took over. I took the hedge clippers—I had never used hedge clippers—and I trimmed all the hedge. I try to keep the grounds up like he did. It was just like a park. I turned around and I was doing like he did. All the things that he did, I just took over and did what he would do. I just dove into it. I did break down, I think from working outside and all the heat. I blacked out and I went right square on the floor. When I felt better I called my son and he came. They kind of think it was because I had driven myself so hard and it was so hot. My son said, "I could never have done what you have done." So then for that month I didn't do a thing. I just rested and took it easy. So from that time on, I do things, but I work in the shade and I take my time. But it was like I was driven. (75-year-old woman)

I'm able to do things I couldn't do before, and if I don't do them it's because I choose not to do them—not because I'm not allowed to, or we can't afford it, or what will people say. It's because I choose not to, and that makes a difference. And, I found out that I'm not really in control of life because I lost the dearest man in the world to me. What hurts the most was that I couldn't save him. No matter what I did, I couldn't save him. I'm through that now, and I know that I really can't control everything. But some things I can, and I do. I don't have to fight for it, I just do. I don't have to explain it or plead for it, I just do. And that's a comfortable place to be, really it is. (56-year-old woman)

I had tried for a divorce, and I wanted so much to get away from him and it wasn't possible. I was praying to let me find a way to get away from him. And just a couple of weeks after, having him diagnosed he was going to die, it's a weird feeling. I was seeing a psychiatrist. I had terrible guilt feelings that I 'm not unhappy about this. He said, "Of course not, you're liberated." I'm doing ok with that. I'm very happy to be alone. At times I think that's selfish, but I had no choice as to whether he was going to die or not. A strange experience. (61-year-old woman)

Men who lost wives often expressed an emptiness that surprised them.

I miss her a lot, a little bit of everything everyday. I don't care if I walk over to water my plants and I see that the orchid has finally bloomed—I just wish she were around so I could show it to her. All those buds coming up on the African violets. She's in my thoughts all the time, but it's not a depressing thought. I really believe that maybe she's better off than I am. She was a good woman. She was a superb mother, lousy housecleaner. She was a superb mother and superb wife, and she's with me all the time. Whether this is healthy or unhealthy, I like it that way, so I'll probably keep it that way. (63-year-old man)

I feel self-reproach because I think I should have taken it harder than I did. I think the big shock was when I went over, after the death, to the house to the family get-together, and not see her as part of the group. There was a certain sense of finality about it. (68-year-old man)

Most women, once single/widowed, live with it, can settle into it a lot better than men. A man can't do everything a woman can. It's a fact. (63-year-old man)

Why did she have to go? It would have been much better if it had been me. She had such a fine mind. Mine is ordinary. She was so smart. We had 40 years of a good marriage. We enjoyed doing things together and we were in business together. We counted on enjoying our retirement years to-gether. We only had 2 years. There is no sense, no justice. She was young.

Yes. All the time, every day, all the time, yes. Yes, just like I told you, it would have been much better if it had been me. My mother in her 90s used to call every week. She would ask, "Why doesn't God take me? I'm old. Why R? She's young." I'm ready to go too, whenever. But it's up to Him [points up]. I don't know why. God decides. We don't. (65-year-old man)

I found I learned a lot about others. I found that there are other people out there like me, that lived and had a good life, and a great marriage, and lost their spouse the same way. And I found that there are people out there that are living terrible lives, and would probably take my position than the one they have right now. We never belittled one another, we never said, "Oh, my old lady, she's not home." If I saw her on the street, we used to pass each other in the car, we'd go crazy. We would stop cars, I would run across to her. We had a love affair going for 43 years. (63-year-old man)

People Who Lost Parents

People who lost a parent sometimes expressed the changes in their attitudes toward themselves that the loss had created.

You kind of feel you've lost your family history when you don't have either parent, and you don't have brothers or sisters. It's like you have no past, all of a sudden. Like I was never a child, I never saw Christmas, all these places I lived where I grew up never existed because nobody remembers them but me. It's kind of a mental thing I found I've gone through. (41-year-old woman)

She had to die. I knew that, and I don't resent that. She was 82. She was a good woman and she had a good life. She was proud of me and she liked me, we were good friends. And that's the part, I guess. I miss her support, rather than the fact that she had to die. I know we all have to do that, so I can handle that. It's just that I miss her. I suppose I handled her death fairly well. I just don't handle the loss of her being there very well. (58-year-old woman)

My self-esteem is down. The whole world seems different. I don't feel like I function very well in any arena. My parents were the only people on earth that loved and accepted me unconditionally and they're gone, which means I have to love me and accept me. That's not easy. (46-year-old woman)

When I notice it the most is when my life goes on, my life is busy, pleasurable, and then somebody will mention, "Oh, I'm going to meet my mother for coffee." Or, like, my husband's parents are still alive, my sister-in-law's parents are still alive. Something here is different for me. I mean I really feel like an outsider. I've been trying to draw a parallel between her life and my life, and her refusal to give in to dying. Also, in terms of my relationship with my daughter, how to make that different, and what is really going on. There was a certain desperateness about my relationship with my daughter that made it impossible for me to feel close to her. When I feel tension between me and my daughter, I look at it in terms of the generational stuff. (50-year-old woman)

I think at first it doesn't feel very real—sort of like they're on vacation and there's all these people around to comfort and support and talk to you. But now the real life is starting. I'm having to go on without her. And I'm having to learn to live without her, to live without her support, and it's very difficult. Sometimes I just wonder how I'm going to do it. There's so much life ahead of me and I think, "How am I gonna do it without her?" But I know that I will be able to. It's just the transition is killing me. It just feels terrible. The transition, but really the whole—the loss of support, the whole loss of the relationship—every factor of the relationship—it just leaves a real big, empty place. (24-year-old woman)

I feel that this is the life that's been given to me, and I have to make the most of it. It's going to be great—I feel as if I have that hope—but for right now, it's tough going. I feel I will at some point feel better, but I feel that I will always miss her. I don't think it will go away, but I will fill my life with other relationships that will be meaningful to me, so I won't have this hole in my life forever. But I think that I can't replace my mother. It'll just be different. (32-year-old woman)

When I stop and feel myself, it's like a piece missing. There's a physical gap. There's an emotional gap. You're forced to look at how you escape your parents' parenting—how you kind of pull away from the parents in actual growth, and then you come back. It forces you to think about all that, and put the change in proper perspective. It was like the universe kicking me in the pants—alright, you don't have Mom and Dad to come back to. So on one hand, it was a release and it was enlightening, and it was a growth process, and my child resented it—I didn't want to have to grow up. I always wanted to be able to go back home, so I always let them be my home, and never found that sense of home within me. (40-year-old man)

The thing is, when you lose your mother, that is basic, because she's there for you all the time. She's the one you talk to. If you had any problems, she was always there to listen. All of a sudden, you're out there on your own. But isn't that what she raised you for? Exactly. That's the question you have to answer. You say, "My goodness, yes. It's my turn." That's the loss of something very close. You don't realize how close it is until your mother dies. (56-year-old woman)

Although our mothers are old, somehow we can count on them. So it's more than your mortality that you're facing; it's this issue of being alone in life. It's upsetting. It's kind of a sad feeling too, but it's more upsetting because it's this recognition that it's not just that you're an adult, but you're an adult who's alone. (45-year-old woman)

I had a much stronger reaction to it than I expected. Now I'm ok, but I knew in my head once it's over, it's over, but I didn't known it in my gut. That's really what I have learned: once it is over, it is over. I've grieved more than I ever thought I would. I have mourned and grieved much more. When my father died, and I loved him, I got it right in my head that I couldn't change anything. But I'm surprised over the period of time that I'm still grieving [over mother's death]. Being an orphan is not a great feeling. I don't think you ever get over it. I'm willing to say that. I'm coping with it because I have no choice. (55-year-old woman)

I still have some anger about it because I feel like she's too young, and how that reflects on me, that maybe I'll die younger than I want to. (50-year-old woman)

I think when parents die early, it's somewhat of a gift to the child, because then the child leads their own life, and is not pulled into caretaking in the older years of the parents, so it's really like a clean break. There's also a real sense that, more than thinking about her death, when I see someone 85 walking down the street or think about my great aunt who is 86, why is my great aunt still living and why is my mother gone? I just believe it was my mother's time. It was her time to leave. It was a process and she also voiced this, that this life, for her, was learning to let go of things. She had to learn how to let go of my father after he died; she didn't do that for 6 years after his death. And then learning to let go of me, because she and I were tied so closely together, very dysfunctionally. With my father travelling all the time, and his death and she moved in with us—I ended up being almost married to my mother. (More thoughts along these lines, how she and mother spent money together, how spending money is now felt as a source of comfort.) I think it's a gift. It's allowing me to make my own decisions for the first time in my life because my sister doesn't interfere at all. She's got enough going on. I'm also learning that her life is very separate from mine. My whole life I was told not to feel that way, or don't say that to that person or don't think that. So I'm really trying to make my own decisions and be my own person now. (37-year-old woman)

If it had been my Mom or my brother, it would be different, but I had already had all that time separated from him, and I had already released him, in a way, as my father. It's just like [he's] this person I knew who died, rather than having the close emotional attachment. Twenty years is a long time, and I had gone through some therapy and I had really worked on it to clear it out and keep the image I had of my father as a young girl—that man. And this man was a different man. He was the same person in the same body, but for me it was different. If it was someone I had a really close emotional attachment to I think it would be very different. (38-year-old woman)

People Who Lost Siblings

She was like a rock and now that rock is gone. For the first time in my life, I'm totally alone, and it's scary. In one sense, it's exciting, like getting to know a friend, getting to know what I like, seeing what I can do. (36-year-old woman who lost her sister)

I'm very jealous of people who have brothers very jealous, very, very, very. Especially when you get depressed—why him, why me, why my family?

Yeah, I'm very jealous of people who have brothers, who get together and talk about their brothers, because I can't say that I have one anymore, and then I don't know whether to talk about it or—. It's still a part of my life, but he's not here anymore. I always want to put that in: "I did have a brother." Because he was very special, and I wish a lot of my friends now had the chance to have met him when he was healthy. (27-year-old woman who lost her brother)

My other cousins and I felt, "well, if B could die, I could die." (39-year-old woman who lost a close cousin)

Grief theories often suggest that people with ambivalent relationships to the deceased have more complicated grief, and some respondents' comments supported this idea. Other respondents felt that the fact that their relationships with the deceased had been very strong made it much harder to adjust to the loss.

I remember during the time he was here, we had such a terrible time with our personality clash, and I wish that we didn't argue so much. And I really feel that we wasted some valuable time. And you know, I don't think either one of us thought of that while it was going on. And I never thought about that until he passed away. And those things were so trivial—weren't really important at all. And the time we could have spent maybe just knowing each other more. Because I felt badly about that. (55-year-old woman who lost her parent)

She was an outstanding woman. I guess that's why I'm grieving so much for her because we had a good relationship, and we went through a lot together. I lost all the rest of my family, and we went through those things together. (59-year-old woman who lost her mother)

Some of our respondents had lost more than one loved one during the period of the study, and expressed the cumulative stress that this put on them.

I had reinforced what I had already figured out—that many of her friends were total assholes, that her family was even worse in the addiction area and in the denial area than I thought. I'm not sure how much, or if I learned very much about myself. I am not surprised the way I dealt with it or the way I held up under it, the way I got on with things, because I went all through that when my Japanese wife killed herself (she was schizophrenic) and I had on-the-job training. I knew what had to be done, I knew how to go about almost all of it, I knew how to keep myself busy, etc. Unfortunately, I suppose the few people who lose more than one spouse in their life—most of us lose two parents, sometimes children—most people lose only one spouse, so there's no track record for doing it. So I suppose in one sense I got a lot of on-the-job training, not that I wanted it, but it was there, I made use of it. I frankly can find no good has come out of her death. (62-year-old man who lost his wife)

Most recently I feel like we've had enough. It's very unusual for me to feel like that; I've just really taken things as they come and rolled with the punches. Now my father-in-law being diagnosed with lung cancer and they've moved here close to us so that we could help them—. My mom's best friend died of cancer a year and a week after my mom died. It's like it's never going to end! It's like seeing my mom die over and over and over again. And I know now what to expect. I saw my mom die and I saw her best friend die who we also helped care for. It's just never going to end. And it's not just the emotional part of it that's going to go on. It's the physical demands, caring for somebody that's dying and watching them deteriorate. That's really difficult to do. I think it's worse when you know what's going to happen, what's next, the pain they're going to have or the uncontrollable pain that you can't control with drugs anymore. (31-year-old woman who lost her mother)

AIDS-Related Losses

Family members who lost a loved one to AIDS expressed a deep sense of dismay and confusion.

He died so young of such a terrible disease. He's gone and I'm here. It's not the natural order of things. It doesn't make sense at all. I've had so many losses in the past couple of years that I feel why J because he was always so interested in health. Sometimes I think that he got his disease because of his lifestyle. He liked to live in the fast lane. I wish something in my life would go well. I kind of think everything I touch is spoiled. I wish I could have talked more to my son, and when he told me he had AIDS I kind of accepted it, but we had a couple bad scenes about it. I thought at the time—we had a falling out. I wish I had hired a cook. He was afraid I was going to poison him because the food in the refrigerator was too old. He felt my cooking habits were such that I was poisoning him. I wish I could have resolved it. (50-year-old woman whose son died of AIDS)

People have told me that they commend me for going to San Francisco and caring for M. But I just feel it was necessary. I felt helpless going through experience. I had hopes for a cure, but more realistic about inevitability. M even recognized this. Me being there helped put M at ease. He could stop the fighting when I was with him. He could focus on going to be with Jesus. (34-year-old man who lost his 38-year-old brother)

He was born gay. I'd like to know why he was gay. If he wasn't gay, at least he'd be alive. I do that thinking a lot. I've learned that I try not to judge people for their differences. B liked the heterogeneity of San Francisco. I've learned from him. We've met a lot of wonderful people because of this—support group—that wouldn't have met if this hadn't happened. When B was diagnosed with AIDS I lived in constant fear that he would die. I thought if he died I'd lose it, I can't handle it, I'd go off the deep end. Surprisingly, I'm still living, working, having a semblance of life. I'm surprised I've been able to cope like I have. I didn't think I could survive if he died.

We're stronger than we think we are. I like to think B is with his friends who died before him and maybe he's there for others. It helps me to cope that he just might be happy, wherever that is. (52-year-old woman who lost her 31-year-old son)

There's not enough information on AIDS because of the rejection/stigma/shame of it. You can't say 'AIDS' in many places, risk a lot. I say it has to be unconditional love to take this on. I'd do it again. When there's love, there's no fear. (45-year-old woman who lost her 36-year-old brother).

3

Coping and Personality

It seems to me that the coping process seems about as different as there are different people who cope, or who lose people. There are similarities in broad forms, but specifically how people carry grief with them through a day seems to be really different (Kyle, 35, whose 68-year-old mother died of cancer)

I never seemed to grieve very much and yet I deny that I don't care for my mother—I did. But I never showed a lot of—I mean, people around me were basket cases, yet I wasn't. I've always wondered about that, what's the significance of that, if any. I even thought that at appropriate times I should be crying along with other people, and I was thinking about trying to make myself cry with people, and I thought, "Well, this is absurd, if you don't feel you shouldn't be ungenuine about it." So I'm quite happy that I'm coping well, but I feel a little guilty about it, that's what I'm saying. I think I should be a little more grief stricken than I am. (Phil, 52, whose 80-year-old mother died of cancer)

I'm not doing as well as other people think I am. I have a fear that I'm not really feeling it and I have a fear that someday I will just fall apart. (Vera, 60, whose 77-year-old mother died of cancer)

I'm having a hard time finding a balance between taking care of things and being a responsible person, and taking care of myself. I want to quit, but there's nowhere to quit to. (Clara, 38, whose 82-year-old mother died of lung cancer)

People often have beliefs about how they or others should be coping in the wake of a loss. Yet, there are wide differences in the specific strategies people use to cope with the emotional and practical consequences of a loss. These differences may be tied to the type of loss people have experienced, their age or gender, and their basic personality characteristics. This chapter examines the strategies people use to cope with loss, and how different strategies are related to adapting to the loss.

CONCEPTUALIZING COPING

Several different typologies of coping have been suggested over the years (Carver, Scheier, & Weintraub, 1989; Lazarus & Folkman, 1984; Moos & Billings, 1981; Nolen-Hoeksema, 1991). Most of these typologies separate coping strategies into two broad categories: *problem-focused coping* and *emotion-focused coping*. Problem-focused coping involves active strategies to overcome a concrete problem in one's life. For a woman bereaved of her husband, this might include finding a job to pay the bills. For a man bereaved of his wife, this might include learning to cook or to care for young children.

Emotion-focused coping includes a broad array of strategies that respond to the emotional consequences of a stressor such as a loss. In our own study, we assessed six types of emotion-focused coping, based on coping theories: support-seeking, emotional expression, reappraisal, distraction, avoidance, and rumination.

Support seeking involves reaching out to trusted family members, friends, and perhaps professionals (clergy, therapists, physicians, lawyers) for emotional and practical support. Teresa, a 40-year-old woman who lost her 43-year-old husband to leukemia describes her belief in reaching out for social support to cope:

You have to find somebody that you can really talk to. If you can't talk to the person involved, you have to find somebody, and just let them listen and listen.

A related coping strategy is *emotional expression*, which involves expressing one's emotions openly, through crying, yelling at people with whom one is angry, and so on.

The sooner you can talk about it, the better it is. Just get them to talk. Talk about the good times. Even if you're gonna cry, talk about the good times. Talk about the death itself, the loss, and how you feel about the loss. It's not easy but it heals. (Sara, 56-year-old woman who lost her 84-year-old mother to leukemia)

Not everyone feels comfortable expressing their emotions openly to others, so some people find other ways to express their emotions. For example, Jonelle, a 45-year-old woman who lost her 65-year-old mother to lung cancer, described:

I remember making a conscious choice, a month or so after the funeral, that I would not discuss it with my friends—they'd heard it, and they didn't need to keep hearing it, although I needed to keep processing it. So that's when I began to write. So, the word processor got used a lot for a while. And that worked. That was fine. What I needed to do was just keep the process going. I felt that I could keep talking and talking, but I wasn't saying anything different, I wasn't offering insights to me or to them. But when I sit down [to write], I begin to go back into the family stuff, and I begin to get in my own mind more understanding and more processing of some of the family problems, and how I wanted to deal with them; how it related to the death; how the resources I learned going through that could help me continue with some of the family stuff, and the estate settlement and so on. So it was like synthesizing the experiences of before. You need the same skills in a different way. That, I think is what the writing did—it helped me bring things forward another step.

Reappraisal involves thinking through one's loss, trying to find understanding and something positive in the experience (e.g., "I tried to remember the positive times with my loved one" and "I looked for the positive aspects of the situation"). *Distraction* involves engaging in positive activities to keep oneself occupied or busy such as hobbies. Priscilla, a 37-year-old woman who lost her 38-year-old husband to a brain tumor, said:

Probably if someone else was in this situation they should go out and try to do something, whether it be go for a walk, take an art class, they need to do something. Whether it's for themselves, something helping someone else, they need to do something, something *different*, not stick with the routine. And sometimes 30 minutes a day—read, garden, a hobby—do *something*.

Avoidance involves denying the loss or engaging in dangerous activities to get one's mind off the loss, such as drinking alcohol, binge eating, or taking drugs. Finally, *rumination* involves passively focusing on the negative emotions aroused by the loss and one's worries about the consequences or meanings of the loss (e.g., "I think about how alone I feel," "I think 'Why can't I get going?'" "I think about the situation, wishing it had gone better.").

Which of these coping strategies should be helpful to bereaved people in adapting to their loss, and which should be harmful? According to the traditional theories of bereavement, adapting to a loss requires working through the loss—confronting the reality of the loss, detaching from the deceased, then reestablishing ties with other people (Bowlby, 1980; Freud, 1917; Lindemann, 1944). The newer cognitive models of grief also suggest that the bereaved person must think a great deal about their loss, searching for and finding meaning in the loss in order to assimilate their loss into their worldview and their view of the self (Horowitz, 1976). Thus, suppressing thoughts of one's loss is clearly maladaptive, according to these theories. This suggests that avoidance coping would definitely be associated with more distress among bereaved people, and perhaps also distraction coping. On the other hand, emotion expression and seeking others to talk with about one's loss would be expected to help in adapting to loss. At her interview 13 months after the loss of her husband to cancer, Flora described the emotional toll that suppressing her emotions took and what happened as she finally started expressing her emotions:

> Before his death, I really had my armor on. I was gearing up for what I had to face. I wanted to get on with it, but I didn't want it ever to happen. So once it happened, when I look back now, I wish I had been more relaxed. I was so tired. There were things that were physically going on for me that stood in the way of being able to ... And it was like an anxiety thing, knowing that this terrible loss was coming. Wanting to deal with it and not wanting to deal with it, all at the same time. So then I became very busy with things I had to deal with, instead of just relaxing, letting all the chores go on. I was running too fast, trying to stay ahead. After he died, I said to my doctor, "I can't talk about it—I'm just blubbering all the time." She said, "Thank God—you're feeling! You're beginning to feel." My expression was, "I've run out of medication. I've run out of being anesthetized by not feeling. Now I recognize the pain, and I do feel it , and it hurts like hell."

Ana, a 47-year-old woman who lost her mother was also conscious of the stress that suppression was causing her:

> I would like to make a big scream. That everybody can hear it. No, no ... then they would take me to the cuckoo farm. (Interviewer: You'd like to be someplace where you could really let go.) Yeah, 'cause I don't think I cry enough. I hold back my crying. I started crying ever since she diagnosed. I would cry at work. And maybe that's why I didn't cry as much after she died. I don't know. I don't want to appear weak in front of my family, so I hold back. Maybe that's why I feel like screaming—I feel like I have a silent scream inside of me.

More recently, however, theorists have been questioning the notion that suppressing thoughts of one's loss is always maladaptive (Rosenblatt, 1983; Ruben, 1993; Shuchter & Zisook, 1993; Stroebe & Schut, in press). Bereaved people may need occasionally to take a break from their grief, and do seem to use suppression to regulate or dose their exposure to emotional pain. There has been remarkably little empirical research on the relationship between suppression of thoughts and emotions about a loss and adaptation to loss. One study found that gay men who tried to distance themselves from thoughts about the loss of their partner to AIDS had more depression over time than those men who did not try to distance themselves from their grief (Folkman et al., 1996). Similarly, a study of men who lost their wives found that those who suppress thoughts of their loss were more depressed months later than those who did not suppress (Stroebe & Schut, 1995). But another study found that bereaved people who tended to avoid thinking about their negative emotions following a loss actually had lower levels of somatic and distress symptoms over time, even by objective measures (Bonanno, Keltner, Holen, & Horowitz, 1995).

Some of our participants talked about their conscious use of avoidance tactics to get their minds off their loss for a while:

> I had to develop in what I could handle at the time, each time. And what I denied was normal and healthy and helped me get to this point. That's why I hate the word "denial." I think sometimes it's the best thing that could happen to people. It's true. If you could handle it, you wouldn't deny it. You're not at a place where you can handle it and denial sometimes *is* the only safe place to be. (Susan, a 37-year-old woman who lost her 40-year-old husband to melanoma)

> I think I consciously avoid the thought that I'm never gonna see her again, that she's gone. Because I think I would be down more, I think I would be having a harder time coping if I allowed my thoughts to drift there. It's very real, it's just that I keep myself busy, not dwelling on it, just to keep myself up and keep myself from thinking of it. (Manuel, a 45-year-old man who lost his 48-year-old wife to breast cancer)

In their dual process model of coping, Stroebe and Schut (in press) suggested there are two quite different orientations that bereaved people must take over the course of adaptation to their loss: loss orientation and restoration orientation. *Loss orientation* involves concentrating on and processing some aspect of the loss. People in the midst of loss orientation recount memories of the deceased, think about the meaning of the loss and their relationship to the deceased, and think about their own self-definition in the wake of their loss. *Restoration orientation* involves focusing on the concrete changes that have occurred as a result of the loss—the need to cook one's own meals, to manage one's finances, to find new relationships. People focusing on restoration are not avoiding grief work but are dealing with the additional tasks that are secondary consequences to their loss. Bereaved people oscillate between loss and restoration orientation, typically being more loss oriented shortly after a loss, and becoming more restoration oriented with time. There may also be differences between people in whether they lean toward more loss orientation or more restoration orientation. One person in our study described dual process coping:

I know I have a great capacity to tolerate pain and all these different things—I'm a survivor—it happened that way. Sometimes I question myself as to whether I'm being very unemotional about things, and then I realize I understand what it is that's happened and I don't try to make it more than it is. When I wake up in the morning, I still have children to feed and things to do. The old life-goes-on saying is true, so there's the reality of it all. You can't just get caught in one thing and dwell on it. I've tried to run away from things, but that's not going to work either. You have to face it sometime. (Esther, a 35-year-old woman who lost her 69-year-old father to lung cancer)

These reconceptualizations of coping with bereavement do not suggest that avoidance coping, as we have defined and measured it, will be adaptive. They do suggest that some use of distraction coping and reappraisal, and certainly problem-solving coping, may be useful in adapting to loss. They also suggest that unmitigated rumination may be maladaptive.

Our own theory and research on emotion-focused coping also suggests that unmitigated rumination is maladaptive (Nolen-Hoeksema, 1991; Nolen-Hoeksema et al., 1994). Again, rumination involves focusing on how badly you feel and your worries that you will not recover in a repetitive manner that keeps you "stuck" rather than moving forward toward greater understanding and acceptance of their situation. When people who are depressed or distressed ruminate, they generate more negative memories from the past and more negative predictions about the future, they interpret their current life situation more negatively, and they have more difficulty engaging in active problem solving (Lyubomirsky & Nolen-Hoeksema, 1994, 1995; Nolen-Hoeksema et al., 1994). It seems that rumination accentuates the negative thinking that is part of depression and distress, and makes it more likely that this negative thinking will be used to understand one's current situation. In turn, this only makes the individual more depressed and distressed. Our previous studies have found that people who ruminate about their depression have longer and more severe periods of depression than those who do not (Morrow & Nolen-Hoeksema, 1990; Nolen-Hoeksema & Morrow, 1991; Nolen-Hoeksema, Morrow & Fredirckson, 1993). People who ruminate may also drive away friends and other supporters, as Avary, a 56-year-old woman whose 49-year-old sister died of ovarian cancer, describes:

Keep your friends. Don't isolate yourself. Put on a good face—not spend the whole time feeling sorry for yourself with other people, because people get very tired if you're always—. Even if they know you're hurting inside, they'll stay with you. But if you're going to be crying and just talking about yourself all the time and your problems, you isolate yourself very quickly.

One form of rumination that may be especially harmful following a loss is *counterfactual thinking*—thoughts about what one might have done to prevent the loss. This type of thinking was even more strongly associated with prolonged distress in people who lost a loved one to a motor vehicle accident than was general rumination about how their lives were going (Davis et al., 1995). As we noted in chapter 2, counterfactual thinking may be especially common among people who lose a child or who lose someone in a death that they think might have been foreseeable or preventable, such as a suicide.

In sum, problem-solving coping involves dealing with the concrete problems that result from one's loss. There are a variety of emotion-focused coping strategies, including seeking social support, emotional expression, reappraisal, distraction, avoidance, and rumination.

RELATIONS BETWEEN COPING AND ADJUSTMENT

How did each of the coping strategies relate to adjustment in our study? The coping strategy that most consistently predicted levels of depression and distress over time was avoidance coping. At each interview, people who were engaging in more avoidance coping were more depressed and distressed than those who were not. In addition, people who engaged in more avoidance coping at the interview 1 month after their loss were more depressed and distressed at all subsequent interviews, even when their initial levels of depression and distress at 1 month were taken into account.[1] Thus, as the traditional coping theories suggest, avoiding thinking about one's loss is maladaptive, both in the short run and the long run.

It is important to note that our avoidance-coping measure included several questions about use of alcohol or drugs to cope, as well as questions about denying or avoiding thinking the loss. Thus, the relation between avoidance coping and poor adjustment to the loss may be due not only to the fact that avoidance copers were suppressing thoughts about their loss, but also because they were engaging in more dangerous activities, like increased alcohol and drug consumption, as a way of avoiding thinking. Indeed, when we divided our avoidance coping scale into these two types of avoidance coping, we found that both were related to more distress. That is, both people who tried to deny their loss and their feelings about it, and those who were using alcohol and drugs to avoid dealing with their loss had greater and more prolonged distress.

---

[1]Avoidance coping was correlated with both depression and general distress at all interviews at $p <$ .05. In addition, partial correlations between avoidance coping at 1 month and depression or distress scores at subsequent interviews, controlling for depression or distress scores at 1 month, and simultaneous regression analysis examining which coping variables measured at 1 month predict depression or distress scores at subsequent interviews, controlling for 1-month depression or distress scores, both confirmed that people who used avoidance coping showed less remediation from depression or distress over time than those who did not. Avoidance coping was a significant predictor of changes in depression and distress even when all other forms of coping were first taken into account statistically.

People who were less emotionally expressive, and thus perhaps suppressed talking about their loss experiences, were more depressed and distressed at all of the interviews. Furthermore, people who were less emotionally expressive 1 month after their loss tended to be more depressed 13 months and 18 months postloss, even after taking into account their depression levels at 1 month.[2] At all but the last interview, people who were less emotionally expressive as a coping strategy were less likely to find something good in their loss than those who were more emotionally expressive.[3] Thus, people who did not feel able or supported in talking about their loss had more difficult adjusting to their loss and more difficulty finding anything good in their loss.

Yet, there also was some evidence that engaging in too much thinking about one's loss was also maladaptive over time. People who were engaging in much rumination were more depressed and distressed at all the interviews. In addition, people who were ruminating 1 month after their loss tended to remain more depressed and distressed over time, even after taking into account how depressed or distressed they were at 1-month post-loss.[4] People who were ruminating also had more trouble making sense of their loss at most of the interviews.[5] Although people who were ruminating were thinking a great deal about their loss and their emotional reactions to the loss, they were not finding ways to understand that loss within their own personal philosophies and worldviews. This fits our previous results that show that rumination is not a productive mode of thought, and instead leads to more negative thinking, more hopelessness and despair, and more depression (Lyubomirsky & Nolen-Hoeksema, 1993, 1995; Nolen-Hoeksema et al., 1994).

Some bereaved people may be reluctant to give up their ruminations, their sadness, their guilt, and their grief because it represents for them their last and final tie to the deceased. They fear that if they no longer think, cry, or mourn, they will "lose" the deceased. There comes a time when most people realize that this is not so, that they can "forget" temporarily, or forget certain aspects or details of the deceased, and they do not lose their connection to the deceased.

---

[2]Emotional expressiveness was correlated with less depression and more distress at all interviews at $p < .05$. Partial correlations (controlling for 1-month self-reported depression) between emotion expression at 1 month and self-reported depression at 13 months and 18 months were marginally significant at $p < .10$.

[3]All correlations significant at $p < .05$.

[4]Rumination was correlated at $p < .05$ with depression and distress at all four interviews. The partial correlation (controlling for 1-month distress scores) between rumination at 1 month and distress at 6 months was significant at $p < .05$. The partial correlations (controlling for 1-month self-reported depression) between rumination at 1 month and self-reported depression at 13 months and 18 months were marginally significant $p < .10$.

[5]The relations between inability to make sense and degree of rumination were significant at $p < .05$ at the 1-, 13-, and 18-month interviews.

Also, they realize that letting go is not a betrayal of the deceased. Thus, people who cling to their ruminations may be, in a way, clinging to the deceased loved one in the only way that is left to them.

On the other hand, people who engaged in reappraisal coping—who actively sought positive meanings and ways of understanding their situation as a way of coping—were less depressed, better able to make sense of their loss, and able to find something good in the loss experience.[6] Reappraisal coping and rumination were very different modes of coping, and were not correlated with each other at any of the interviews. Whereas ruminating involves going over things you wish you had done differently and worries about how bad you feel and whether you will ever recover, reappraisal involves the search for a positive way of framing one's experience. People who engaged in reappraisal as a coping strategy were also more likely to use active problem solving to cope with the concrete problems they faced as a result of their loss. In turn, people who focused on solving problems as a coping strategy were also more likely to be able to find something good in their loss experience.[7]

Seeking social support is a coping strategy that people used often, and was associated with lowered levels of depression and distress at each interview. Yet, seeking social support was not as strongly related to depression or distress as the other coping strategies we already discussed, and did not predict changes in depression or distress over time. It also was related to finding something good in the loss at only two of the four interviews.[8] Although reaching out to others may be helpful for some people, the success of this strategy obviously depends on the response of others, as Hazel, a 72-year-old woman who lost her husband, describes:

I'm taking each day as it comes and doing the best I can. Maybe I'm wrong in not asking for help. I sometimes think that. But I can't see where listening to other people tell about how unhappy they are, or even how they've overcome it—I can't quite see that that would help me. I recently talked to an acquaintance who was recently widowed. I helped her. I didn't feel that much better when I left. I thought, "Oh, she's got so much to go through."

---

[6]Reappraisal coping was significantly related to being able to make sense of the loss at the 1-, 13-, and 18-month interviews at $p < .05$. Reappraisal coping was significantly related to finding something good in the loss experience at all four interviews at $p < .05$.

[7]Reappraisal and problem solving were significantly correlated with each other at all the interviews, and problem-solving coping was significantly correlated with finding something good in the loss at all the interviews, each correlation significant at $p < .05$. Problem solving was significantly correlated with lowered depression and distress only at the 18-month interview, however.

[8]Seeking social support was correlated cross-sectionally with depression at all four interviews, and with distress at $p < .10$ at all four interviews. Partial correlations and regression analyses showed it was not significantly correlated with changes in depression or distress from 1 month to the subsequent interviews. It was significantly related to finding something good in the loss only at the 1-month and 13-month interviews.

It was good for her to have someone to talk to, but I didn't feel any better talking about it because I felt that the worst is yet to come. She's still in a state of shock. I felt badly because I knew she has to go through that. I talk about my husband, but other people don't, which is strange to me. Maybe his sister will say something once in awhile. I mention him all the time, but other people don't. I don't know whether they're afraid. I found that out about people. They don't know how to deal with it, and some people stay away because they don't know how to deal with it. I understand that, and I don't—well, I *do* resent it a little bit. I think, well, you don't like to go to a funeral, but it's something you do. Some people disappoint me because I think that they should overcome that, and they don't.

As we discuss in chapter 4, friends and family members often do not respond to bereaved family members in helpful ways. This may be why seeking social support is a coping strategy that is not as reliably associated with positive adjustment to loss as some other coping strategies.

We mentioned earlier that there are conflicting predictions from older and newer bereavement theories about the adaptiveness of using positive or benign distractions to take a break occasionally from one's grief. In our study, using positive distractions as a coping strategy was not associated with the degree of depression or distress people expressed at any of the interviews. It also was not related to finding meaning or something positive in the loss at any of the interviews. Thus, neither engaging in little or no distraction nor engaging in much distraction, interfered with adapting to the loss. Instead, the other coping strategies proved important to adjustment.

HOW COPING CHANGES OVER TIME

Bereaved people may change their coping strategies over time. We looked for such changes in the coping strategies measured in our study, and found significant changes in two coping strategies. First, the degree to which bereaved people sought support from others as a coping strategy declined significantly with time among both men and women (see Fig. 3.1).[9] As discussed in chapter 4, over time, people may be less and less willing to respond in a supportive manner to a bereaved person. They may be weary of listening to a bereaved person talk about the loss, or feel that the bereaved person should be over the loss, making the bereaved person feel he or she cannot reach out as a coping strategy. Bereaved people may feel they should not burden others with their grief as time passes, and thus be less likely to reach out. Finally, as the most severe pains of grief subside, bereaved people may not feel the need to reach out to others as much.

---

[9]Repeated measures analysis of variance on support seeking scores showed a significant main effects of time, $F(3, 648) = 2.50$, $p < .06$ and gender, $F(1,216) = 7.28$, $p < .01$.

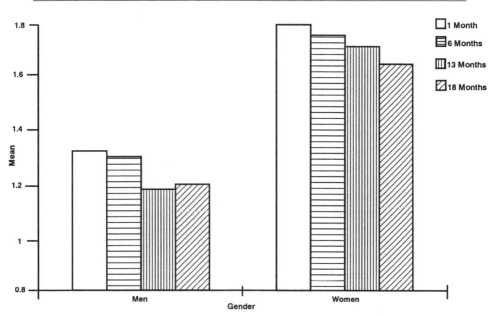

FIG. 3.1. Changes in seeking support as coping over time among men and women.

Second, bereaved people were using relatively little distraction coping at the interview 1 month after their loss, but reported much more use of distraction as a coping strategy 6 months after their loss (Fig. 3.2).[10] As time passed, their use of distraction declined. Bereaved people may feel it is unwise or may feel uncomfortable using distraction immediately after their loss. But by 6 months, they used distraction more as a way of taking a break from their grief. As their symptoms of grief decline with time, they may find it less necessary to use distraction to cope. Penny, a 36-year-old woman who lost a parent, described the types of distractions she felt were helpful in her coping with the loss:

> I've gone through some real serious depression and didn't even know it. I've gone through some great times. I know that when somebody that you love and is close to you dies, it's like it's cutting off an arm or a leg. It's hard to fill that hole. And when you go to fill that hole, make sure you fill it with things that are really important to you and not just empty things like work and activities. Try to occupy yourself with things that really mean something to you. And try to spend more time with God. You know how people will do things to kind of fill time. Do something that you really enjoy. If you enjoy needlepoint, then do needlepoint. Don't do idle things. Don't do

---

[10]Repeated measures analysis of variance on distraction scores showed a significant main effect of time, $F(3, 648) = 3.14$, $p < .05$, and a significant interaction between time and gender, $F(3, 648)=3.34$, $p < .05$. The gender interaction is discussed later.

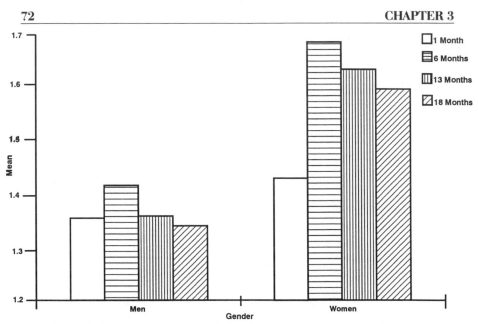

FIG. 3.2. Changes in use of distraction coping over time among men and women.

things to fill time. Do something that's going to bring you joy or feelings of contentment or completion or something like that. I've never had time to do cross stitch before. I made these cross stitch projects and I gave them to people I really liked, and it was therapeutic for me. I didn't just go out and weed the yard, but I did something that meant something to me, and I gave it to somebody that meant something to me. Now when I see that, I think that was a good time for me to do that. It was a good time. We all fill time. When you're going through grief, every once in a while you feel you have to do something just to be doing something.

It was interesting that we did not find significant changes across time in any of the other coping strategies—rumination, emotional expression, avoidance coping, reappraisal, or problem solving. These strategies may be more traitlike—they are consistently either used or not used by individuals.

GENDER DIFFERENCES IN COPING WITH LOSS

Men and women seem to cope differently with loss. Several studies of bereaved parents and spouses have found that more women than men want to talk about their loss, and women, more than men, seek out other people to talk to and for support (Bohannon, 1990; Carroll & Shaefer, 1993; Feeley & Gottlieb, 1988;

Smith & Borgers, 1988). Women are also more likely than men to ruminate and be preoccupied with thoughts about their loss (Bohannon, 1990; Feeley & Gottlieb, 1988). In contrast, men appear to engage in more denial or avoidance of thinking about their loss than women, and often try to keep busy or take on extra workloads as a coping strategy (Bohannon, 1990; Smith & Borgers, 1988).

The results of our study parallel those of previous studies. In our study, the women were more likely than the men to report using rumination and support seeking, whereas men were more likely than women to be using distraction.[11] The differences between the ways men and women cope can cause tremendous friction between husbands and wives, partners, or male and female members of a family. We witnessed a couple in therapy whose teenage son had been killed in an automobile accident. The wife coped by expressing her emotions. Although she had family and friends around each day who were supportive of her expression, she still needed to talk about the loss with her husband each day. He, on the other hand, wanted to avoid thinking about it and move on, and used work and golf to distract himself from the loss. Two weeks after the son's death, the husband announced unexpectedly that he had arranged for the couple to go to Hawaii to "get away." The trip was a disaster because the pain went right along with the wife, and the husband felt frustrated in his attempts to "distract" her from her grief. This couple's different coping strategies continued to clash until they dropped out of therapy unable to accept their differences.

Men and women often feel that they would like to cope in a way that is not expected for their gender. In particular, men talk about wanting to express their emotions, but feeling it is unacceptable to do so. Jose, a 72-year-old man who lost his wife, described eloquently how the expectations for how he should cope as a man interfered with his coping as he needed.

> Nobody told me it was ok to cry—would have helped if they had. The hospice chaplain told me—that was such a big help. I needed some religious advice. The hospice chaplain very helpful to us. Most men get such a strong message that it is not ok to cry.

Age was also a factor in how people coped. Older people were less likely than younger people to be engaging in avoidance coping and rumination. Interestingly, older people were also less likely than younger people to be using

---

[11]The repeated measures analysis of variance on rumination scores did not show a significant main effect of gender, but we had a strong a priori hypotheses about a gender difference in rumination based on our previous studies. Thus, we examined the data separately for each interview for a gender effect on rumination scores, and found women to have higher rumination scores at all but the 1-year interview (p's < .05). A main effect of gender did emerge in the repeated measures analysis of variance on support seeking, $F(1, 216 = 7.28, p < .01$ and a significant gender by time interaction emerged for scores on distraction, $F(3, 648) = 3.34, p < .05$.

emotional expression to cope. In turn, they were less depressed and distressed than the younger participants.[12]

Older people grew up with a different set of social rules than younger people for coping with negative emotions. Rumination about the loss and expressing one's feelings in public may not be seen as acceptable ways of coping for older people. Clearly, using alcohol or drugs is not seen as acceptable. In contrast, younger people may feel more free to focus on and express how they feel because they have grown up in an era of open expression of emotions, in the media, among their friends, and so on. In addition, younger people may not have learned to control their impulses to drown their grief in alcohol or drugs.

HOW DIFFERENT FAMILY GROUPS COPE WITH LOSS

Different family groups might cope differently with loss, either because the circumstances around their loss differ, or because their ages and upbringing might differ. We found that spouses were significantly less likely than the other family groups to ruminate about their loss or to use avoidance coping at each of our interviews.[13] These differences between spouses and other family groups disappeared, however, when we took into account differences in the ages of the family groups. That is, in general, older people tended to use less rumination and avoidance coping. Because the bereaved spouses tended to be older than the other family groups, when we controlled for their ages, there no longer were any differences in coping strategies between the family groups. Thus, it seems that it is not the type of loss you experience, but your age or generation that influences the type of coping you use.

RELIGION AND COPING

Alone you cannot do it, but with God nothing is difficult. (Gerry, 74-year-old woman who lost her husband)

Most religions have rituals for responding to death and doctrines that explicitly address the meaning of death. Thus, it is reasonable to expect that people who subscribe to a religious doctrine or who are part of a religious community would cope differently with loss from those who are not.

---

[12]Correlations between age and avoidance coping and rumination were significant at $p < .05$ at all four interviews. The correlations between age and emotional expression were significant at $p < .05$ at 3 of the four interviews. Older people were significantly less depressed and distressed than younger people (by bivariate correlations) at all interviews, p's $< .05$.

[13]Analyses of variance of rumination and avoidance scores at each of the interviews revealed significant main effects of relationship to the deceased (all p's $< .05$). Spouses scored lower than the other groups at all four interviews.

In our study, people who considered themselves spiritual and who attended religious services regularly tended to use more adaptive coping strategies. First, they were more likely to use social support and active problem solving to cope. Indeed, their religious organizations were an important source of social support and problem solving, as fully described in chapter 4. Second, they were more likely to engage in positive reappraisal of their situation. Often, they were able to use their faith to reappraise their loss:[14]

> My faith has given me everything I need to cope with it. That's why I don't need support groups. I have the greatest support group—God—He's there. I was able to use my faith as the greatest way of coping with it, and then dealing with it after , of understanding and acceptance, and to realize that I could. (Cora, a 56-year-old woman who lost her 74-year-old mother to cancer)

In turn, those spiritual or religious people who did attend religious services at least occasionally had lower levels of depression at 13 and 18 months following their loss than those who never attended religious services.[15] Thus, people who had faith and a religious organization to turn to seemed to cope more adaptively with their loss and were less distressed after their loss (for similar results, see Bahr & Harvey, 1979; Bornstein et al., 1973; McGloshen & O'Bryant, 1988). As Darlene, a 56-year-old woman who lost her sister, expressed

> My belief in God has been my saving grace, really. In years gone by, if something happened, I'd ask God, "Why did you do that!?" Now, meeting priests and people who believe in God, that has helped 90% of the time. I'd go to the church when it's quiet, chat with God. It was very consoling. My belief in God is terribly important.

Because religions have doctrines that explain the meaning of death, religious people might find it easier to make sense of the loss—to find some way of understanding it as having purpose or meaning (McIntosh, Silver & Wortman,

---

[14]Repeated measures analysis of variance on seeking social support scores showed a significant main effect of spiritual interest, $F(2, 212) = 18.08$, $p < .001$, and a significant interaction between spiritual interest and attendance at religious services, $F(1, 212) = 5.11$, $p < .05$. Repeated analyses of variance on reappraisal scores showed significant main effects of spiritual interests, $F(1, 212) = 19.08)$, $p < .001$, service attendance, $F(2, 212) = 3.75)$, $p < .05$, a significant interaction between spiritual interest and service attendance, $F(1, 212) = 12.24)$, $p < .001$, and a significant interaction between spiritual interest, service attendance, and time, $F(3, 636) = 5.45)$, $p < .001$. Repeated measures analysis of variance on problem-solving scores showed a significant main effect of spiritual interest, $F(211) = 6.45)$, $p < .05$, and a significant interaction between spiritual interest and service attendance $F(1, 211) = 8.15)$, $p < .005$.

[15]Repeated measures analysis of variance on interviewer-related depression scores showed a significant interaction between religious/spiritual interests, service attendance, and time, $F(3, 201) = 3.61$, $p < .05$. No significant effects of religious/spiritual interests or service attendance were found on the other psychological or physical distress measures, however.

1993).We found that religious or spiritual people in our study were more likely to say they had made sense of their loss, even shortly after the loss (Davis, Nolen-Hoeksema, & Larson, in press). Most often, the way they made sense of the loss was to say that God had needed or wanted their family member, or more generally that the family member's death was a part of God's plan.

Religious beliefs did not always help people find meaning, however, and some people found themselves deeply questioning their beliefs in the wake of their loss:

> Why me? My answer is Christ loves me and He'll do what He can to get me to go in His direction. I was angry at Him for the longest time. But He lost His son, and if I had, I would've been tremendously angry. So I talk to myself in that way about dealing with me. (Serena, 42, whose 66-year-old father died of renal cancer)

> For a while I was mad at God. Why did He give me this marvelous person, then take him away. (Jasmine, 56, whose 59-year-old husband died of sclaraderma)

> It's harder if you're deeply religious. I went to a rabbi with the question of why people suffer when they die. He didn't give a good answer. (Barry, 59, whose 55-year-old wife died of peripheral neuropathy)

> The part of the death that I had a hard time making sense of was—here was a woman who spiritually had a God that she believed in very strongly. She lived her life according to what she felt were good religious beliefs. She was known as everybody's angel, always there for people. Why she suffered as she did, and why she had to experience death in a slow, painful way was the think I couldn't accept. It deepened my questioning of spiritual belief, whether there really is any spirit out there looking over you, taking care of you. He certainly didn't do it for her. But, as one of my friends said, "You never question God." So we'll have to rely upon that. (Geoff, 38, whose 68-year-old mother died of a brain tumor)

PERSONALITY, COPING, AND ADJUSTMENT

There has been relatively little research on the relationship between basic personality styles and either the coping strategies people use following a loss or their adjustment to loss (Sanders, 1993). The traditional grief theories suggest that people who are more dependent on others for their self-esteem will be more at risk for poor adjustment to loss. The few studies directly testing this hypothesis have supported it (Parkes & Weiss, 1983; Sable, 1989). More generally, some studies have found that people who are emotionally unstable, neurotic, insecure, or anxious tend to cope less adaptively and adjust more poorly to loss (Parkes & Weiss, 1983; Stroebe & Stroebe, 1987; Vachon et al., 1982). One study found that people who had low self-esteem prior to a loss engaged in more maladaptive coping strategies and had higher levels of distress following the loss than those with higher self-esteem (Lund et al., 1985).

In our study, the personality characteristic we measured was dispositional optimism, the tendency to be optimistic in most circumstances (Carver, Scheier, & Weintraub, 1989). Not surprisingly, we found that people who were dispositional optimists were less depressed and distressed at each of the interviews. They also showed greater declines in depression and distress from the interview 1 month after their loss to the 13-month and 18-month postloss interviews. Finally, they were better able than pessimists to find meaning or something positive in their loss.[16]

Dispositional optimists also used more adaptive coping strategies. They engaged in more problem solving, reappraisal, and emotional expression, and less rumination and avoidance coping, than pessimistic people.[17] Being better copers is probably one way that dispositional optimists adjust more quickly to their loss. Christine, a 74-year-old widow who scored high on our optimism scale, said,

> It's a pretty normal part of living. Everybody lives, everybody gets sick, and everybody dies. We were really lucky because he didn't suffer a lot of pain. He only took morphine the last 2 days. So with all those millions of things to be grateful for, all you can do is, when you get down, kick yourself in the rear end and say, "Get going!"

Optimism may help in its own right in adjusting to loss, however. We found that optimists were still less depressed and distressed than pessimists over time, even when we accounted for the differences between optimists and pessimists in coping strategies.[18] A general sense of optimism may help one understand and shape one's experience of loss in ways that make it easier to cope and to adjust. Joy, a 48-year-old widow who scored high on our optimism measure said:

---

[16]Dispositional optimism was significantly correlated with lower depression and distress at all four interviews (p's < .05). Partial correlations showed that dispositional optimism, measured at 1 month, significantly predicted (p's < .05) depression and distress scores at 13 months and 18 months, controlling for depression or distress at 1 month. Finally, cross-sectional relations between dispositional optimism and finding meaning in the loss and finding something positive in the loss were significant at $p < .05$ at all interviews.

[17]Cross-sectional correlations between these coping variables and dispositional optimism were significant at all four interviews. Dispositional optimism was significantly correlated with seeking more social support and using positive distractions only at the 1-month interview.

[18]Regression analyses showed that dispositional optimism measured at 1 month still predicted significant variance in depression and distress at the 13-month and 18-month interviews when we controlled for depression or distress at 1 month, and avoidance coping, emotional express, problem solving, reapprasial, and rumination at 1 month, (all p's for dispositional optimism < .05).

I think that when you lose a loved one, it's a rebirth for yourself. You can't always dwell on the loss of the loved one. You have to look forward to what you are going to do with your life now—who you are as a single person, which is very disturbing. Many people have been married much longer than I was, and they have to find out who they are. And it's a whole new experience, learning who you are, knowing who you are as a single person. That's one of the hard parts about being a widow or widower. A lot of people don't have time to think of who they are because they're always attached to someone. And it's exciting. I mean, it's not bad, but it's exciting and it's also a little fearful to have to do that. Every day's a little learning experience for myself, of doing new things and learning new things as a single person.

SUMMARY

Many of the predictions of grief and coping theories about what types of coping help people adjust to their loss were supported at least partially in our study. People who expressed their emotions more and did not engage in dangerous activities to avoid thinking about their loss were less distressed over time. Yet, people who perhaps were too focused on their emotional reactions to their loss—who ruminated about those emotions and the consequences of their loss—were also more distressed. Thus, as recent theories of coping with grief suggest, there may be a "happy medium" between too little and too much attention to one's grief-related emotions.

Women were more likely to ruminate and less likely to distract than men, but also more likely to reach out to others for social support. Older people were more likely than younger people to engage in adaptive coping strategies. And religious people and optimists tended to use more adaptive strategies and were less distressed than nonreligious people.

One surprising finding was that people who reached out to others for social support as a way of coping did not adjust better than those who did not reach out. Chapter 4 explores evidence that other people can be an important source of support, but also can create conflict and burden for bereaved people.

_____

Voices

The respondents described many ways they had been trying to cope, and sometimes described things they wished they could do to cope.

I think the only thing positive, you keep going on. And try not to make a big ass of yourself. I remember when my mother died when I was 14, we really didn't know what to expect with her also. She died in stages, so we were ready; it was tragic and everything. But her best friend came in and just wailed and threw herself down on top the coffin, and we just weren't expecting—we didn't know that she would react like that. And then I watched one of Bob's daughters, just threw herself down on top of him and screamed, and the next day she was mad at me for not sharing everything I owned with her. But they've never experienced any deaths. At that time I thought maybe they thought—that that's how they felt. ... But I just try not to throw myself down on top of anybody. (51-year-old woman who lost her spouse)

I don't know if it's cause it happened so fast, but it just doesn't seem real. I think it's hitting me more now. I think I was numb for a long time. I was so strong for her, I held everything inside, and now, it's just hitting me. (30-year-old woman who lost a parent)

I can't believe that I went through what I went through. It does not seem that I went through 5 months of my husband's illness, and living with it day in and day out. It's like a blur. I don't realize that I did it, and now looking back, I realize how awful it was—not just for me, but for anybody that would have done it. But I think it's a mechanism that you have so you can get through it. It's like you just react. It's almost like an out-of-body experience—it's not you doing it, but it gets done, until you can step back and when it's all over say, "No, I was the one who really did that, and it was really hard." That's what I really see looking back, I can't believe it because I wasn't feeling anything during the time I was doing it. That's how you get through it. (48-year-old woman who lost her spouse)

Don't predetermine how you're going to do something. Let it happen, and if you have the strength to handle it don't be a martyr about it. If you reach the point you can't handle it, don't feel guilty. (58-year-old woman who lost a parent)

I've been trying to go to church more and pray more about it. I've been trying to find some peace with—understand it. But honestly I don't know that I've gotten there yet. I don't understand it. I still have thoughts that it isn't fair, and why ... I believe in God. The church tells me, the Bible tells me, it's His will, and I try to find some peace in that kind of a thought, but it's hard. It's hard for me to find the faith. I want to believe that, I want to accept that, but it's hard. (45-year-old man who lost his wife)

By 6 months postloss, many people had advice for others as to how to cope with the impending death of a loved one, and the aftermath.

The more open the dying person is, easier for person who's living. Be honest with yourself, do what you need to do because you need to go on. Reach out, be open, talk, seek support. The world is going to go on and the world gives you a very finite time to grieve. Because everyone expects you to be fine—come on, it's been 3 months!—I think that period becomes much more difficult. Allow yourself however long it takes. One of the things that comes up is anger—it's easy to lash out at the people you love. It's important to be open about that. I would say to my husband, "I know I'm lashing out at you." That made it easier for him because I wasn't personally attacking him.

Be very direct in asking for what you need, be very clear. It may not even make sense, what you need. I did some really bizarre things—I decided to redecorate the house in the midst of my parents' dying. I did it because it was one way of proving to myself that I wasn't afraid to go on. I needed the visible proof that that was true. Also I needed to change things. Also, as I went through this, my head became more and more cluttered, and it meant that my environment needed to be less and less cluttered. Not to panic—am I crazy? (45-year-old woman who lost a parent)

Just say, "Life as usual." Carry on the way you did before. Because they wouldn't want to take that away from you. They lived their life, now it's your turn—that's life as usual. All the memories are held within. Sitting home and thinking about morbid things is not going to help you. And let's face it, when you lose somebody it's easy to become morbid. So get out and live your life like you lived it before. I had good friends who got me right back into the mainstream of life. So I have had all these lovely people who have been a true support system. (56-year-old woman who lost a parent)

The main thing I would tell them is not to take any of the negative behavior patterns that are exhibited by the ill person personally. Because nine times out of 10 it probably doesn't have a damn thing to do with you. I'd also tell them to make a point to say all the good things that they ever wanted to say, so that after they're gone you'll never have to worry about—Oh man, I meant to tell them I felt this way, and I never did. (34-year-old woman who lost a parent)

My general advice would be to take the focus on themselves and to make sure that they do take care of themselves, physical care of themselves. To stay healthy, to be able to be of whatever help they could be, but to stay tuned into themselves. (46-year-old woman who lost a parent)

I guess I would say get some professional help over time. What was so helpful for me was I saw my therapist at least once a week, and it was a time I could just address the terrible stuff that was going on in my life. Because you can't be addressing it all the time every day because you really got a lot of work to do. But to take time out for yourself, and get the help that you need to keep yourself going. Because not only does it help you, but also it helps the person you're caring for. It helps you deal with the terrible thing they are going through. (24-year-old woman who lost a parent)

Don't react as you think people want you to. There is no "right" way to handle it. Just let your heart run free and do what your heart tells you. This is no time to do the right response. This is not one of those moments in life. (38-year-old man who lost a parent)

Be totally honest with yourself. Don't think person is going to get better. Don't pretend. My sister did—it caused her and mother a lot of grief. *Let go*. Let the person who is dying accept and just spend time loving them. Let the dying person know that you're going to be ok and everything is ok. You don't have to worry about anyone but your [family member who is dying].

If she was tired, let her go. Think about the person who is leaving and reassure them that you love them and that you'll be ok so that they can go on their way. After the loved one is gone, allow the person who is grieving to talk about it until there is no more talking. Then keep a journal to talk to the person who is lost. Express—get it out. Feelings are like a cut—you have to open it up to air so it can heal. You don't want it to fester. (57-year-old woman who lost a parent)

Be nice to yourself. Get a massage. Pamper yourself. As you're taking care of the dying, also find time to take care of yourself. Write it in your notebook: "I'm taking this time off for me. I'm going to this class. I'm going to meet this person." Normally I wouldn't go to this class. Normally I wouldn't meet this person. Normally I wouldn't eat at this particular point or go to the show or do this massage. But let's label this "Taking Care of Myself." And I would actually label it and book it—5 hours for Mom, 1 hour for me. I think it's so, so important. It will help to have that sense of peace about the letting go. Because when someone's really dying, it demands more time. It demands more energy. It demands more money. It demands more sacrifice. When people demand a lot ... part of you begrudges it on one level. And the guilt!—how can I possibly do that when she's dying? So I think by doing what you need to do and being as clear and honest as you can and taking care of yourself, then you won't be as obsessed as I was, trying to juggle relationships to escape. (40-year-old man who lost a parent)

First of all, accept it. Don't feel as if you're guilty because they'll die because that's not up to us to make that decision. We have no decision over life and death. Accept it because nobody's at fault. Talk about the loss of your loved one as soon as you can, often. To fight it, you're hurting yourself. They were a part of you, you are hiding a part of yourself. You talk about them; you had a main part of your life with this person. They haven't disappeared. They still live within you. Cry when you have to. If you get angry, shout. Let it all out. Don't hold it all in because it's not beneficial. It just isn't. (56-year-old woman who lost her parent)

I kind of regret that I didn't probe, kind of go into my husband. I kind of stayed away from the subject at that time, because he never discussed cancer with me. He never even told me the doctor said it. He told it to his roommate, and he told my daughter. But for us to talk about it—I just never could pull myself into something that I seemed to have stayed away from because I felt that it would be upsetting for him. I know he didn't ever like for me to know when he was feeling worse—one thing—because he knew I would tell the doctor if there was any change. But I do wish I had gotten into the conversation with him, for him to tell me more about how he felt and what have you. I would feel really better about it had I known more about his feelings and what he thought about it. He always seemed to avoid it, so I would leave it at that. (60-year-old woman who lost her husband)

What D did, and what was great, was, first, he accepted the fact that he was dying—we both did. We took care of everything he wanted to take care of as far as "I want this kid to have that." He talked with all the children. He really accepted that he might die any second. And then, he went on with living. (63-year-old woman who lost her husband)

Don't listen to anybody. Listen to your inner voice and do what you feel is right, irregardless of what people around you say. The only advice is between you and that loved one, and what you feel is right. And that is a very hard thing to do. Family, friends will say "If you eat right, if you do this, if you do that." You're not the one in that body that's dying. That person—what they want is what's right. The person taking care of them will have to tell that concerned person, "Will you shut up? This is the person that's going to decide what's good for them at this moment." To take on that battle and to become that protector without losing yourself because you're losing this other person, you really have to stay true to your inner voice. What's important is the person who's dying—the time that you have with them right then can never be brought back. That do-gooder, you have to tell them, "No!" and maybe hurt their feelings for your own sanity and for the sanity of the person you're taking care of. You must do what you feel is right. Sometimes that's even concerned with the person that's dying. They might be demanding so much where you have to say, "I'm sorry. I've got to go do this." You must be true to that inner voice, and you will hurt a lot of people when you do, but you will not destroy yourself. That's a hard thing, a very difficult thing. I think a lot of people don't realize that. (37-year-old woman who lost her husband)

There's nothing you can do so accept each day as it comes along. The wheels are in progress, and you can't turn them back. The best thing is to just go ahead and face it head on and not hide you head in the sand. This is it. There's nothing you can do, so let it happen. I think you can deal with it better if you're realistic about it. (58-year-old woman who lost a close personal friend)

I wish I would not have pressured my father to take his pills, eat the right foods, behave himself, be good, because a good part of it was selfishness. I didn't want him to die, I didn't want him to lose his faculties, and I thought if he would just do it right, things would be better. A few times, my husband had to tell me, "Lighten up and leave him alone—it's his life." That was a good thing for me to hear because I didn't even recognize the pressure I was putting on him. That was very helpful. I think if somebody's lucky enough to have a neutral observer, that would be a good thing. It did open my eyes. There were some times I simply had to say, "Take the pill now." And there were other times where I could just say, "ok." And I didn't know that at first. I thought if I did everything the doctor said, we would have an optimal situation. I realize now it was for my own benefit I was doing it. I wanted a comfort level that wasn't there when I could see how ill he was, and when I felt like I had to do his thinking for him, which was partially true. (45-year-old woman who lost a parent)

Be very patient with yourself because you're going through things that you don't even understand. I'd say no matter what you're feeling, just take it easy, be patient with yourself. Give yourself pep talks. Say, "You're doing just fine." I feel you will learn and grow and be different because of it and not to judge yourself at the time. The thing that helped me the most going through my sister's illness and then the death was just doing whatever I could to take care of me. I would treat myself a lot of times, as a way of getting through things. Even if it was a New York Peppermint Patty, it was something to say I was still ok although it seemed my world around me was crashing down because I depended on her for a lot things. Maybe in another situation, another individual isn't so dependent on their loved one that's just passed away, where I was very dependent on her. I know it's different for everybody. The only advice I could say is be very patient with yourself, and *do* things for yourself. (36-year-old woman who lost a sibling)

4

Social Support

I found out how to treat other people when they lose someone—what to do for them—what helped me, and what I can do in return. Like, he died on a Thursday night and the next day my friend from work brought over a lot of food. We had enough to eat all weekend. 'Cause I couldn't think about cooking. The next day I just laid in my bed and watched TV, which is something I'd never do, and the kids got in bed with me, these great big kids, you know. Cards and phone calls—not to be afraid to contact the people 'cause you really need that contact. You need someone to say they're there if you need them. (Perry, 50-year-old woman whose father died of prostate cancer)

We had incredible support from family and friends, unbelievable from our church and our pastor. And even school friends. We anticipated some negative response to our caring for a person with AIDS, particularly with children in our home, and nothing negative was ever said to us during or since. That was quite amazing. He was very touched by the expressions of concern from friends of ours who would come in and visit him. It was a very close time for my family, that is, my husband, children, and my parents. My mother and I worked in tandem, and our relationship was altered as a result of this. We kind of emerged from this experience as peers. We're much closer. That has been absolutely wonderful. (Fran, 39-year-old woman whose cousin died of AIDS)

As far as getting through her death, I feel I came through it with flying colors only because I had such great support through friends and family. It seemed like when situations would come up that I didn't know how to handle or didn't have the answers to, when things were really the darkest, the very next day there would be someone there, a phone call or someone would stop by or I'd run into someone in the store. Whatever that problem was, the next day someone was there with an answer and solved my problem for me or at least showed me how to handle it. Someone who has, you might say, little faith—in those dark times, it was neat to see how those things were solved for me. It seemed like it would build up from a crisis—I'm desperate, how am I going to handle this?—and the next day, there would be someone there to save me. (Jan, 36-year-old woman whose 40-year-old sister died of breast cancer)

After living with somebody for 50 years and you're left alone, it's very frightening. It's the aloneness that's frightening, losing someone to share things with. My husband was very strong and I relied on him. (Bess, 72, whose 73-year-old husband died of cancer)

My husband probably doesn't feel very comfortable talking about her death with me. Neither do my friends. They can't handle if I start talking about it and get upset. My friends couldn't possibly understand how it affected me. Most of them couldn't even imagine losing their parents. I know I could never imagine losing my mother. It was always a big fear for me when I was growing up, because I knew that they were older than most of my friends' parents. At 29 you're supposed to be mature enough to where you don't feel like teenagers would feel if they lost their parents. But I think it hurts the same no matter how old you are. I'm grateful to have had her as long as I had her. (Donna, 29, whose 52 year-old-mother died of breast cancer)

One of my sisters said that she felt the family had gotten closer, but I don't feel that way at all. In fact, I feel the opposite, that if anything it made things more stressful, because Mom was always like the catalyst, as I'm sure most Moms are. They kind of pad things between you and you could always use her as a sounding board, so you never got as mad at your sister because your Mom was listening to what you were saying. So to me there's nothing positive at all. (Candy, 31, whose 60-year-old mother died of lung cancer)

Bereavement has been called a "social network crisis" (Stylianos & Vachon, 1993, p. 397). The person who died may have been the bereaved person's primary source of social support. Friends tied to the deceased may withdraw from the bereaved person now that the deceased is no longer present. If the death occurred after a prolonged illness, family and friends may have already withdrawn from the bereaved person's life, unable to bear the chronic stress of the illness.

Yet, having the support of others can be critical to coping positively with loss (Lopata, 1973; Sanders, 1993; Stroebe & Stroebe, 1987; Stylianos & Vachon, 1993). Said one daughter in her 20s who had lost her mother to pancreatic cancer:

Nobody can replace her or be her—it's not the same. But I can surround myself with supportive, loving people that can help me get through life. It's really hopeful.

The meaning of good social support turns out to be complex, and varies from one person to another. This chapter explores the various meanings of social support and examines the role social support plays in helping people cope with loss. We also examine whether different groups of bereaved people—spouses, adult children, parents, siblings, men, women, those who lose a loved one to a stigmatized illness—need and receive different amounts and types of social support. We consider whether people who belong to religious organizations have more social support following a loss than those who do not. And we ask whether support groups formed to provide social interaction and support for bereaved people are helpful.

WHAT IS SOCIAL SUPPORT?

Just what does it mean to have good social support? Social support is generally divided into two types: *emotional support* and *material support* (Cohen & Wills, 1985; House, 1981). Emotionally supporting a bereaved person involves allowing and encouraging the person to discuss the loss. Bereaved people often feel the need to repeatedly tell the story of their loss as they try to understand and make sense of it. They may want their listeners to affirm that their way of making sense is right or good. They may want to be told that they made the right decisions about the medical care that their loved one received, the rituals that were followed after the death, the handling of the deceased's estate, and the many other matters that arise because of a loss. Talking with supportive people about the thoughts and images around the loss helps the bereaved assimilate the loss into their worldviews and feel affirmed for the decisions they made and for their understanding of the loss (Lepore, Silver, Wortman, & Wayment, 1996).

Bereaved people may have secrets they need to tell, or acts for which they need absolution—lies they told the deceased or others, ways they feel they let down the deceased, perhaps even ways they feel they hastened the deceased's death. Some bereaved people need to express their grief openly, by crying or expressing anger at the deceased or at othes associated with the loss (such as physicians, emergency room personnel, unhelpful family members). Others may need just to sit quietly, perhaps occasionally remembering pleasant times with the deceased. They may need to confide their fears about living without the deceased. They may need to admit that they are glad that the deceased is dead, either because he or she was suffering terribly or because their relationship with the deceased had been difficult. These kind of thoughts are often not socially acceptable, however, and the bereaved person can feel isolated and guilty because of his or her thoughts.

Material support consists of the things people can do to make everyday living a bit less complicated and burdensome for bereaved people. Material support is often divided into instrumental support and informational support (House, 1981). Instrumental support can include assisting with funeral arrangements, wading through piles of bills or papers, dealing with insurance companies or the social security office. It can mean providing money to pay medical and funeral bills, living expenses, the expense of relocating surviving family members, or other financial burdens falling on the survivors. It also can include taking care of surviving children while the adults cope with the aftermath of the loss, providing transportation for family members, or simply providing housecleaning and food in the early days and weeks following the loss. Informational support is often provided by professionals—social workers, hospice workers, lawyers—who help the bereaved deal with the complicated legal and financial issues often left behind after a loss. Eventually, material support may involve helping the bereaved person find new ways of integrating into society and changing social roles (by finding a job, learning to care for dependent children, etc.).

It seems obvious that the larger the social network, the more likely the bereaved will be to have available all these forms of social support, and from multiple sources. On the other hand, people who have little or no social network, who are isolated and perhaps estranged from others, may not receive any of these forms of social support. For many bereaved people, the deceased, particularly if he or she was a spouse or longtime partner, may have been the only person who provided support to them. Now that this person is gone, they are left literally with no one. Historically, people grew up and lived in the same communities throughout their lives. Their extended families were nearby, and community members knew each other well. Today, even people living in urban environments, surrounded by thousands of people, can feel alone and isolated.

When it comes to social networks, however, quantity does not always mean quality. Some people have large extended social networks that, at the time of a loss, act as burdens rather than blessings (Rook, 1984; Vachon & Stylianos, 1988). A bereaved widow may be faced with children who are fighting over the estate left by their deceased father. A bereaved daughter may be criticized by her siblings for the decisions she made about her deceased mother's medical care. A bereaved parent may be questioned by others in ways that imply that the parent should have been able to prevent his or her child's death. Laura, a 36-year-old woman whose father died 6 months previously and whose mother was dying after a prolonged illness said:

I think the stress that it puts on a marital relationship (is great). My husband has never experienced the death of a parent, or the illness of a parent, so he's not really good with compassion. He doesn't have the foggiest idea. He says, "Well, it's been 6 months. You should be over this now." I felt invalidated by him along the way quite a bit.

And Maria, a 47-year-old woman whose 50-year-old husband died of AIDS said:

> After the death, we went through about 2 months of us all tearing up on one another in rage, fighting, and I wish I would have done that differently, but I don't know that you can. Everybody's in such pain. You are lashing out in anger. But out of that came a great deal of growth, I think. I have such a good relationship with my daughter. But the boys still haven't come to terms with [their father's death].

Even when people are trying to be helpful, they may say or do things to the bereaved person that hurt rather than help (DiMatteo & Hays, 1981; House, 1981; Lehman, Ellard, & Wortman, 1986; Thoits, 1982). In the heat of the moment—when faced with a distressed bereaved person—friends and family members often feel anxious and tongue-tied. They may fear saying the wrong thing or simply not know what to say. As a result, they may say nothing, or what they do or say may be delivered or taken in ways that are unhelpful. For example, bereaved family members are often told, "She has led a full life," "Be thankful you have another son," or "You shouldn't question God's will" (Davidowitz & Myrick, 1984). The aunt of one of our former clients greeted the client the first time they met after the death of the client's 12-year-old daughter in a traffic accident, with "You're so lucky! You have an angel in heaven!"

In our bereavement study, one woman whose mother died of cancer said:

> Everybody gets their share of, "You should be doing this." Don't let it get to you. And they don't mean it probably. People that were there all the time for you before this happened, disappear. They can't deal with it—too much about their own mortality, I guess. It's understandable, but it's real hard not to be really bitter.

Veronica, a 55-year-old woman who lost her 99-year-old mother recounted:

> I got real angry when she died, but people would tell me to look at the other side—she had been just laying there, just wasting away. I got angry at that!

Harold, a 74-year-old man, who lost his wife, talks about the silence that ensues when others just don't know what to say:

> Apparently people feel that I would rather not talk about her. I went out to dinner with my number two boy, his wife and two girls, and nobody said anything about M. I think maybe they do it because they figure I don't want to hear about it—being unpleasant, you know. That sure as hell ain't so. It has come to me over the months that they really don't talk about her that much. (Group of retired friends who meet periodically for lunch) will say, "How are you doing?" and you know what they mean, but they don't get around to talking about it. I think it's, "Ok, this guy lost his wife. That's an unpleasant subject. I won't bring it up."

And Juanita, a 64-year-old woman who lost her husband said:

> People don't really understand your dilemmas about certain things. I cry alone. People care, but they don't ... they don't want you to feel badly. So I try not to embarrass myself and everybody else.

The comments bereaved people most often find unhelpful include giving advice (e.g., "You should clean out all the clothes right away, just get rid of everything that reminds you of him"), encouragement of recovery ("Just put this behind you and get on with your life"), minimization or forced cheerfulness ("You should be thankful that she went so quickly"), and identification with feelings ("I know just how you feel" ; Lehman et al., 1986). These comments most often come from other family members who truly want to be supportive. On the other hand, supportive expressions that bereaved people often do find helpful include expressions of concern, the opportunity to ventilate their feelings, being included in social activities, getting in contact with people who have had similar losses, and simply having another person be around (Lehman et al., 1986).

Friction within a family is often created when family members grieve out of sync with one another according to their own personality and coping styles. One family member might try to impose his or her style of coping on others, or criticize others for their styles of coping. Some may accuse certain family members of not caring, or not missing or loving the deceased because these family members are not grieving "as they should be." Or, other family members may have angry outbursts when some people begin talking about or crying for the deceased.

When the bereaved person reacts with annoyance or continued distress to unhelpful comments by others, family members and friends may become annoyed or frustrated at having their well-intentioned efforts rejected. At this point, they may simply withdraw. Or they may push their advice and encouragement a bit harder, perhaps infusing it with thinly veiled frustration or criticism. This may be met with more resistance and increasing anger by the bereaved person, who may accuse family members and friends of not understanding or making it worse. A negative interactional cycle may be set up that is very difficult for either party to break (Coyne, 1976).

The next sections examine our own data and data from previous bereavement studies, focusing on four aspects of social support, following the literature just described. *Emotional support* was defined in our study as receiving support from others for expressing one's grief as one needed, feeling affirmed by others for one's actions and ways of thinking about the loss, and feeling loved and respected by others. *Material support* included receiving instrumental help (money and other resources) and information helpful in coping with the consequences of the loss from others. *Social isolation* was the experience of being separated and isolated from others, and wanting more interaction with others. *Social friction* was the experience of being criticized by others, burdened by others' problems, and generally in conflict with family members and friends.

WHO RECEIVES MORE SOCIAL SUPPORT, AND WHO RECEIVES LESS

Some types of bereavement may be easier for others to respond to, and thus some groups of bereaved people may receive more social support than others. That is, people may find it easier to deal with or think about certain types of loss, and thus may be better able to respond in a supportive way to people experiencing those types of loss.

Loss of a Child

One type of loss to which people may have difficulty responding is the loss of a child (Edelstein, 1983). Some parents feel there is a "conspiracy of silence" among their friends and other family members—everyone steadfastly avoids even mentioning the child's death. This may be because others do not know what to say to parents or because they do not want even to consider the possibility that any child could die. Friends and family members may think, "I don't want to remind them of their loss and their pain" as if the grieving person has forgotten the loss for a moment. Tom, a 28-year-old man whose infant son died of congestive heart failure said:

> For me, one of the things that's bothered me is—because it is a sensitive subject, because it is a child—people tend not to want to talk about it. We talk about him amongst ourselves. There's probably some people out there who would be more than happy to talk about it, but I don't know them very well, and the friends that are closer tend to shy away from it. I can understand that because I'm typically a person who has a tough time finding words. I never can forget him. None of my brothers and sisters bring it up, ever. It's surprising. They all have kids—maybe it's just too painful for them. They think maybe it could happen to them because it happened to me.

Parents who lose a child late in the mother's pregnancy or shortly after birth often feel isolated and dismissed in their grief (Benfield, Leib, & Vollman, 1978; Helmrath & Steinitz, 1978; Kirkley-Best & Kellner, 1982; Nichols, 1986). People have actually been heard to say to parents who lose a newborn, "You're young, you can always have another one" (Helmrath & Steinitz, 1978, p. 788). Even when they do not voice such thoughts, others often feel it is inappropriate for parents to grieve the loss of a fetus or newborn for an extended period of time, assuming that because the parents "didn't know" the child, they could not have developed an attachment to the child.

Parents who lose an older child—one in middle childhood or adolescence—also face social isolation because other people do not want to talk about the loss. In addition, these parents lose the social network of other parents and children that had revolved around their own child's activities—the other "soccer moms and dads" (Edelstein, 1983). Parents who lose an adult child often feel overlooked by medical and mental health professionals, who are concerned and intervene with the spouse and children of the deceased, but may not attend to the bereaved parents (deVries, Dalla Lana, & Falck, 1994). It can be difficult for parents who lose an older child or adult child to find support groups. There are nationwide organizations for bereaved parents, but these groups are usually oriented toward parents who lose infants and young children.

Loss of a Parent

Losing a parent is not expected to be as difficult as losing a child. Because we often consider the loss of an elderly parent to be part of the natural order of things, however, bereaved adult children can feel ashamed and rejected when their grief goes on "too long" or appears to be "too intense." Terri, a 31-year-old woman who lost her mother to cancer said:

> I took a lot of time off (when my mother was ill). My immediate supervisor said something that I've thought about a lot. She said, "You're a big girl now. You don't have to be down there all the time." She didn't mean it in a mean way, but she felt like maybe I was taking it too hard.

Clearly, this woman felt invalidated in her choice to spend her mothers' last days with her, and was put in the position of quitting her job or leaving her mother alone. Many of our respondents who lost a parent said that other people had criticized them for reacting so strongly to the loss, and had encouraged them to "get over it" more quickly than they felt they could.

Loss of a Sibling

People who lost a sibling also often felt that they did not receive the support they needed. Many people had not even told coworkers and other friends that they had a sibling who was terminally ill, or who had died in recent months. They expected that they should be able just to go on with life as if the loss had not happened, and they noticed that other people expected that of them as well. Yet as we discussed in chapter 2, the loss of a sibling hit many people hard because it broke an important attachment bond, and because it raised issues about their own age and mortality for them.

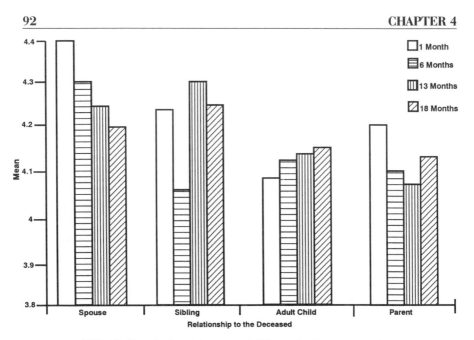

FIG. 4.1. Perceived social support of different family group members.

Loss of a Spouse

In our study, the group that felt best supported by others were bereaved spouses (Fig. 4.1).[1] Bereaved spouses were especially likely to report being less socially isolated and experiencing less friction in their social network than other family groups.[2] Their children, their siblings and the rest of their extended family rallied around them after their loss, shielding them from conflict and helping them feel connected to others. This difference between bereaved spouses and the other family groups came primarily from support from family members. Bereaved spouses reported significantly more satisfaction with the support they received from family members than the other groups, particularly shortly after their loss.[3] In contrast, there were no differences between the bereaved groups

---

[1]Repeated measures analysis of variance on overall social support (all social support variables averaged together in one scale) showed a marginally significant main effect of relationship to deceased $F(3, 14) = 2.23$, $p = .085$ and a significant interaction between time and relationship to the deceased $F(9, 632) = 2.92$, $p < .01$.

[2]Repeated measures analysis of variance on social isolation showed a marginally significant interaction between time and relationship to deceased, $F(9, 629) = 1.71$, $p < .10$. Repeated measures analysis of variance on social friction showed a significant interaction between time and relationship to deceased, $F(9, 629) = 2.21$, $p < .05$.

[3]Repeated measures analysis of variance on satisfaction with family support showed a significant interaction between time and relationship to deceased, $F(9, 620) = 2.06$, $p < .05$.

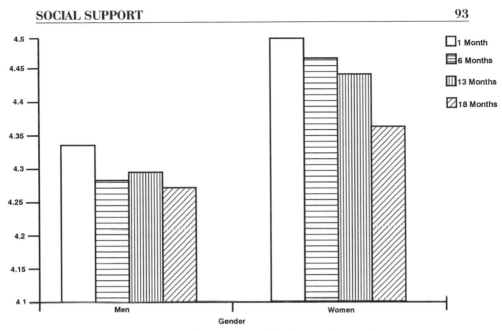

FIG. 4.2. Emotional support reported by bereaved men and women.

in satisfaction with the support received from friends. Thus, it seems that bereaved spouses enjoy particularly strong support, compared to other bereaved groups, from their family members.

Gender Differences in Social Support

One reason why women adjust better to loss than men may be that women have broader and deeper social networks that support them after a loss (Morgan, 1994; Stroebe & Stroebe, 1997). Women not only have more people in their social network than men, but they also feel more comfortable openly expressing their emotions—including their grief—with others than men, and this may help them adjust to life without their loved one (Perlman, Gerson, & Spinner, 1978; Stroebe, Stroebe, Abakoumkin, & Schutz, 1996). We found that women reported receiving more emotional support than men at all but the 18-month interview (Fig. 4.2).[4] The women probably felt much more comfortable reaching out for social support than did the men. Recall that in chapter 3 we found that women sought social support as a coping strategy significantly more often

---

[4]Although repeated measures analysis of variance on emotional support did not show effects of gender, we undertook comparisons of men and women at individual interviews nonetheless because gender was of great theoretical interest. These individual t tests showed women to report higher emotional support than men at $p < .05$ at the 1-, 6-, and 13-month interviews.

than did the men. Women may have a way of responding to the support of others that makes it easier for them to garner support, as well. That is, women may be able to receive a variety of kinds of social support from others and make others feel appreciated for their support. Men may have more difficulty in responding positively to the support offered by others, because they are not comfortable in being supported or in showing their emotions. That is, a man who is typically taciturn and stoic may be difficult for others to respond to and may seem not to appreciate the responses that others try to make.

Thus, it seems that bereaved spouses may feel they receive more social support than other groups of bereaved family members, probably because we recognize and accept the grief process for bereaved spouses more than we do for other family groups. In addition, the terrifying prospect of losing a child may make it especially hard for people to respond appropriately to bereaved parents. The next section explores another type of loss that may be difficult for people to respond to in a supportive manner—loss due to the stigmatized illness of AIDS.

AIDS-Related Losses

The stigma of AIDS can lead traditional family members of persons who die from AIDS to hide the cause of their loved one's death and feel ostracized and isolated. These family members may not be part of a community that accepts homosexuality and thus feel isolated because of their loved one's homosexuality as well as the cause of the death. Said Kate, a 58-year-old mother who lost her 32-year-old son to AIDS:

> I'm still very upset over T's death. The fact that he died of AIDS and was gay has put a big stigma on the way people have treated his death and have reacted to it. I just wish people could be more educated when it comes to someone who is gay, and what the lifestyle is all about and how it isn't something that people embrace; it's the way they were born. I think that's really been the hardest part with T's death. I always knew he was gay and never had a problem with it. But then when the AIDS epidemic broke out, people seemed to blame it on the gay community, which really wasn't fair, isn't fair. It's been very hard for me to accept the way a lot of people feel, because unless you're in this situation, unless you have a son who is gay, unless you have a son who has AIDS, or are involved with anyone who had AIDS, I don't think there's any way anyone can really understand what it's all about, I really don't.

Gay men have it doubly hard. They are rejected by the larger society because of their sexual orientation. In addition, their relationships with their partners who die of AIDS are not sanctioned or even acknowledged by society. As a result, they may receive even less support from family members, colleagues, and the religious community, than traditional family members of AIDS patients (Sowell, Bramlett, Gueldner, Gritzmacher, & Martin, 1991). Their friends, particularly their gay friends, may be very supportive of them during a loss. But many of these friends may have died in the last 10 years as part of the AIDS epidemic, or may be burdened with their own recent losses, or their own HIV infection (Martin & Dean, 1993; Schwartzberg, 1993).

In our study, the gay men who lost their partners to AIDS reported the greatest sense of social isolation of any group, followed by the traditional family members of AIDS-related deceased; family members of people who died of non-AIDS illnesses reported the least social isolation.[5] Thus, although we conducted our study in the San Francisco Bay area, where the gay population is large and their community is strong, gay men who lost partners still felt isolated and alone. Some of this aloneness came from the fact that many members of their social group had already died of AIDS. It also came from feeling that, even in one of the most open communities in the world, they were still estranged from family and from the larger society.

However, when it came to reports of social friction—conflict and tension with other people in one's family and network of friends—it was the traditional family members who lost someone to AIDS who reported the greatest level of social friction.[6] Some of these family members talked about problems within the family in acceptance of their loved one's homosexuality or the means by which the loved one contracted AIDS. For example, if the loved one had been injecting drugs and contracted AIDS by sharing needles with other drug users, there was often much blame of the loved one by other family members, or questions about whether the drug use could have and should have been stopped by the surviving family members. Some people who lost a sibling or a child to AIDS had not even told more distant family members or their own circle of friends of their loved one's illness. One participant, a mother of a man who died of AIDS, went to San Francisco from her home in the midwest to care for her son in his last weeks. She had not told anyone in her hometown of her son's homosexuality or his illness. She nursed him until he died, buried him, then went back to her midwestern home, feeling unable to share anything about her experience and loss with the people she interacted with daily.

Thus, the stigmas surrounding AIDS can create a context of low social support for family members who lose a loved one to the disease. On the other hand, social support is at least as important for people who are left in the wake of this illness as for people who suffer any other type of loss.

---

[5]Differences between the three groups were significant at the 1- and 6-month interviews, but not at the 13- and 18-month interviews at $p < .05$ in analyses of variance done separately for each interview.

[6]Differences between the three groups were significant at $p < .05$ at the 1 month interview, and at $p = .08$ at the 6-month interview, but nonsignificant at the 13- and 18-month interviews in analyses of variance done separately for each interview.

HOW SOCIAL SUPPORT INFLUENCES
DISTRESS AND COPING

Social support helps. Numerous studies have found that people who have family members and friends who provide them with emotional and material support report less distress both shortly after and long after a loss (Bass, Bowman, & Noelkerm 1991; Clayton, Halikas, & Maurice, 1971; Dimond, Lund, & Caserta, 1987; Norris & Murrell, 1990; Schwarzer, 1992; Stroebe, Stroebe, Abakoumkin, & Schut, 1996; Vachon & Stylianos, 1998; Windholz, Marmar, & Horowitz, 1985). Again, it seems that it is not the quantity of social support but the quality of social support that is important. The relationship between the simple number of family members and friends a bereaved person has consistent contact with and that person's level of distress following a loss is weak (Zisook, Shuchter, & Lyons, 1987). The relation between the quality of the emotional and material support others provide and the bereaved person's level of distress are strong, however.

In our own study, people with more emotional and material support, and who were less isolated and had less friction in their social networks, were less depressed and distressed than people with less emotional and practical support, or who were isolated or experiencing friction in their social networks. Of all the social support variables, isolation was the most consistently and strongly related to depression and distress over time. Thus, people who felt they were alone and without caring others to talk with and be with showed the most persistent depression and general distress over time.[7]

People with good social support used more adaptive coping strategies than those without good social support. Not surprisingly, they reached out to others as a coping strategy more than people who did not have good social support. But they also were engaged in more problem solving, positive reappraisal of their situation, expression of their emotions, and in less rumination and

---

[7]Cross-sectional correlations between each of the social support variables and measures of depression and general distress were all significant at $p < .05$. Partial correlations between emotional support at 1 month and depression or distress at 13 and 18 months, controlling for depression or distress at 1 month, were significant at $p < .05$. Partial correlations between social friction at 1 month and depression or distress at 6 and 13 months, controlling for depression or distress at 1 month, were significant at $p < .05$. Partial correlations between isolation at 1 month and depression at 6, 13, and 18 months, controlling for depression at 1 month, were significant at $p < .05$, and partial correlations between isolation at 1 month and distress at 6 and 18 months, controlling for 6 distress at 1 month, were significant at $p < .05$. Partial correlations between material support at 1 month and depression at 13 and 18 months, controlling for depression at 1 month, were significant at $p < .05$. Simultaneous regression analyses examining which social support variables measured at 1 month predicted depression or distress at subsequent interviews, controlling for 1 month depression or distress scores, showed that only isolation was a significant predictor of depression or distress (for both the 6- and 18-month depression and distress scores), once all the other social support variables were controlled.

maladaptive avoidance coping.[8] Part of providing good social support is helping bereaved people solve the problems they must face (such as problems with the estate or with caring for small children). Having supportive others who will allow you to express your emotions can also help to quell ruminations and to stop engaging in maladaptive coping strategies such as drinking heavily.

People who had more positive emotional support, and less friction and social isolation, also seemed to find it easier to make sense of their loss in the first 6 months of their bereavement than people with less social support. Indeed, one consistent theme among people who found meaning in their loss was that the loss brought family members together and/or caused the bereaved to appreciate the importance of his or her relationships with family members or friends:

> We definitely learned a lot about ourselves and about each other within the family circle. There was a rallying of support, and a camaraderie that I think only shows itself, truly shows itself, when something like this occurs. I think you always assume that it's there, but it was tested, and we were pleasantly surprised, very pleased with how each one took their role, and no one was ever left to feel as though they were abandoned. (Wayne, 38-year-old man who lost his mother to pancreatic cancer)

> We learned a lot about our family—how we rallied round, and had a sense of real love and support. And friends that were very supportive, even some that we might not have expected to come through the way they did, unsolicited help and encouragements—those kind of things. (Val, 59-year-old woman who lost her 38-year-old son to melanoma)

> One positive thing it showed me was the best in my sister. She just took charge because she had the knowhow and the resources and because she loved my dad so much. And for me, the positive thing was seeing that—seeing that full capability in my sister. (Carrine, a 48-year-old woman who lost her father to pancreatic cancer)

> I came to know my stepdad better than I had known him when she (the mother) was alive. And it's been a real positive experience. It was like her going-away present, you might say. Her death brought us together. In fact, he even said that at one point he apparently never even knew me. Now he's totally open, he shows all of his feelings, and it's amazing to me, because he was a crusty old blue-collar worker. He turns out to be one of the most sensitive, feeling people I've ever known. (Gene, 51-year-old man who lost his mother to pancreatic cancer)

It is easier for people to give good social support to bereaved people who seem to be coping well. That is, having good social support may be a consequence, as well as a cause, of good coping (Hobfoll & Freedy, 1990; Sarason et al., 1991). Bereaved people who are coping well may give better signals as to what kind of social support they need. They may be more tolerant when

---

[8]Correlations between all the social support variables except practical support and the coping variables were all significant at $p < .05$.

others provide inappropriate social support, not reacting with anger when a family member or friend gives unwanted advice or encouragement. One of our clients, a man bereaved of his wife, felt terribly uncomfortable with the support that women from his daughter's school were trying to provide in the wake of his wife's death. These women had organized themselves to provide meals three times per week for the next 2 to 3 months. The client was so uncomfortable with accepting this support that he was ready to turn it down.

In our study, people who were more distressed at the 1-month interview lost social support between that interview and the 6-month and the 13-month interviews.[9] Thus, it seems that people who are highly distressed shortly after a loss risk a withdrawal of family and friends, feeling unable and unwilling to provide continued social support.

But even taking into account that it is easier to support someone who seems to be coping well with their loss, bereaved people who had more positive social support from others fared better over time. People really did "get by with a little help from their friends."

DIFFERENCES BETWEEN BEREAVED GROUPS, AND CHANGES OVER TIME, IN TYPE OF SUPPORT NEEDED

The type and amount of support people need following a loss may change with time, and different groups of bereaved people may need different types of support. One study of widows found that emotional support and empathy was most helpful to them just after their loss, but over time, material support focused on helping them form new social roles was most helpful (Walker, MacBride, & Vachon, 1977).

In our study, neither emotional nor material support was strongly related to levels of distress among the bereaved spouses. Instead, the experience of friction in their social network and social isolation were significantly related to levels of distress, and became more strongly related over time.[10] Thus, widows and widowers who felt that others were creating conflict in their lives at the

---

[9]Regression analyses were done predicting changes in overall social support scores from 1 month to 6 months, 13 months, and 18 months using distress scores at 1 month. The standardized beta weights for the effects of distress on changes in social support were significant using the 1- to 6-month data, $B = -.13$, $p < .05$ and the 1- to 13-month data, $B = -.16$, $p < .05$, but not for the 1 to 18 month data, $B = -.08$, ns. Other regression analyses predicting changes in social support from 6 to 13 months using 6-month distress scores, and from 13 to 18 months using 13-month distress scores showed no significant effects of distress on changes in social support.

[10]Among the bereaved spouses, emotional support and material support were not significantly correlated $p < .05$ with overall distress at any interview. Friction and isolation were significantly correlated with distress at all interviews, with the correlations increasing from about $r = .35$ to $r = .56$ from the 6-month interview to the 18-month interview.

very time they needed positive social support were faring significantly worse than those who did not experience much friction in their social networks. Having other people be critical or create tension in the family can create a sense of betrayal in the bereaved spouses. Just when they need their children to support them in their loss, these children may be bringing up old family feuds, or arguing over the settlement of the deceased parent's estate. Just when they need their own siblings to support them, these siblings may be pushing them to start dating, or to move out of their home into a smaller home, or do something else that the widow or widower does not feel prepared for yet.

The isolation that widows and widowers feel comes from losing not only their partners but also the social network of couples that they and their partners were part of. Several widows and widowers in our study talked about being dropped from the circle of couples that they and their partners had spent years socializing with. They would occasionally be invited to dinners or outings, but always felt like the fifth wheel, no longer part of a network that had been a vital part of their lives before their loss.

In contrast, for people who had lost a child, the emotional support of others was critical to their psychological well-being, and became more critical with time.[11] For bereaved parents, the emotional support of others can help them come to grips with the shock, the sense of injustice, the vacuum created by the loss of a child.[12] And, as we saw earlier, bereaved parents often feel no one wants to talk about their loss, so having even a few people who can bear to talk about the loss of a child can be a rare and tremendous gift.

Similarly, emotional support was the most critical aspect of support for people who lost a parent. Losing a parent can mean losing a major source of affirmation and support. As one woman whose mother died said, "The unconditional support, your number one fan is your Mom—how important that is all through a person's life, even when you're not still a child." Having others who love and respect you, who affirm your ways of thinking and ways of doing things, and who will listen to whatever you need to tell them, can help a great deal for people who have lost a parent to whom they were close.

Among all the bereaved groups, the relationship between distress and friction or isolation increased over time, suggesting that these issues become more salient as the time since the actual loss passes.[13] Other family members and friends are probably on their best behavior in the first weeks and months

---

[11]Correlations between overall distress and emotional support among bereaved children and parents ranged from .33 to .70, all $p < .05$.

[12]Adults who lost a sibling were also more distressed if they had lower emotional support, but the relationships were significant only at 1 month and 18 months. The instability in correlations among the adult siblings may be due to the small size of this group ($n = 17$ by 18 months).

[13]Correlations between overall distress and friction or isolation among all groups ranged from .34 to .80, all $p < .05$.

following a loss. With time, old conflicts arise again, and perhaps the bereaved person is less tolerant of these conflicts, more sensitive to the criticisms and annoyances of others. As Nikki, whose brother died of a brain tumor said, "I've never suffered fools, but now I suffer them even less." Also with time, family members and friends tire of hearing the bereaved person talk about his or her loss and subtly, or not so subtly, give the bereaved person messages to stop talking and get over it. The sense of isolation and suppression that the bereaved feel can be enormous. In our study, several participants told us that they looked forward to participating in our interviews, particularly the 13-month and 18-month interviews because our interviewers were the only ones who would listen as they talked about their loss.

The amount of material support that others provided—instrumental support such as bringing food or lending the bereaved person money, and informational support—was less strongly related to levels of distress than emotional support, friction, or isolation for all the bereaved groups. In addition, material support was only significantly related to distress in two groups, the people who lost a parent and those who lost a child, and even in these groups, at much lower levels than the other forms of social support. Yet, in our society, providing material support is one of the primary ways people reach out to the bereaved after a loss. People often feel comfortable "doing" for bereaved people, but do not feel comfortable "sitting" with their grief. But, as one woman said, "I don't need a casserole, I need someone to talk to, someone who will let me cry."

RELIGIOUS COMMUNITIES
AS SOCIAL SUPPORT NETWORKS

Religious communities or groups may be more active than most other social groups in responding to the losses experienced by members of the group. When a bereaved person is an active member of a religious group and subscribes to the doctrine and rituals of the group, he or she is likely to receive considerable support from other members of the group (McIntosh, Silver, & Wortman, 1993). Many religious or spiritual people also feel they receive much support directly from God or the deity in which they believe:

Man cannot comfort another man, although there are many comforters. The Lord is the real comforter. God can speak peace to a soul—then you are helped. (Joe, an 84-year-old man who lost his 82-year-old wife to melanoma)

In our study, people who said their were religious or spiritual had overall levels of social support that were higher than those who were not religious or

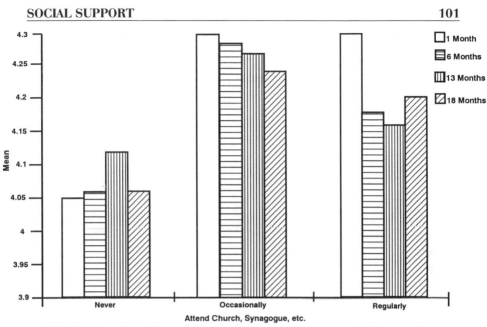

FIG. 4.3. Overall social support for people who do and do not attend religious services.

spiritual (Fig. 4.3).[14] Among the participants in our study who were religious or spiritual, those who attended religious services (church, synagogue, etc.) at least occasionally also reported more overall social support, particularly practical support from others, less social isolation, and less social friction than those who did not attend religious services.[15]

> The first thing they should do is reach for the church because you need the support. The spiritual support is so important for the sick and for the well. It is very important. You don't feel alone. My husband was very comforted

---

[14]Repeated measures analysis of variance on overall social support (all forms of social support averaged together on one scale) showed a significant interaction between time and religious/spiritual interests, $F(3, 210) = 2.83, p < .05$, and a significant main effect of attendance at religious services, $F(2, 212) = 2.44, p < .05$.

[15]Repeated measures analysis of variance showed a main effect of service attendance (never, occasionally, regularly) on practical social support, $F(2, 211) = 3.32, p < .05$. Repeated measures analysis of variance on social isolation showed a main effect of service attendance, $F(2, 211) = 3.24, p < .05$, and an interaction between service attendance, religious/spritual interests, and time, $F(3, 211) = 2.57$, $p < .06$. This three-way interaction suggested that the effects of service attendance on social isolation held for those who were spiritual, but not for those who were not spiritual. Similarly, repeated measures analysis of variance on social friction showed an interaction between service attendance, religious/spiritual interests, and time, $F(3, 209) = 2.41, p < .07$. This three-way interaction suggested that the effects of service attendance on social friction held for those who were spiritual, but not for those who were not spiritual.

by visits from church people. Right after he died there was all kinds of moral support. Even food they brought! It's not the food they brought, but the fact that somebody cared, somebody's caring! (Tess, 58-year-old woman who lost her 60-year-old husband to cancer)

The only time I really feel comfortable is Sunday morning, go to mass, and then it's a little better. (Raul, 65, whose 62-year-old wife died of a brain tumor)

As noted in chapter 3, religious or spiritual people, particularly those who attended religious services, coped more adaptively and were less distressed following their loss than those who were not religious or spiritual and did not attend any services.

DO SUPPORT GROUPS HELP BEREAVED PEOPLE?

One solution for bereaved people who have little or poor social support might be to join a bereavement support group. Bereavement support groups can focus on activities, a class, a spectator event or entertainment—anything in which the people who get together share the common denominator of bereavement. Support groups do not have to involve only sitting and talking, although that is the most common form and what we most often think of as a support group.

When bereaved people are asked what they have perceived as helpful in their recovery, they often mention talking to other people who have had similar experiences (Lehman et al., 1986).

I just know it's been really helpful to talk to other people who have lost their husbands, and just talk about how things are going for them now. I think hooking up with people is important. (Flora, 47-year-old woman who lost her 50-year-old husband to cancer)

Thus, joining a bereavement support group can provide such experiences for people who do not have friends or family members who they feel truly understand their loss.

One of the most important functions of support groups is to normalize and validate bereaved people's experience. Despite gains in the last couple of decades, there is still much confusion and ignorance about the experience of grief. Bereaved people are often relieved to find out that their experience is normal and appropriate, whether it's a stomachache, that they have had more colds since the death, that they cannot concentrate or remember things, or that they feel like they are going crazy.

Proponents of bereavement support groups suggest that these groups can provide a number of other resources to participants as well (Hopmeyer, & Werk,

1994, p. 245; see also Gottlieb, 1986, 1988; Videka-Sherman & Lieberman, 1985):

1. Help participants develop and strengthen informal support networks.
2. Help participants gain hope, receive new ideas for solutions to problems, receive information regarding other sources of help, improve skills in developing social relationships, and become less lonely and isolated.
3. Give participants a sense of belonging as well as feelings of fellowship and solidarity.

Comments by people who have attended bereavement support groups suggest that they do serve these functions and more (Hopmeyer & Werk, 1994, p. 253):

> You are not alone in your grief. You can share the pain, discuss, cry, help each other. This releases the guilt. You can ask questions and realize there are no answers.

> The contact with another person in the group who had experienced things very similar to me gave me the feeling that I am not alone.

> I made a commitment to myself to get better, to learn more; I made a commitment to living a fuller life. If I didn't have this group, where would I go? I would be stumbling around in the dark; isolated.

People who have lost a loved one to a stigmatized death, such as AIDS or suicide, may be particularly needy of finding others who have shared their experiences and can understand their thoughts and feelings (Hopmeyer & Werk, 1994, p. 253):

> In the group I felt a sense of acceptance, of being more among others who understand and therefore don't expect more of me than I can do. Especially the reassurance that I am part of a very diverse and normal group of people who have in common the loss of a loved one by suicide. The reassurance that I am still a good—ok—person, not a pariah. Our common experience of helplessness before another suicide allows me to believe that I am not to blame—none of us are—and that I can go on with my life.

Nongay family members and friends of people who die from AIDS often find their only support among the gay or lesbian community. For example, Sally, who lost her 31-year-old son to AIDS said:

> The whole time he was sick, very few people called to say "How is he?" I'm sure if he had cancer, I would have been getting phone calls right and left. It was very hard. That's why this support group is so helpful. It's really for gay and lesbian people, but it's broken up into different groups, like

significant others—we went to that one, the bereavement group, the HIV-positive group. They have facilitators in each group. It's great. Now we're into the bereavement group. There are other parents in that group as well as wives, significant others. Everyone is just able to talk about their feelings. It's the only place I can really talk and feel at ease. I know they'll understand. They're not judgmental. They've gone through it. So it really is a big help. It's just a wonderful group.

Many self-help groups for widows are based on the pioneering work of Silverman (1972, 1986). Silverman viewed widowhood as a transition from one role to another: from wife to widow to woman on her own. In her Widow-to-Widow program, widows receive assistance from another widow who can help them redefine their roles and find positive ways of adapting to their new role. In a controlled study of such a widow-to-widow program, researchers found that widows in these programs did adapt faster to their loss—in terms of their levels of distress - than those not in such programs (Vachon, Lyall, Rogers, Freedman-Letofsky, & Freeman, 1980). Widows who did not have good support from their family and friends benefited most from the program. Some other studies have found that support interventions help widows (Constantino, 1988; Lieberman & Videka-Sherman, 1986), but still other studies find that widows or widowers who attend these groups do not fare better than those who do attend (Barrett, 1978; Marmar et al., 1988; Videka-Sherman & Lieberman, 1985)

About one in four of the participants in our study were members of support groups one month after their loss. With the passage of time, fewer people participated in support groups, so that by 18 months postloss, only 16% of our participants were in a support group. Bereaved parents were the most likely to seek out support groups (43% at 1 month postloss), followed by bereaved spouses (25%), bereaved siblings (21%), and bereaved adult children (17%). Although there were no differences between those who joined support groups and those who did not in levels of distress over time, 75% of the people who joined support groups said that they had been helpful.

It's funny working with a support group. Because you see people coming in that are where you were 6 months ago or whatever, and as you see the progress, you see yourself, too, so you know you've changed. It's good—it's an additional support tool. (Jessica, 35-year-old woman who lost her 69-year-old mother to cancer).

Support groups clearly are not for everyone. Some people find listening to other people's stories makes their pain worse. Some may feel uncomfortable sharing their stories with others or may fear losing it in front of others. These people may tolerate activities-oriented groups, but may not tolerate the traditional talk-oriented groups. Support groups can vary in personality as a function of the leader and the constellation of participants. Bereaved people may feel like they fit with one group but not with another. In general, the more narrowly focused the group (on people who lost a loved one to cancer, to AIDS, to suicide, etc), the more participants feel helped (Yalom, 1985).

Thus, support groups may be one way that people can find support after their loss, especially when they are not getting the support they need from family members and friends. The fact that these groups are made up of people who share a similar type of a loss can make participants feel that they are understood more than can ever be the case with people who have never experienced that type of loss. Some members of support groups bond with each other so tightly that they continue meeting years after the loss. The issues they share change over time, but they change together, so they are able to provide ongoing longitudinal support to one another.

SUMMARY

The loss of a loved one truly can be a social network crisis. It can mean the loss of one's only confidant and close friend. It can mean the loss of a group of friends who were tied to the deceased. It can mean the silence of others who cannot face the meanings and fears that the loss arouses.

Fortunately, many people feel very well-supported after a loss. They receive strong emotional support from others, and feel affirmed for who they are and the way they handled the loss. They receive material support from others—food, money, babysitting, and so on. Their friends and family members do not let them become isolated and do not create new friction in their lives. These people clearly experience less distress over the long term than people who do not have positive social support.

Voices

People often expressed deep appreciation to those who had supported them through their loved one's illness and death. The growth in their relationships with others was sometimes one of the few bright spots in their experience of loss.

> I've always been close to my sister, but we became even more close. We've always had good feelings toward each other, but (with Dad's cancer) we became closer. We relied on each other. We aligned against my Mom. It's carrying on even after Dad's death. She makes me laugh, she makes me feel good. It's great. She's been there for me during my real down periods, and she'll understand, but she doesn't always give me great sympathy, which is exactly what I need—she comes right out there with it, punches me in the nose with it, and that's great too. (48-year-old woman who lost a parent)

My husband—I have a lot to thank him for because he never said one word (about) the house or "me"; he said, "your mom comes first." So we were free in a way. (He never put himself first.) Neither did my brother-in-law. That's very beautiful. That gave me all the freedom. I didn't have that guilty feeling. (66-year-old woman who lost a parent)

I believe it probably brought family relationships along to another level. Some are better, some are not as good, but they certainly advanced from where they were before—where things were just allowed to be what they were. This really forced some issues, not only for me but for other family members also. I could see everybody was making some life decisions. People showed at their best and at their worst, I would say, throughout this. (45-year-old woman who lost a parent)

Many respondents discussed the friction that had arisen in their social networks, and the problems other people had in responding in a helpful way to their loss.

There seems to be a hole. I feel that the public needs to be educated about what to do, what specific—how to help people that are in this situation. People just don't know what to do. They feel like they're intruding or they're bothering you. Like friends and neighbors—they're sitting in their homes and they want to help, but they don't know what to do. They're capable of really helping (but they just say), "call me if you need me." What they really should be doing is bringing over cooking. (I could have called for help but) I didn't even know WHAT I needed. But people need basic things. They need dinner on the table every night, lunch, breakfast. Some people who've been through it know what to do—they reach out in a tangible way. (32-year-old woman who lost her parent)

I find that other people are afraid to talk about it to you when they shouldn't be. If there was some way to get to people's friends so that they're not so threatened ... maybe a lot of help should be with friends and acquaintances and family. (72-year-old woman who lost her husband)

Such a personal thing—some break up, others stoic. Death is very personal. I don't think we should interpret responses or lack of responses. People try to make comforting statements, but it's hardly ever appropriate—I've even done it against my principles, especially at a funeral. If you're going to go, what are you going to say—I've done it myself. People use cliches, expected thing. It's ok, not a bad thing. Maybe we just don't have a lot of experience or know how to do it. (51-year-old man who lost a parent)

I get angry when I listen to these talk shows once in awhile. I hear these celebrities where they had a little adversity in their life or they recovered from alcohol or addiction to drugs. (They say,) "I'm a survivor!" No one forced them to become alcoholics or drug addicts, and then they're so proud, they say, "I'm a survivor." I get so mad, I say, "You son of a bitch, if you went through half the stuff we have, how much of a survivor would you be?!" You know, they can go into a health clinic, $20,000.. I used to listen to people at meetings with little trivial adversities that caused them to become addicts. You don't know what problems are! I used to leave those meetings so depressed. (59-year-old man who lost an adult child)

Some people—friends—I've gotten a lot closer to because of it, and I've learned about the values they have. Other friends, I've realized that they have nothing to give, and they weren't there for me at all. It really sort of shakes out a lot of conclusions. (33-year-old woman who lost a parent)

Respondents who had joined social support groups generally found them very helpful.

You can bring more to it if you can get away. I did a fair amount of feeling sorry for myself because I couldn't get out. It wasn't until I joined a support group and talked out some of these things that really I felt better about it. It was really great. In the group, I saw women who dealt with very difficult mothers; mine was sweet and gentle. So I said, "Gee, I don't have it bad." That was the surprising, beneficial part of it for me—listening to them. About the grief, it's going to happen—prepare yourself. Be realistic.

At first I was so sad. I couldn't believe I would ever be happy again. I thought it was such a horrible waste. I missed her so much, 'cause we were kind of buddies. The groups really helped. You see people who had lost their spouse of 50 years and they were coping fairly well. At least then I could see that I was gonna be ok. 'Cause at the time I just felt so horrible. 'Cause it was such a shock. (39-year-old woman who lost a parent)

I think an emotional support group would be a very important opportunity. Specifically for women in the middle—you've got your kids, and your husband, and your frail, elderly parents. Those women need support, because the quality of life for the husband, kids and frail parents depend on that woman. If we could at least keep her feelings acknowledged and validated. (Also help for practical things—how do you do their income tax, etc.) And not just when they're dying. Sometimes you just need "peer hugs" (from someone going through the same thing). (44-year-old woman who lost a parent)

A caregiver's job is very difficult. If any kind of support group is available, I think that would be a great help. You get to a point where you're tired, worn out, not as patient as you could be, not quite as loving as you might want to be, so it's very difficult. Today there's more emphasis put on the caregiver's role than there used to be. The first couple of years N was sick, it was never, "How are you feeling?" It was always, "How is N?" Sometimes I wanted someone to ask how I was, and on the occasions when they did, it was a great help to me. It made me feel as if I were visible and not just an invisible entity revolved around taking care of N. (71-year-old woman who lost her husband)

Find a support group. I used 12-step, but any of the groups—survivors of terminally ill patients with other people going through similar situations that you can talk to—to know you aren't alone and that there are other people who have gone through this. They can kind of help you out, understand feelings. I was really fortunate. During that time in my recovery a lot of people came into my life that had gone through some of these circumstances, lost someone close to them—father or mother, brother or sister. They lost somebody due to a terminal disease right while they were in recovery or before they got in recovery. So I had a lot of different experiences—we did a lot of talking together. It helped me get through some of the different stages that I was going through. You can have family that's really close to you, have friends, but to have someone else that's gone through a very similar experience, that's helpful. (27-year-old man who lost a parent)

I was in a support group with eight women. Don't go through it alone. I can't imagine going through it alone. If you can't talk to your family, seek it out on the outside. (60-year-old woman who lost an adult child)

5

Children and Grief

People need to know when we are sad we need to be taken care of. (J.P. age 9)

It was very hard to see my dad, a muscular man who loved to run and exercise, go from that to skin and bones and barely be able to walk. (Kate, age 12)

I was alone with my mom at one of my sisters' softball games when she told me my dad was ill. All I remember was fear. I was never exposed to an illness as serious as this. I was afraid of the unknown. I didn't know what was to come. (Jim, age 15)

You miss out on a lot! Your childhood is cut short and you are forced to grieve when young people should be happy. Everything that you could've done with your parent you can't. (Meg, age 18)

My father and I loved an old Harry Chapin song, "Cats in the Cradle." It tells the story of a father who waited until tomorrow to choose to spend time with his son. If my father had waited, we would have missed everything because tomorrow never came. (Joe, age 20)

To have a child survive the loss of his parent and to grow to adulthood and be a together person who is totally functional without baggage, is close to a miracle. The loss can become tolerable but if you think it ever becomes acceptable you're going in the wrong direction. (Chris, mother of J.P., Kate, Jim, Meg, and Joe)

Sometimes, children must cope with bereavement. They may survive the death of a parent, grandparent, sibling, neighbor, classmate, friend, or pet. In our culture, we do not like to acknowledge that children are touched by death. Society's taboos against openly talking about death and grief are even stronger when it comes to children. Parents and other significant adults may avoid the topic with children because they are, themselves, anxious and uncomfortable. Or they may refrain from discussing death in a misguided attempt to prevent the child from feeling distressed (Becker & Margolin, 1967). Rando (1988) described the negative effects that can result when well-intentioned adults attempt to protect children from death and grief. Silence and isolation can lead to feelings of insecurity and abandonment. In the absence of factual information and open discussion, children will develop fantasies that are often much worse than reality. Without the opportunity to experience and deal with death and grief, children cannot learn healthy coping skills for managing their grief and other serious life challenges.

Attempts to protect children from the topic of death seem counterintuitive. Death is found in children's literature, television programs, movies, games, humor, and songs (see Corr, Nabe, & Corr, 1997). And sometimes death occurs in their personal experience. We know that young children think spontaneously and readily about death (Fox, 1985; Webb, 1993), and there is no evidence to support the notion that discussing death with children causes undue distress. Given the opportunity, children are curious and interested in talking about death and dying.

Supporting bereaved children often means educating and supporting the significant adults who are in a child's life on a daily basis. In order to respond effectively and appropriately to children who are coping with the loss of a loved one, and inform and support their significant adults, it is important to understand as much as possible about the subject of children and death.

RESEARCH ON CHILDHOOD BEREAVEMENT

Although much has been learned from clinical observations, systematic studies of bereaved children are few and yield conflicting or inconclusive results. Most childhood bereavement research is conducted with children who have lost a parent. Rando (1988) suggested this is because the loss of a parent, compared to other childhood losses, poses critical physical and psychosocial survival issues. Comprehensive literature reviews (Baker & Sedney, 1996; Berlinskey & Biller, 1982; Silverman & Worden, 1993) reveal that studies lack consensus on whether the death of a parent in childhood leads to depression and behavioral problems, and increased risk for subsequent problems in adulthood. Berlinsky and Biller suggested that the inconsistencies and confusion result from over-simplification of outcome measures (usually psychiatric symptoms or behavior problems) and the use of a single-event model.

The death of a parent represents a series of events that precede and follow the event of the death itself, and a host of other factors must be considered before concluding that a child is at risk. Evidence suggests that risk is influenced by the way the surviving parent responds, the availability of social support, subsequent life circumstances, and continuity in the child's daily life (Berlinsky & Biller, 1982; Brown, Harris, & Bifulco, 1986; Elizur & Kauffman, 1983; Norris & Murrell, 1987; Reese, 1982). Silverman and Worden (1993, p. 301) proposed that "bereavement outcomes need to be conceptualized in more dynamic terms that emphasize change and adaptation rather than merely the presence or absence of symptoms or signs of psychological disturbance." They further suggested that what is needed is "understanding the interaction among the social context, the family system, and the personal characteristics of those involved."

The Harvard child bereavement study (Silverman & Worden, 1992a) was designed to respond to the deficits in previous studies of childhood bereavement. Semistructured home interviews were conducted with 125 bereaved children and their surviving parent 4, 12, and 24 months after the death. Standardized assessments of locus of control (Nowicki & Strickland, 1973), self-esteem (Harter, 1985), and the child's understanding of death (Smilansky, 1987) were administered to the children. Standardized instruments measuring family structure and coping (Olson et al., 1983), family changes (McCubbin, Larson, & Olson, 1987), depression (Radloff, 1977), impact of events (Horowitz et al., 1981), and for each child a Child Behavior Checklist (Achenbach & Edelbrock, 1983) were administered to the surviving parent.

Results of the Harvard study revealed that although the event of a parent's death is indeed stressful, and its impact pervades most aspects of a child's life, most children were not overwhelmed by these stresses. One month following bereavement, 22% of the children showed some form of dysfunctional behavior, as reported by parents. These behaviors included (but not excessively so) restlessness and sleep disturbances. Somatic symptoms were high, confirming the belief that grief is often somaticized in young children. Despite the manifestations of grief observed, Silverman and Worden (1993) also "saw children who were carrying on by going to school and by maintaining relationships with their friends and in their family. Clearly, these children were grieving, but the majority did not express their grief in prolonged crying periods, aggression, or withdrawal behavior, as has been traditionally thought" (p. 314).

An important finding of the Harvard study concerns the ways in which children maintain a connection to the deceased (Silverman, Nickman, &

Worden, 1992). Previous accounts of these behaviors have been described as symptomatology that should be terminated, implying that disengagement from the deceased is desired, if not necessary, for successful grief resolution. Silverman (1987) and Anderson (1974) have reported evidence that although a parent has died, the child's relationship with that parent does not die, and is in fact reformulated constantly as the child ages. Finding a way for the dead parent to continue living in the experience of a child does not preclude accepting the reality of the death (Rubin, 1985; Silverman & Silverman, 1979; Worden, 1982, 1991b). Children may maintain a relationship with their dead parent by talking to the parent, dreaming about the parent, or feeling that the parent is watching them. The crucial point illuminated here is that maintaining an attachment to thoughts and memories of a dead parent is not a sign of pathology but a sign of healthy adaptation. Even so, more than half the children interviewed reported emotional self-protection, choosing not to discuss their dead parent with their friends.

> There are quiet ways my children grieve and show a need to remember in other ways. One of my sons writes Rick's initials on himself all the time and wants to have a tattoo with his dad's initials within a baseball because baseball was his life with his dad. Each of the kids have areas in their room where they put pictures of Rick, and of themselves with Rick. All of them have written stories in school or just essays about their dad. (Chris, the mom)

The Harvard study found that most children understood the concept of death in the abstract but lacked sufficient vocabulary and communication skills to talk about it. This finding suggests that young children need assistance in developing a vocabulary to use in talking about death and grief. Children need clear, unambiguous, honest definitions and words that can label their experience and the experience of their family. Parents in the Harvard study tended to underappreciate the fact that absence of overt emotional expression in their children did not mean that they were not successfully coping with their grief, and that having conversations about death and about the dead parent were just as importantly and legitimately a part of their child's "grief work."

Baker and Sedney (1996) concluded, based on their review of the literature, that research to date "provides a provocative but incomplete picture of children's bereavement reactions" (p. 115). Silverman and Worden (1993) made a strong argument in favor of an approach to studying childhood bereavement that encompasses the child's social and family systems, and for the need to include measures of resilience and good adaptation as well as poor adaptation. Silverman and Worden proposed that a more appropriate model is one that "sees death as a normative life-cycle event and grief a response to loss to which all people must learn to adapt" (p. 316).

RESEARCH ON ADOLESCENT BEREAVEMENT

A comprehensive review of research on adolescent bereavement can be found in Corr and Balk (1996). Until only recently, adolescent bereavement received little sustained attention or recognition as a serious life event (Balk, 1991a). There has been much confusion regarding the definitions of adolescents used in the research. Most researchers have regarded adolescence as either an extension of childhood or as part of adulthood. As with research on childhood bereavement, the vast majority of adolescent bereavement studies have dealt with parental and sibling loss. Inconsistent use of assessment tools and methodological flaws have yielded inconsistent results. There has been little, if any, attention paid to adolescents' reaction to the death of a friend, death resulting from suicide, AIDS, violence, or adjustment to multiple losses.

Balk (1990) found that among the bereaved adolescents in his study, high self-concept scores were correlated with less depression, fear, loneliness, and confusion; average self-concept scores were correlated with more depression, loneliness, and anger; and low self-concept scores were correlated with more confusion but less anger. An inverse relation between self-concept and intensity of bereavement was reported by Hogan and Greenfield (1991).

Gray (1987a) determined that bereaved high school students scored higher on a depression inventory than nonbereaved students, students without religious beliefs, and students who scored low on perceived social support. Balmer (1992) found that younger teens were more likely to experience physiological distress and were less likely to talk with their friends, whereas older teens were more likely to talk with friends and to experience psychological distress.

As with children, there is evidence that school performance can be affected by the death of a loved one (Balk, 1981; Balmer, 1992; Gray 1987b) manifested either by a drop in grades, or reported difficulties with concentration, focus, and memory. Yet, bereaved adolescents do not necessarily suffer a drop in self-esteem following a death, and in many cases experience feelings of increased self-worth and personal growth. (Balk, 1981; Davies, 1991; Martinson & Campos, 1991).

> Although I'd give it all up to have him back, I've gained a sense of perspective on life. I put things in perspective when they happen. I also think I'm independent and I'm a stronger person. (Meg, age 18)

> My dad's death made me stronger emotionally, and more independent. I had to learn how to do things on my own. I believe in some way or another something positive comes out of everything. (Jim, age 15)

> Although it may be true that I am more independent, or have more responsibility, or I am more mature, or I have achieved more because of this, I don't see that as positive. I don't think learning how to swim is necessarily a positive thing for someone thrown into a pool. It comes out of necessity. (Joe, age 20)

There is evidence that family dynamics can either mediate stress or create stress, and this may be particularly true when families are coping with bereavement (Bell, 1978; Walsh & McGoldrick, 1991a), however few empirical studies have investigated this issue. Gray (1987a) reported lower depression scores in parentally bereaved adolescents who felt they had a good relationship with their surviving parent compared to those who reported a poor relationship. Balmer (1992) found that a positive family climate acted as a protective factor in sibling-bereaved adolescents. Adolescents may find their family to be helpful in adjusting to a death when the family is cohesive, low in conflict, and permits emotional expression. Balmer (1992) also found that mothers tend to be perceived as the most helpful in grief-related support, especially when mothers are emotionally expressive about their own grief. Fathers were perceived to be somewhat less helpful, and Balmer found no evidence that siblings support and comfort one another after a death in the family.

Peers are often the most important people in an adolescent's social network. The sibling-bereaved adolescents in Balmer's study rated those friends who were flexible and available as needed as being the most helpful. Also, friends who knew the deceased sibling were more likely to be sought out for comfort and support. Teachers are also important to adolescents, and adolescents are disappointed and perceive their teachers to be indifferent or uncaring when they fail to acknowledge the death.

> At first my teachers were just like the kids, they ignored it as well. They treated me as if nothing had happened. But later on, they realized that it was the biggest struggle anyone could have, and started looking out for me. (Jim, age 15)

> My teachers were really supportive and treated me differently, but rightly so. I remember all of them being extremely supportive. (Meg, age 18)

CHILDREN'S UNDERSTANDING OF DEATH

Children's understanding of the concept of death has been systematically studied since the 1930s and began to proliferate in the 1970s (Speece & Brent, 1996). Yet, despite this proliferation, Speece and Brent reported surprisingly slow progress. Methodological inconsistencies have yielded "a confusing array of results" (Stambrook & Parker, 1987), thus comparisons between studies are difficult. According to Speece and Brent's comprehensive review of the literature, methods of assessment have included interviews, essays, drawings, play activities, children's stories about death, questionnaires, reactions to stories about death, definitions of the word "dead," descriptions of death-related pictures, multiple-choice responses to hypothetical death situations, ratings of death-related statements, group interviews, thematic apperception tests, sentence completions, and sequencing ordered death-related pictures.

Focusing primarily on studies using interviews, Speece and Brent developed the most contemporary view of children's understanding of death. Their analyses led to the identification of five logically distinct components, most consistently studied empirically, that comprise the concept of death in children: *universality, irreversibility, nonfunctionality, causality,* and *noncorporeal continuation.*

Universality refers to the understanding that eventually every living thing dies. A child achieves this understanding when he or she realizes that death is all-inclusive, inevitable, and unpredictable. In order to determine whether a child has grasped this concept, the following types of questions might be asked:

Will everybody die someday?
Will you die someday?
Do children ever die?
Is there something I can do so that I won't ever die?

In general, younger children are more likely than older children to indicate that death is not universal—they will exclude themselves, children in general, their immediate family, teachers, and other familiar people. Nagy (1948) determined that younger children are more likely to conclude that death can be avoided by the clever and the lucky. Several researchers determined that younger children are more likely to regard death as something that only occurs in the distant future (Candy-Gibbs, Sharp, & Petrun, 1985; Derry, 1979; Lee, 1987; Swain, 1979). Speece and Brent reported that recent research, in direct contradiction with earlier beliefs, suggests that most children understand their own personal mortality before they understand that all people die. When children exclude themselves from the vulnerability of death they almost always exclude other individuals as well, an indication that personal mortality is not the last aspect of universality understood. Children may understand that death is not likely to occur until some distant time, but the concept of universality includes the realization that, whether death is likely to occur, it is possible for death to occur at any time.

Irreversibility, as defined by Speece and Brent, refers to the understanding that when someone's physical body dies, they are unable to come back to life again. Fox (1985, 1988) offered a similar definition that death is "when the body stops working." These definitions allow for the belief that some kind of continuation beyond physical existence (e.g., spiritual immortality, reincarnation, resurrection) is possible. The advantage of this definition is that it is concrete, observable, and allows for any religious or spiritual orientation embraced by the child's family.

Speece and Brent proposed that the concept of irreversibility comprises two aspects: process irreversibility and state irreversibility. Children must understand that the processes that occur in the transition from living to dead (e.g., decompensation) are irreversible, and that the state of being dead is a permanent state. Questions that help elicit children's understanding of irreversibility include:

Can a dead person become alive again?
Can you come back to life after you die?
If I gave some medicine to a dead person, could he become alive again?

Younger children are more likely than older children to view death as temporary and reversible. Young children will typically equate death with a sleeping state from which one can awaken. Other common beliefs of younger children are that the deceased has gone somewhere, as on a trip, and can return at some future date, that death can be reversed spontaneously by wishing, praying, or as a result of magical or medical intervention (Speece & Brent, 1992).

Nonfunctionality refers to understanding that, once dead, the physical body cannot walk, talk, eat, hear, feel, see, think, or perform any other functions that define physical life. Children's understanding about nonfunctionality can be assessed by questions such as:

Can a dead person still hear?
Are people different after they die?
Is there anything a dead person can do?

Younger children are more likely than older children to believe that a dead person can still hear, or see, or perform other various living functions (Fox, 1985; Hoffman & Strauss, 1985). Kane (1979) determined that children more readily understand nonfunctionality in terms of "external," or observable functions (e.g., walking, talking) than "internal," or nonobservable functions (e.g., thinking, dreaming).

Causality is an aspect of understanding death that appears to have achieved little, if any, consensus among researchers who seek to define the concept of causality in markedly different ways (Devereux, 1984; Kane, 1979; Karpas, 1986; Koocher, 1973; Robinson, 1977; Smilansky, 1987; Wass et al., 1983). Synthesizing the various definitions found in the research, Speece and Brent(1996) proposed that understanding causality "involves an abstract and realistic understanding of the external and internal events that might possibly cause and individual's death" (p. 36). Children achieve a mature understanding of causality, based on this definition, when they no longer restrict their explanations to particular individuals but can describe classes of causes that are generally accepted by adults as valid, and that apply to living things in general.

Children's understanding of causality can be revealed in their responses to questions like:

Why do people die?
How do people die?
Can people die because they are bad?
Can people die because someone wishes it so?

Younger children will be more inclined than older children to offer unrealistic, specific, external causes. Older children will be more likely than younger children to understand that death is the result of an internal bodily organ or system that ceases, for whatever reason, to function.

Noncorporeal continuation is an important fifth component of understanding death that resulted from Speece and Brent's (1993) research and their extensive review of existing literature. This aspect of understanding allows for the belief in some form of personal continuation after the physical body dies. Such beliefs are often held by children as well as mature adults, despite the fact that it has been largely ignored in empirical studies to date. Thus, Speece and Brent argued that more research is needed. To determine a child's belief and understanding, one might ask:

What happens after death?
When the body dies, what happens to the person's spirit/soul?

There is insufficient information to date regarding this aspect of children's understanding of death. Children may give references to concepts like heaven, or that a deceased parent is now an angel or is "watching over me," but it remains for further investigation to provide a clearer picture of when and how children understand noncorporeal continuation, and how that understanding changes as a child grows and matures.

DEVELOPMENT OF UNDERSTANDING
AND RESPONSES TO DEATH

All children eventually come to understand that death is irreversible, inevitable, and universal. Some may achieve a mature concept at younger ages (Wass & Stillion, 1988), especially if they have experienced the death of a pet, friend, or family member (Yalom, 1980; Kane, 1979). The natural evolution of children's cognitive abilities leads gradually to a full understanding of death.

Infants and Toddlers

Most researchers believe that children's first awareness and understanding of the concept of death begins in the preschool years (Anthony, 1940; Ferguson, 1978; Lonetto, 1980; Nagy, 1948). Maurer (1966) suggested that the roots of understanding may begin much earlier. For example, a toddler's game of "peek-a-boo" (translated literally from Old English, it means "dead or alive"), and of tossing items over the edge of a high chair might be the toddler's earliest cognitive experiments with "here" and "not here," or "being" and "not-being." Infants may react with distress to the removal of a source of nurturance, but they are usually comforted relatively quickly and easily when nurturance is returned to them.

Preschool

There is consensus among researchers and clinicians that preschool-aged children actively attempt to understand events of death when they encounter them. Many preschoolers, however, believe that death is reversible and temporary. They tend to explain dying as going to another place. Thus, they believe it is possible to visit that place, or at least telephone the person who has gone there. Children at this age might request a vacation trip to heaven to visit Grandpa instead of the usual beach house or relative's home.

Explanations by adults can reinforce misconceptions by telling children that death is like going on a long journey, or that death means the deceased loved one is "with God." Even simple, accurate explanations can cause confusion and concern to the young mind. When children are told, or observe, that the person's body is put in a coffin and buried in the ground, they will become concerned about how the person will perform life functions in such confinement. Because children at this age do not fully understand death, they will wonder and worry how the person will eat or go to the bathroom. Will they get wet when it rains? How can they see inside the box? Won't they get lonely?

Religious beliefs that comfort adults often confuse preschoolers. When a young child is told, "God needed your Mommy," The child may become confused and angry at a God who does not understand that the *child* needs a Mommy, too. And what if God needs the child's father and siblings, too? Resolving the dilemma of how a person can be buried in the ground and, at the same time, be "up in heaven" is a daunting task for the preschool mind.

Whether they understand that death is permanent, children do react to loss and to the change in the emotional atmosphere in the home. Because children openly exhibit their grief intermittently, adults sometimes conclude they are not affected by their loss. Or, they do not realize that the grief is being expressed in other ways. Children at this age may become irritable, demanding, or clinging. Regressive behaviors such as thumb-sucking and bedwetting are common. Separation anxiety may result from a fear of losing the surviving parent. Young children may have difficulty sleeping and find comfort sleeping with the surviving parent or a sibling. Children may ask repeatedly where their deceased parent is, and when they will return, then protest in anger when the deceased does not return. Not uncommonly, this anger is directed at the surviving parent or siblings.

One notable characteristic of preschool children is their literal thinking. Fox (1985) provided an excellent example of how this causes confusion and concern. It serves as a beautiful reminder that adults need to remain mindful of the child's perspective and be watchful of the following kinds of distortions:

> A psychologist tells of a child she had talked with for many months prior to the death of his beloved grandmother. Timmy wanted to be a part of the various funeral rituals and understood them to be an opportunity to say good-bye to his special friend. One day his grandmother died and, much to his family's surprise, Timmy vehemently rejected all invitations to the rituals he had planned to attend. Even the psychologist who he had talked to for so many hours could make no sense of this sudden turn of events until Timmy sobbed: "I don't want to see Nanna with her head cut off!!" When questioned further, he continued: "You told me that when Nanna died, they would put her body in a casket." No one had thought to tell Timmy that his grandmother's head would be there, too, nor had he been able to ask! (p. 10).

Latency

During elementary school years, children begin to have a more complex understanding of death and its implications. They realize that death is not just another form of life or sleep, that death is final. Although children come to understand that death is final, they are not yet ready to understand that it is universal. Their increasing sense of power and control in life makes it difficult for them to believe that such a thing as death could happen to them. Thus, younger children in this age range make the best sense they can by externalizing and personifying death. Death may be described as a ghost, an angel, a space creature, skeleton, an old man with a white beard, and so on. Death, in whatever form, comes to get people and takes them away. Children believe that death can happen to others, especially for helpless, old, or handicapped people who cannot outrun death. Children commonly believe they can escape death because they can run faster than death can.

Children's curiosity and concerns at this age reflect their natural developmental issues regarding body integrity. They will ask graphic questions that can be disturbing to supportive adults. They want to know about how the body works, why it becomes cold when it dies, and details about decompensation. Asking questions is the way children learn about themselves and their world, and they deserve direct, honest answers. When adults recoil in horror, children are given the message that death is a scary and taboo subject and will become inhibited about asking for the information they need.

Children in this age group begin to understand death more fully, but typically have little capacity to cope with significant loss. Denial is an expected primary defense. Children may behave as if nothing has happened, they may hide their feelings and concerns, and they may fear loss of control and dependency. They may cry only in private. This kind of response can be amplified if adults around them demand emotional containment or are inhibited in their own emotional expression. Children need repeated, gentle encouragement and permission to deal with their feelings.

> I coped with it by trying to ignore the seriousness of it all, which after he died, I realized was the wrong way. The only way to cope with anything is to talk about it. (Jim, age 15)

Preadolescence

Around the age of 10, children begin to know that death is permanent, inevitable and universal, and that it is not a personification but the end of physical life. Although they have little difficulty understanding the biological and physiological realities of death, children at this age are far from ready to cope with significant loss from a psychological aspect. Gains in independence are fragile, thus the loss of a parent or other close person can bring up feelings of helplessness that children interpret as childish. Children may put on an appearance of independent coping.

According to Rando (1988), children of this age may find anger an easier emotion than the longing and helplessness that accompanies their loss. An increase in arguing and fighting with siblings, irritability, and oppositional or other "difficult" behaviors may be one way their grief finds expression. However, such expression is often unrecognized as grief and may incur reprimand or punishment when understanding and support are needed. Even when this behavior is recognized as an expression of children's grief, it can be extremely taxing on the surviving parent or other supportive adults.

> About a year after Rick died, we drove to Los Angeles to visit his mother and family. We all knew this might be the last time we saw her, her health was failing fast. Everything went great while we were there. But all the way home, the kids fought and argued and picked on one another. I know now that it was their grief. First their father, now their grandmother. But, those 7 hours in the car were the longest hours of my life! (Chris, the mom)

Although striving for independence, children at this age still rely on guidance from adults and may be unable to determine for themselves what is appropriate expression of the sadness, longing, anger, or guilt. For vulnerable children, a well-intentioned comment can be very costly.

Adolescence

Adolescents are capable of thinking about death in the same way adults do—in a mature, formal, conceptual, abstract, or scientific way. However, the capacity to think abstractly about death does not necessarily mean that they actually do think about death in those ways (Corr, 1995). Cognitive capacity cannot be isolated from the rest of the adolescent if we are to fully understand the differences between adolescent and adult understanding of death. Moreover, there are developmental differences within the span of adolescents that must be considered.

According to Fleming and Adolph (1986), younger teens are more likely to be concerned with achieving emotional separation from their parents. Middle-aged teens are likely more concerned with mastery, control, and striving for competency. Older teens are most appropriately faced with issues that revolve around autonomy, intimacy, and commitment. It is generally agreed that all adolescents share the developmental task of establishing a relatively stable sense of personal identity. In coping with bereavement, adolescents can be expected to manage their grief in different ways, according to their life circumstances, their personalities, and the specific developmental issues that challenge them.

Noppe and Noppe (1991, 1996) have proposed that, for adolescents, certain death-related tensions arise from biological, cognitive, social, and emotional factors, and that these tensions significantly influence their understanding of death. First, according to the Noppes, as a result of rapid biological maturation and sexual development, adolescents become aware of the loss of their more innocent, perhaps simpler, childhood. In addition, they become aware of the inevitability of physical decline that will ultimately lead to their death and to the death of others. Second, the Noppes suggest that adolescents' cognitive maturation enhances their ability to think about the future, including both the positive and negative components, and about life and death. Embracing the inevitability of death requires that they confront the fact that, as they strive to form their own identities and reevaluate parental values, there are aspects of life that are out of their control. Third, tension is created as social relationships within the family and among their peers change. Such change, on the one hand, represents growth and opportunity, but on the other hand a series of "lost" relationships. Tension is created in the challenge to develop a viable social life outside their family and the fear of becoming socially isolated. Fourth, the process of separation and individuation gives rise to affective tensions. The Noppes observed that adolescents' feelings about development and death are often intertwined. Achieving autonomy, and all that encompasses, can threaten an adolescent's self-esteem and purpose in life.

In general terms, adolescent grief may be expressed as confusion, crying, feelings of loneliness and emptiness, sleep and appetite disturbances, and exhaustion (Balk, 1983). Adolescents are also inclined, according to Jackson (1984) to believe that their grief is unique and cannot be understood by others. Adolescent grief may be suppressed out of fear of losing control or fear of how they will be perceived by others. Not uncommonly, adolescent grief is expressed in brief outbursts. There may be a kind of paradoxical ongoing and intermittent quality to their experience and expression of grief (Hogan & DeSantis, 1994; Raphael, 1983).

The hardest part was watching him get sicker and sicker. I couldn't handle the thought of losing him. I just hid myself from it. I became really busy and found things to take my mind off it all. I pretended like everything was normal. I denied anything was happening. (Meg, age 18)

COMPARING CHILDHOOD GRIEF AND ADULT GRIEF

"Grief does not focus on one's ability to 'understand,' but instead upon one's ability to 'feel.' Therefore, any child mature enough to love is mature enough to grieve" (Wolfelt, 1983, p. 20). Although some similarities exist, it has been well documented in empirical and clinical literature that there are marked differences between the grief of children and the grief of adults (Rando, 1988; Webb, 1993).

The central concerns of bereaved children are appropriately different from adults. Worden (1991a) identified three issues that are common among young children: (a) Did I cause the death to happen?; (b) Is it going to happen to me?; and (c) Who is going to take care of me? The emergence of these issues is largely dependent on the child's degree of egocentricity and level of cognitive development. Young children may imagine that their bad behavior or unkind thoughts caused the death. The fact that parents and doctors could not prevent the death may leave children wondering and worrying if death can happen to them, also. This may be an especially important issue in the death of a sibling or peer who is close in age. Particularly in the case of parental death, children may fear for their safety and welfare and will wonder who will now provide for their needs (Donnelly, 1987; Krementz, 1981).

Children understand and make sense of death very differently than adults do. Their cognitive development influences their ability to understand and make sense of death, which in turn influences their grief. If children have not grasped the concept of irreversibility, they may understand that their parents are not here, but won't understand that her parent cannot return. Due in part to the immaturity in their thinking, children tend to take things literally. They can be easily confused by euphemisms that indicate a dead person is "lost," "sleeping," or "was taken to heaven by an angel." Less than honest explanations can instill unnecessary fearfulness in children: "If I go to sleep, I will die?" or "Can I get lost and never be found?"

Like adults, children can be expected to demonstrate a wide variety of reactions to bereavement. They may experience some of the same physical, cognitive, and affective symptoms as adults, and may have many of the same needs and issues. Unlike adults, children are limited in their ability to *verbalize* their feelings. Their vocabularies and experience are limited, thus they may have difficulty articulating their thoughts, feelings, or memories.

Children are limited in their capacity to tolerate very intense emotions for long periods of time. It is not uncommon for bereaved children to actively avoid talking about their loss. Most often, children grieve in intermittent "spurts" for many years. Children may alternately approach and avoid their intense feelings, and in this way protect themselves from becoming overwhelmed. In addition, children may manifest their grief by being boisterous, mischievous, or irritable instead of being sad or despondent. Adults often misinterpret this aspect of childhood grief. They may assume incorrectly that because a child is behaving "normally," the child does not understand or is not affected by the death. Most likely, the child is merely grieving in the manner and timing that is most appropriate for him or her.

Children differ from adults in their use of play as a coping strategy. Play is the most natural means of communication for children, and an important activity for working through strong feelings and problems. Children's play is the equivalent of an adult's discussion and processing of feelings. The younger the child, the more the child relies on play as a means for understanding loss, working through grief, as well as for taking needed breaks for mourning.

Children and adolescents fear being different from their peers (Webb, 1993). Returning to school following the death of a parent can be difficult. Children may welcome the condolences of teachers and peers, or they may dread them. The discomfort of others and unhelpful, even hurtful, comments can be a source of additional distress and pain. Children who regard crying as "babyish" may hide their feelings from others and cry only in private (Furman, 1974). During latency and adolescence, in particular, children strive to gain control over their emotions, therefore they may not want to talk with their friends about their loss or their pain.

It was hard going back to school. My teachers kept on asking me questions. (J.P., age 9)

It was very awkward going back to school. I was the only one who had lost a parent. My friends never said anything really. My dad died 2 days before the first day of school. It was hardest being the only one, and not being able to talk to other kids. (Kate, age 12)

I liked going back to school because it got my mind off everything, but kids did treat me differently. I felt people being fake, and treating me better than they normally would. (Meg, age 18)

Because children are dependent upon their parents for their physical and emotional needs, children are especially vulnerable to some of the "secondary losses" that accompany a death. In particular, if the surviving parent is over-whelmed by grief, the child may "lose" important contact, comfort, and support. Financial difficulties following the death of a parent sometimes force surviving families to move—the loss of the familiar home, neighborhood, and playmates can be more difficult for a grieving child. A bereaved wife may be required to return to work following the death of her husband, leaving less time available for children. Unless an adult surrogate for the deceased parent is available, a bereaved child may also "lose" the role model she required for normal healthy development. In a very real sense, the death of a parent represents the death of a way of life for a child. The future will be forever changed and colored by a child's bereavement experience.

The pain will never go away. It may get easier to cope with, but the pain of a close death is scarred for life. (Jim, age 15)

FAMILY DYNAMICS

Family dynamics play a crucial role in the development and adjustment of children. When a death in the family occurs, children are affected not only by the loss of an attachment figure, but also by the changes in the family's functioning that occur in response to the death (Walsh & McGoldrick, 1991). Understanding children's responses to bereavement and assisting them in coping require an understanding of the family dynamics that influence their grief.

Imbalance in Role Relationships

The interlocking role relationships in a family are disrupted by a family member's death (Walsh & McGoldrick, 1991). The entire family system must respond and adjust to reestablish the lost balance. A surviving sibling may seek to replace the "role" occupied by the deceased child. In case of parental bereavement, the surviving parent must assume, to the extent possible, the role of both mother and father. An older sibling may attend father–son functions, or become a confidant and consultant to the surviving parent.

I think the hardest thing about losing parent is seeing the toll it takes on the other parent. Dealing with a mother or father who has to change to fill both roles and do it without the person who promised to be there with them. (Joe, age 20)

Communication

Communication patterns within family systems are complex and intricate. When a death occurs, communication patterns can be seriously disrupted, or may undergo significant adjustment (Silverman & Silverman, 1979). The fact of the death removes one family member's influence on communication. For example, if a father is the one who usually mediates disputes, and the father dies, conflicts may escalate until new methods of mediation are developed. Sometimes, family members attempt to contain their intense emotions and thereby refrain from communicating what they are feeling. This can leave a child feeling that emotional expression is forbidden, or result in confusion about the impact of the loss on the rest of the family. A child's responses are strongly affected by the quality and kind of information she received, and the language used to impart relevant information. Family members who avoid mentioning the dead person or the circumstances of the death provide an opportunity for the child to develop often inaccurate ideas about the death and deprive the child of opportunities to talk about the deceased (Baker, Sedney, & Gross, 1992).

Overprotectiveness

The death of a parent or sibling can evoke strong feelings of protectiveness in the surviving parent. Just as children can become more fearful of losing the surviving parent after a death, the parent can become more fearful of harm coming to her children. Initially, the increased protectiveness can be a source of comfort and reassurance to both parent and child, but if overprotectiveness continues over time, it may undermine a child's sense of self-sufficiency, mastery, and safety in the world. Continuous, excessive protectiveness may also instill feelings of generalized fearfulness and anxiety.

Compromised Parental Control

Even bereaved children require, and depend on, limits set by parents and other significant adults. The surviving parent, overwhelmed by grief and efforts to reestablish family stability, may have difficulty setting necessary limits or enforcing preestablished family rules. Without the familiar support of the deceased parent, and feeling sorry for the child's pain, a parent may develop a habit of leniency. As a result, children may feel anxious that no one appears to be in control and develop subsequent behavior problems.

Changes in Parent's Behavior

Children are egocentric by nature, and need adult support and assistance to cope with serious loss. They can easily feel abandoned, sad, and lonely if a surviving parent withdraws emotionally. Irritability or angry outburst that are sometimes part of grief can leave a child feeling anxious or guilty. The child may withdraw in fear, or might become overly "good" and compliant in an effort to prevent future outburst, believing he or she is to blame for the anger.

> When a parent dies, sometimes it's hard to explain to someone younger all the emotions everyone is feeling. J.P. and Kate especially didn't know how to feel and could not explain the way others felt. (Joe, age 20)

Religious and Cultural Factors

Children absorb and interpret the religious beliefs and cultural customs of their family. They will ask questions about what they do not understand, and come to their own conclusions when explanations are vague or incomprehensible. A comprehensive overview of death-related practices and customs is not possible here, but in order to fully understand a child's grief and mourning behavior, it is important to have accurate information regarding the cultural or religious beliefs of the child's family, and then to determine how accurately the child has incorporated these beliefs into his or her own understanding. This task becomes even more complex in the case of families comprised of more than one religious or cultural background. (For information in depth, see Berger et al., 1989; Coles, 1990; Grollman, 1967; Johnson & McGee 1991; Ryan, 1986.)

FACTORS THAT INHIBIT GRIEF

Rando (1988) outlined the following factors that can inhibit a child's grief. These factors apply not only to parents, but to other significant adults in a child's world:

- A parent's inability to grieve
- A parent's inability to tolerate the pain of the child and to allow the child to mourn
- A child's fear about the parent's vulnerability and desire to protect the parent
- A child's concern for security, which may not allow the child to give in to grief because it is too frightening
- Lack of the security of a caring environment
- Lack of a caring adult who can stimulate and support the child's grief
- Confusion about the death and the child's part in it
- Ambivalence toward the deceased
- Unchallenged magical thinking
- Lack of opportunities to share longing, feelings, and memories
- Instability of family life after the loss
- Inappropriate reassignment of roles or responsibilities
- Secondary losses

TASKS OF MOURNING

Fox (1988) identified four tasks of mourning for children of all ages. Each task is accomplished according to a child's age level, individuality, and other factors discussed earlier. The first task, *understanding the death and making sense of what happened*, is a cognitive task that requires simple, honest information. Children can become easily confused by events and explanations surrounding the death of a loved one. Children must also understand and make sense out of the intense emotions of the adults around them. Fox's second task, *grieving*, addresses the emotional component of the child's mourning. Children must be allowed expression of their feelings as they arise, and have those feelings validated by trusted adults. The third task, *commemorating*, is a behavioral task in which children perform some kind of act or ritual that helps them to remember and memorialize the person who died. Fox's fourth task, *going on*, involves incorporating the loss into their lives, and developing a life philosophy that allows them to go on with their lives without their loved one.

The focus and relative significance of each childhood task of mourning changes over time (Baker, Sedney, & Gross, 1992) as children grow. This observation led Baker and Sedney (1996) to further develop Fox's tasks of mourning by identifying early, middle-phase, and late tasks of childhood mourning.

Early tasks include *understanding* the event and circumstances of the death, and *self-protection*. A child needs to know that the family is safe and that the child will be cared for in the aftermath of the death. Middle-phase tasks include *emotional acceptance* that the person is gone and cannot return or be replaced, *reevaluation of the relationship* through recounting positive and negative memories and qualities of the deceased, and *bearing the pain* in slow, intermittent, and tentative increments. Late tasks include *forming a new sense of personal identity* that incorporates the experience of the loss, *investing in new relationships* without constant comparison to the deceased loved one and without excessive fear of loss, *constructing a durable internal relationship to the deceased*, incorporating both the absence of and a new kind of attachment to the person who died, and *coping with periodic resurgence of pain* which commonly accompany developmental milestones, transitions, or significant anniversary dates.

HELPING CHILDREN COPE WITH GRIEF

Helping children cope with death and bereavement encompasses many of the same principles as those for helping adults. Children need honest, factual information, and they need to have their experience normalized and validated. Children need safe adults and places where they can remember the dead person and discuss their feelings and ideas about the death and their grief. Helping children cope with grief is "more a matter of attitude than one of technique or easily definable skills" (Corr, Nabe, & Corr, 1997, p. 327).

Helping children is an ongoing process, not an isolated act in response to a single event. Children will return over and over again to certain issues as they work through them. Children will also readdress their bereavement and grief issues as they grow and mature, as they meet new transitions and challenges, and as they gain a more sophisticated understanding of death and its implications for their lives.

Help for grieving children and their families may take many forms, both formal and informal (Cook & Dworkin, 1992; Crenshaw, 1991 ; Masur, 1991; Webb, 1993). For children under the age of 2, and for children who appear to be experiencing little distress, parental guidance and support may be the only intervention needed. School-based intervention or support groups may be useful for older children. For children who are clearly having difficulty coping with their grief, or exhibit some form of complicated response to the death, a referral for individual psychotherapy is needed. The goals of helping bereaved children include: a) facilitation of the mourning process; b) ensuring that the family is able to provide for the child's material and emotional needs; and c) prevention of the development of disturbed grief, or treatment for disturbed grief it is occurs (Masur, 1996).

Education and Preparation

Even very young children encounter death-related events in everyday life. A dead fish in the aquarium or the discovery of a dead bird in the yard provide "teachable moments" in which adults and children can converse about death. The more opportunities children have to explore the meaning of death and discuss issues related to the subject, the better equipped they will be to cope if a significant loss occurs in their life. Excellent curriculum materials are available for death education in the schools (O'Toole, 1989). There are many excellent books available, for all ages, on many aspects of death and bereavement. Reading a story with a child is a particularly good way to introduce the topic of death in a safe and nonthreatening way.

To the extent possible, children are helped when they are prepared ahead of time for the event of an anticipated death (Crase & Crase, 1976). They should be told honestly and simply what is happening and what to expect. Too many details can overwhelm a child's ability to process information, they will generally ask for the information they are ready to receive. Regarding hospital visits and memorial or funeral services, children are less distressed and fearful when they are given a clear description of what the place will look like, who will be there, and what will happen.

I found out about my dad's illness by my mom telling me. I was very confused and scared because I was very young. (J.P. age 9)

I asked everyday. They sat me down in their room and told me he had a tumor and it was malignant. I had no idea that meant "cancer." I remember thinking nothing of it because I hadn't known anybody who had died of cancer. From what I knew, they went in there, and cut it out, and you were done. Boy, was I wrong. (Meg, age 18)

My mom told us that our dad had cancer. I wasn't very worried about this because I didn't know what cancer was. Mom tried to tell us what it was, and to tell us what was going to happen. Joe and Meg took it the worst because they knew what cancer was. (Kate, age 12).

Communication

Effective communication with children is an essential and crucial component of supporting bereaved children. Children know when they are in the presence of an adult who is uncomfortable or fearful about discussing death and the painful feelings of grief. Adults create a safe environment for children when they speak clearly and honestly about death and grief, using language that children can understand given their age and abilities. Asking children what they think can help to illuminate misconceptions they may have, and provide opportunities to clear any confusion.

Keep eye contact when you talk with a child. Talk softer, but not in a baby voice, in a compassionate gentle tone. Don't hesitate if a hug is appropriate. (Joe, age 20)

Information

Children need reliable, dependable information to develop a foundation for healthy grief work. The first task of mourning is to understand and make sense of the death. As much as adults may want to soften the facts and protect young children, myths and fairy tales about death are unhelpful or even harmful. Young children who cannot understand that death is irreversible and permanent can understand that death is like a broken toy. The person who died does not work anymore, and even though we want very much to fix it, the person will not work again (Rando, 1988). Young children need to be told very specifically that the deceased person cannot eat, walk, move, breathe, can no longer feel sad, mad, hurt, or cold, and cannot come back.

Be brutally honest. Children understand more than they get credit for and they deserve to know what's going on. Protecting them or making promises are difficult to explain later. When kids ask questions about how much time they have left with their father, I wouldn't want to hear, "We hope he lives for a very long time." If it's unclear, then say that. Maybe something like, "Your father might only have a couple of weeks but we are doing the best we can." (Joe, age 20)

Avoid Euphemisms

The use of euphemisms for death assist adults in distancing themselves from unpleasant feelings. Some commonly used euphemisms include lost, passed away, expired, resting in peace, left us, gone to heaven, and asleep in Christ. Young children who think literally will believe that a lost person can be found, that if someone is resting or asleep they will wake up, and if they have gone to heaven (or somewhere else) they can return. It is important to tell children that someone has "died" and be mindful to choose words that will not lead to misconceptions.

Repetition

Adults need to be aware that children often use repetition to integrate information and work through difficult emotions or problems. They may ask the same questions over and over, even moments after an adult has given an excellent and honest answer. For very young children, repetition may signal their struggle to integrate difficult concepts that they are not yet able to understand. Another function of repetitious questioning can be to test the reliability of the explanation—will the adult give the same answer as last time, or will different adults answer the same way? Repetitious symbolic play is a common method children employ to grasp the reality of the situation and discharge the feelings they cannot verbalize. Such repetition can be exhausting, and for a grief-stricken adult, extremely painful. Adults need to remember that this is the child's grief work, remain patient, and resist the inclination to discourage this behavior.

Secondary Losses

Children experience a myriad of secondary losses when someone they love has died. Adults can assist children in identifying and acknowledging secondary losses. Getting a great report card, performing in the school play, or going camping with the scout troop are all positive events, but there can be a component of sadness because the deceased parent is not there to offer congratulations or share in the event. Simply inquiring, "I wonder if you were missing your father," helps the child to understand the experience and lets him or her know that someone is noticing and cares. When children lose a parent, sibling, pet, or other close loved one, they lose their future with them, and secondary losses can surface over the course of a lifetime.

> I miss my dad more than usual when I go through a change in my life. Like when I graduated from high school, and when I left for college I really missed him more than usual. When I learn something I would've loved to

share or ask him about, I miss him. Also, any father–daughter event makes me miss him. (Meg, age 18)

The hardest thing about having a parent die when you're young is the fact that you can't show him the kind of person you turned into, and the things you accomplished. (Jim, age 15)

Impact of Other Losses

Many life experiences can represent loss to children. The death of a family member, friend, or pet are among the most obvious and significant kinds of loss. But children can also have grief experiences due to a separation or divorce, relocating, a favorite teacher leaving, a friend moving away, loss of a favorite toy or other possession, changing schools, graduation, or leaving for college. A bereaved child may be even more vulnerable to the pain of the "necessary losses" encountered as part of life, and even a minor loss (losing a toy, for example) may bring a resurgence of grief, sadness, and longing for the deceased person. Children are well-served by adults who can recognize and honor that these are legitimate, important losses and can provide understanding, comfort, and an opportunity to talk about the new loss.

Many of our friends, including the kids' friends, have not known how to cope with our loss so they back off from us and are nowhere to be found. My kids would all say that the severe drop off of kids who could talk about it with them was something that made it all hurt worse. There seems to be a very short period of time that they were allowed to share their pain. (Chris, the mom)

Memories

Memories are every bit as important to children as they are to adults. For children who are bereaved at a very young age, they will have fewer memories of the person who died. Particularly in the case of a parent's death, the absence of memories and the missed opportunity to "know" the deceased person can be painful for years to come, and may resurface in adolescence and adulthood. A caring adult can help the children construct a legacy that they can carry with them throughout their life. Children love to hear stories about the deceased, particularly if they are included in the story. Even simple remarks like, "Remember how much Dad loved chocolate ice cream?" or "Mom would have hated that lightning and thunder!" help to keep the memory vivid. Looking at photograph albums or videos are also helpful. Many children enjoy making "memory collages" or "memory books." Surviving parents can create memory books for their children as commemorative gifts.

The hardest part is I didn't get to spend as much time with him as the other kids did. A good memory is playing catch in the backyard. My mom tells me stories about my dad to help me cope. (J.P., age 9)

I think the hardest thing is you don't have very many memories about your parent. The ones you have, you cherish, but you don't have many. Joe and Meg had many more memories than Jim, J.P., and I did. (Kate, age 12)

You need to not forget the person, but you must celebrate the life that person lived, and move on. They might be gone physically, but no one can ever take away the memories you have. (Jim, age 15)

Commemoration

Memorialization/commemoration is one of the tasks of mourning for children that is often overlooked or underappreciated. A common question asked by concerned adults is whether it is helpful or harmful to take a child to a funeral (Corr, 1991; Weller, Weller, Fristad, Cain, & Bowes, 1988). Although there is clinical evidence to suggest that children who are excluded without choice may become very angry, there is no evidence that allowing a child to attend a funeral is harmful (Furman, 1970; Kastenbaum, 1991; Kubler-Ross, 1983; Lamers, 1965; Silverman & Worden, 1991; Wolfelt, 1983). Silverman and Worden (1992b) have demonstrated that taking part in funeral planning and funeral ritual can help children with their grief work. Children should be allowed, not forced, to attend services. A trusted adult should describe as specifically as possible what to expect and what will happen, that some people may be crying. For very young children, a visit to the funeral home prior to the service can ease apprehension and they can familiarize themselves with the surroundings. If a child chooses to take part, an available, trusted adult should accompany him or her through the entire event, and be available to leave early should the child need to. After the service, adults should discuss what happened and encourage the child to ask questions and describe his or her own thoughts and responses.

Children are often curious about the various means of disposing of dead bodies. Adults are often uncomfortable with this topic, especially in answering questions about cremation. As with all other aspects of death and grief, children deserve honest answers and receive information easily from an adult who can deal with the topic matter-of-factly. Fox (1985) suggested telling children that there are a variety of ways that people from different cultures or religions go about disposing of bodies. One way is to put the body in a special box and bury it in the ground. Another way is to turn the body to ashes that are then put in the ground or the ocean. Fox (p. 35) offers a particularly good explanation of cremation used by one family:

When the body is placed in a box and into the ground, it will eventually—after a long, long time—decay and turn into dust. By heating the body, as hot as the warmest part of the sun, we are speeding up that process of turning the body into ashes or dust.

If children ask how the body is heated or turned to ashes, they can be told it is done with flames or a fire. Children will need to be reminded and reassured that when a body is dead, it can not feel anything.

Beyond the memorial or funeral services, children benefit from commemorative activities as they grow. Children can be very creative and inventive when they are invited to participate in the planning and execution of rituals or events in memory of a deceased loved one.

It's important to do things in the name of their loved one who has died. Plant a tree and have a community low-scale planting ceremony. Decorate that tree on holidays and anniversaries. Include a little plaque. Have things named for the person who died. Help organize one day a year that *something* is done to remember the loved one—dinner, a softball game with friends, a golf tournament. (Chris, the mom)

HELPING BEREAVED ADOLESCENTS

Adolescents need the same things that children need: honesty, validation, permission to grieve in their own way, and understanding adults and friends who can offer appropriate support. Because adolescence is a time of differentiation and individuation, and because adolescent grief is paradoxically intermittent and ongoing, it can be difficult to determine when and how to best support a bereaved adolescent. Although direct comfort might be rejected, there are some indirect ways to help grieving adolescents.

One important way to indirectly help a bereaved adolescent is to teach and model good coping skills. Adolescents appear to be helped by activities that reduce stress, such as sports, playing a musical instrument, dancing, drama (Balk, 1991b; Balk & Hogan, 1995; Hogan & DeSantis, 1994). Adults can also model healthy expression, and recovery, of intense emotions like sadness and anger. Adults can also model healthy use of social support and encourage the adolescent to do the same. Most importantly, keeping lines of communication open, and maintaining and active interest in all areas of the adolescents' life will increase the likelihood that they will reach out and receive help and comfort.

Bibliotherapy and journaling are often utilized by adolescents to assist in the processing of their loss and grief. Both fiction and nonfiction resources help adolescents understand their experience and decrease feelings of isolation and alienation. Happily, the range of literature is wide and diverse, and excellent guides are available (see Bernstein and Rudman, 1989; Corr, 1993). One grief counselor we know invites adolescents to read certain books and advise her on the appropriateness, or helpfulness, of the book. In this way, the adolescent is less likely to feel like they "have a problem" and more likely to feel that they have something valuable to contribute. Many adolescents will respond positively to writing poems, essays, letters, or keeping a journal, memory book, or scrapbook.

> What helped me was a good support group of friends, teachers, and family. Absolute expression of emotion in tears, exercise, and writing was invaluable. Good perspective on life helped. (Joe, age 20)

SUPPORT GROUPS FOR CHILDREN

The professional literature has focused on individual support for bereaved children and adolescents. Hospice and similar organizations have recognized the need for bereavement groups for young people and have implemented groups for children and adolescents. Not every child will want to attend a support group, but for those who do, there are a number of benefits (Cook & Dworkin, 1992).

Children often report discomfort around feeling "different" from their peers following the death of a loved one. A support group provides a place to be with other children who have also experienced the loss of a loved one. In this place, they can share their feelings and experiences, and learn that what they think and feel is similar to what other children their age think and feel. Merely being in the presence of the other children helps to diminish feelings of alienation and isolation. Young people will often share more readily with peers their own age, and willingly offer one another emotional support.

> It helped playing with my friends. (J.P., age 9)

> Nobody knew what I was going through, so I had no one to talk to, until my counselor made a group with other kids who had lost a parent. Which helped a lot in that they know what you're going through. It helped in that you didn't feel alone in your struggle. (Jim, age 15)

> Knowing that there are other people out there has helped me cope with my dad's death a little better. I have a group of kids, and three teachers at school whose parents have died. It's easy to talk to them. I know that I'm not alone through it all. I like knowing that other people know how I feel when they talk to me about my dad's death. Most say they do, but the don't really have the fondest idea of how I feel. (Kate, age 12)

Children will often try to protect their parents and other family members. Observing that their surviving parents are coping with their own grief, children and adolescents may not look to them to get their own needs met. Children, especially older children, may feel the need to take on adult concerns and responsibilities to support the surviving parent. A group is a private place where children can discuss their feelings without fear of upsetting or burdening a family member.

> I can be a great older brother and a fantastic son, but I can never be my mom's husband. We'll never retire together, I can't make it up to her on Valentine's Day or their anniversary or her birthday. I'll never be 'dad.' I can teach baseball and carry someone on my shoulders or walk someone down the aisle, but it doesn't mean the same thing. For me to be proud isn't enough. It is a deeply sad thing for me to do my very best at something and know it isn't good enough. (Joe, age 20)

Many adolescent peers may not have experienced a significant loss them-selves, and therefore cannot truly understand their friend's pain, or know what consolation or advice to give. But sometimes adolescent peers have a natural sensitivity and can listen nonjudgmentally, thereby assisting with the grief process. Schools, churches, and other organizations are beginning to understand the value and effectiveness of adolescent peer support, and are providing training for adolescents who want to provide peer support to others in their community (See Baxter, Bennett, & Stuart, 1987; Cunningham, 1990). In these self-help groups adolescents can find information about coping with loss, and a place to share their grief. For some bereaved adolescents, providing support to newly bereaved peers helps them their own growth and helps give some meaning to their loss.

Bereavement support groups for children can take many forms. They may be time-limited or open-ended. They may follow a specific agenda or be relatively nondirective. They typically provide a time for discussion paired with opportunity for other forms of expression that are important means for children to processes feelings: play, art, puppets, clay, drama, books, creative writing, and music.

One particularly good model for bereavement support groups can be found at the Dougy Center in Portland, OR. Founded in December 1982, the Dougy Center operates on the principles that grief is a natural reaction to loss, that each person has within them the natural capacity for healing, that duration and intensity of grief is unique for each individual, and that caring and acceptance assists in healing (Corr et al., 1991; Knope, 1989). The Dougy Center offers groups for children ages 3 through 19, and provides groups for children who have experienced all kinds of loss. Concurrent groups are offered for adults caregivers of the children in the program. Many support programs have been fashioned after the Dougy Center's model. The Center has developed a training program, manual of activities, and other resources (Whitney, 1991).

SUMMARY

Children and adolescents cannot avoid encounters with death, loss, and grief. Their reactions and responses to bereavement are influenced by a multitude of factors including, but not limited to, their age, cognitive and emotional development, developmental understanding of the concept of death, personality style, prior experience and education, family dynamics, and quality of available support.

Children take their cues from adults, and need adult assistance and guidance to cope effectively with bereavement and grief. Adults can best support children by becoming well informed about children and bereavement, by honoring and supporting children's unique grief processes, and by creating an atmosphere of safety where children can learn about death, experience and express grief, and be supported and encouraged in their efforts to integrate the loss into their lives and to go on without their loved one.

> What I've noticed about the individual grief processes of my children is that each has their own timing, their own style, and that all of it can come and go for no reason at all. There are times when there's a withdrawal from social activity and a quietness consumes them. Then there are times when they are socially outgoing and fine with talking about losing their dad and quite demonstrative with their feelings. There are numerous ways the kids have chosen to remember Rick—some more positive than others, some more productive as well. All their ways, however, are their individual ways to cope with their deep loss.
>
> The other thing that I've noticed about their grief processes is that they can each go for long periods of time and seem perfectly stable with their loss and then something will rock them and then it's followed by a period of time when they spend time putting it all back together again. When done, they are ready to go on with life again.
>
> Supporting children in grief is a full-time job that is never done, and something to always keep on the lookout for. The healing is not a process with a set "end." It's much closer to say "healing is really learning coping skills that need to be sharpened from time to time, and at other points need all out overhauling." The advice I'd give to other parents whose spouse has died is: a) pull up the draw bridge; b) fill up the moat, put in the alligators; c) be with your kids, be with your kids, be with your kids.
>
> In more sound words, counseling at all costs—not on a short-term basis where you expect to feel healed, but more where it's a built-in support to lean on when needed. Plan events to be done in the spouse's name so that the kids *feel* their legacy, and keep identifying what their heritage *was* and *is*. Spend time with other families who've had similar sadness to help each other. Devise activities that help them remember their parent. Show them it's ok to be devastated and that someday you will feel better, and it doesn't mean you have to love your dad less at all. Follow their lead. Listen. (Chris, the mom)

Voices

The participants on the Bereavement Coping Study were adults, and so we asked the Goethals family to talk with us about children coping with bereavement. Rick Goethals was diagnosed with cancer and died 1 year later at the age of 43. He is survived by his wife Chris, and five children Joe, Meg, Jim, Kate, and J.P. At the time of his death, the children were 16, 14, 11, 9, and 6 years old, respectively, representing a nearly full developmental spectrum. We are grateful to them for their contributions to this chapter.

I've learned to deal with my sadness and how to take care of myself. (J.P., age 9)

When we went out to swim, my dad knew that I was scared of the waves, so he would take me by the hand and take me out to the ocean with him. He would take me under the waves so that I couldn't get crushed by the wave. I felt safe with my dad. I also loved just sitting with my dad. (Kate, age 12)

I think that my dad was an angel who maybe was only allowed down here on earth for awhile. Even if he wasn't a real angel, he still is one to me. (Kate, age 12)

On holidays and special occasions it's harder than usual. But sometimes, it just hits me harder than usual. Maybe I saw my friend with her dad, or I watched a sad movie. Sometimes it hits me hard for no particular reason, I just really miss him. (Kate, age 12)

I believe that everything that happens is meant to be. In some way or another, someone or something will turn out for the better. I think that from my dad's death, each one of the kids as well as my mom have bonded and become stronger. (Jim, age 15)

I miss him the most when my brother tries to fill in for him at a father–son event. First, because my brother didn't ask for this job. Second, I can't enjoy the event when I'm supposed to have a dad there. I never got to share a whole lot of life with him, and would do anything to do so. (Jim, age 15)

When I was a little girl, whenever I had trouble sleeping, or had a nightmare, my dad would sing me to sleep. The song he would sing was Silent Night. It would put me right to sleep. (Meg, age 18)

Seeing him get sick at the dinner table, lose his hair, lose weight, and lose strength hurt a lot, but through it all, he never lost his smile, great spirit, or generosity. (Meg, age 18)

I still wake up some days and think, "Why me?" I never found an answer, nor do I think I will ever find an answer. It's just one of those things there is no answer for. (Meg, age 18)

An illness such as cancer is a painful wake-up call and reminder of our mortality. The time spent with someone who has cancer is twice as important, twice as appreciated, and only half as enjoyable. (Joe, age 20)

When he got sick again, a stroke and now the cancer had spread to his brain and his bones, just about everywhere, I got to the hospital the next morning and he was heavily drugged. They let up a little on the medication and he woke up. Everyone let me be alone with him for awhile and I tried talking with him. He didn't recognize me or anyone. I could write volumes about that one moment. In that one moment I believe I grew up more than I had in the previous 18 years. For a parent not to recognize his child is something I wish on no one ever. He later felt better and began to recognize me, but it was never the same after that. (Joe, age 20)

I will continue to struggle with meaning and order for the rest of my life. There's absolutely nothing wrong with that. (Joe, age 20)

The most helpful thing for my children has simply been time—not just time, but more time, and what they have done with that time. They have struggled to find ways to demonstrate their love for their dad and their commitment to not forget him, and to become a better person for knowing him. This is why time has helped them. Time was necessary, but it could not have done it alone. You need works of love in your father's name, events when you can profess your pride and love of your dad, and numerous activities where you can write about your feelings for him. All these things help and when added to time they represent *healing*, but not *forgetting*. (Chris, the mom)

We asked what advice they would give to other children who were coping with the death of a loved one, and what people need to know about children who are grieving. Here are some responses:

Ask your parent to tell you things you didn't know about the parent you lost. (J.P., age 9)

I would tell them to remember the good times they had with their parent instead of when they died. If I think about my dad during his last night, it's hard for me, but if I think about the good times when we went in the ocean, it is a bit easier. Easier because you didn't have to think about him at his worst stage, but more his best stage. Harder, because then you don't have those moments anymore. (Kate, age 12)

I think people should know that there is no attitude that every kid has who is grieving. Some kids want space and to be alone, others want to be open about their grieving and need to talk to somebody. Whatever somebody's attitude is, you should learn it quickly, and try to follow it. Instead of always trying to talk about it with somebody who needs space, let them have their space, then maybe that's how they heal their grieving. (Kate, age 12)

People need to know that the pain will never go away. You need to let them know that they will always have a shoulder to cry on, someone to talk to, or someone will just listen. (Jim, age 9)

The only advice I could give someone is to do what *you* want. Don't let anybody tell you how to grieve or what the "best" thing to do is. The "best" thing to do is whatever the best thing for you is. (Meg, age 18)

People need to know that children are extremely vulnerable when they are grieving, and one little thing could set them off. The only thing you can do is *be supportive*. (Meg, age 18)

I would sit facing the person and say nothing. I would ask nothing of the person and probably suggest nothing. If appropriate, I would give the person my phone number and tell them if they ever want to get together, just give me a call. I would answer the person's questions with absolute honesty and if asked I would share my experiences, what helped me, without giving any advice. (Joe, age 20)

Don't *disappear*!! Don't not mention the person who died. Don't leave the children out from your family outings—include them when you go somewhere. Invite the family over, not necessarily for the big formal dining situation, but more for the loose pizza gathering. Follow their lead, you don't need to lead them. Remember the holidays stink forever. Mention how it must be hard and how you miss the person, too. Listen. Listen. (Chris, the mom)

My grandfather sat me down the day my father died
He told me a story I'd heard a thousand times
I drank some beers and he sipped on some gin
Then he told me God takes the best of us when we're young men
Memories aren't forgotten when pictures go up on the wall
And heroes live forever cause in our hearts they can never fall.
My dad was my hero
I thank God he was my dad
But now he's gone forever
And his memory makes me sad
I wish I could have known him better
He was the best dad any boy could have
Sitting in my front room watching baseball on TV
Dodgers and the Braves were tied in the fifth when my son said to me
Dad, whose that man on the wall, the one in black and white
The one you like to look at and then sit there and cry
Was he your coach or an army general
What was he that makes that man so special
That man there was my hero
That man there was my dad
But now he's gone forever
And his memory makes me sad
I wish you could have met him
I really wish you had
He could have been the best granddad you ever had
Dad, you are my hero
I thank God you were my dad
Now you're gone forever
Your memory makes me sad
I wish you could have stayed longer
Sometimes I get so mad
You were the best dad any boy could have.

Joe

Memories of the Greatest Father of the World

I remember when my father held me in his hands and when he would try to do my hair with rubber bands
I remember when he would do anything for me no matter how loud I yelled at him and when he would play catch with me no matter how dim
I remember when my father would take me and my sister to the park and when he would rent a movie for us no matter how dark
I remember how his heart was so full of love and care and how he told us never to stare
I remember how he would never swear and how he would let us play with his hair
I remember how he coached all of our teams and I think he was the greatest father of the world so it seemed
I think he had a heart bigger than Europe

Kate

An Angel

If I had the power to bring someone back to life I would choose my father. I would obviously choose my father because I knew him pretty well but I wish that he could watch me, my brothers, and my sister grow up into mature adults, to see me become president of North school, to see me become a lawyer and to see my brother become a doctor. I wouldn't just bring my dad back for myself but I would also bring him back for my mom because she really needs a husband, for my older brother because he is in college and he wanted to have my dad be right there when he walked up and got his diploma for not only college but also from high school, for my sister because she really needs a father to love and to talk to, for my other brother because he really needs a dad at this point of his life, for my little brother, J.P. because he only got to have my dad for six years and that my dad only got to be a part of six years of his life. J.P. is just learning how to read and also for my dad's family and for the many, many friends that he made during his life.

I feel that my dad was sent to us from heaven and that he is a saint. My dad was 43 and he was a tall handsome man with dark hair and tan skin from living in L.A. and running every morning. He never swore in his life. He was a gentleman and a great father. I would give the world to have him back right now.

Kate

The Sad Time

It all started one ordinary day after school. I went over to my friends house and played with my friend, when I got a call that my dad's in the hospital. When I got the phone call, I didn't know what to say but, "Let's go." It was so scary. It was the scariest thing I've ever gone through. Every second I wanted to be with him. When I finally got there, I couldn't stand looking at him in the hospital bed. I'd rather eat brussel sprouts than look at him be so sick. It was just so scary looking at him and listening to him talk. I just didn't want to be here anymore. I really didn't. It killed me to look at him like that. My only wish was to have him come out of it. In a couple of days later he came home. He was up and around playing football and baseball. One day he started to get sick again. We brought a hospital bed in Kate's room so he could sleep at our house. He was still able to get to our games. Soon he had to stay in bed 24 hours a day and everybody was really scared. I was probably the most scared because I was only with him for so short and they were with him for so long. I cried every day and I still have so many more questions. It was fun when he was still with us but then he started to really get sick again. So we took a couple of days off of school to stay with him.

On those couple of days we were at home, mostly we stayed in the room with my dad. We were all very sad. When he started to get really sick we wanted a nurse to help us. Then everybody went back to school. That's everybody but me. I went to the hospital when he got check ups at Stanford.

I always got a little toy. It was so fun at the time, until he had to go back to the hospital. It was scary seeing so many sick people. A lot of times I just needed some one to talk to.

Finally the day came when he passed on to a better life. We all cried for a long time. The next day [I was] in first grade. Ever since he died we all look at pictures of him. But the most important thing is we still love him.

J. P.

Life

Life is like a rose.
It starts out as a bud,
and slowly it will bloom.
When it is full grown,
it will be more beautiful than ever.
For awhile it will bring love;
but when its petals start to fall,
you will too.
They will fall,
One;
After another;
After another;
Until they are gone.
When they are all gone
it will die,
and so will you.
With no rose,
there is no love;
With no love,
there is no life.

Jim

6

Growth and Resilience
Following Loss

Thinking back on it, if I had not done this, look at all I would have missed—all this growth, all this understanding. (Vera, 65, who lost her 90-year-old father to leukemia)

I tend to look at it generally as if all the things that happen in my life are a gift, for whatever reason, or however they happen. It doesn't necessarily have to be only pleasant gifts, but everything that happens ... there's a meaning. I've had a lot of suffering in my life ... and through that I've learned a great deal. While I wouldn't want to go back and relive that, I'm grateful for that because it makes me who I am. There's a lot of joys and sorrows, but they all enrich life. (Alicia, 50, whose 70-year-old father died of cancer)

I like who I am now because I find at 44 that I really like myself. If I didn't go through a lot of the hardships that I had, I wouldn't be who I am. So in a lot of ways, it's been an ok journey. And if I hadn't had people like that in my life, I wouldn't have a good sense of humor, which is one of the things that helps get through, right? I feel extremely fortunate lately. (Norma, 44, whose 60-year-old father died of cancer)

Although the loss of a loved one is one of the most difficult experiences people have in their lives, over and over again we have heard people say that they felt they grew and gained something positive in the experience. Many said they would never wish the experience on anyone else, but they were glad that they had the opportunity to go through it. This chapter explores the idea that the loss of a loved one can be a watershed experience, leading to positive change and growth in many people.

We begin by describing the various ways the people in our study said they had grown or found something positive in the loss of their loved one. Then we address the question, "what does it mean to grow following a trauma?" by reviewing the writings of theorists and researchers who have contemplated this question. Next we look at the relationship between perceiving something positive in a loss and one's psychological adjustment (in the form of symptoms of depression, anxiety, distress, etc.) following the loss. Finally, we investigate who finds it possible to grow in the wake of a loss and who does not.

WHAT WAS POSITIVE

When we first considered asking the people in our bereavement study if they had found anything positive in their loss, we were somewhat reluctant to do so. We were concerned that we would cause them further distress or offend them. Yet, our review of previous studies on bereavement and other major negative life events and our own clinical work suggested that many people do find positive aspects in their experience and report having grown from the experience (see Frankl, 1963; Miles & Crandall, 1983; Tedeschi & Calhoun, 1996). For example, studies of cancer patients, myocardial infarction patients, bone marrow transplant patients, stroke victims and their caregivers, and men testing positive for HIV find that, as a consequence of their experience, they now value relationships more, have gained important self-knowledge, reorganized their priorities, and developed new attitudes toward life (Laerum, Johnsen, Smith, & Larsen, 1987; Michela, 1987; Tedeschi & Calhoun, 1996). And previous studies of bereavement find that the majority of people say they have found something positive in their loss (Lehman et al., 1993). Thus, we cautiously asked the participants in our study the following:

> Sometimes people who lose a loved one find some positive aspect in the experience. For example, some people feel they learn something about themselves or others. Have you found anything positive in this experience?

Although some respondents reacted negatively to this question (one man said, "No. Make that HELL NO!"), the overwhelming response to the question was affirmative. Even just one month after the death of their loved one, 73% of the respondents said they had found something positive in their loss experience, and 81% of the respondents had found something positive by the end of the study 18 months after their loss. Just what they found positive varied greatly.

Here, we describe several themes in the answers people gave to the question, "Have you found anything positive in this experience?"

Reprioritizing One's Life and Goals

The loss of a loved one can cause people to completely reevaluate their priorities, their goals, and their lifestyles. The most common response people in our study gave to the question, "Have you found anything positive in this experience?" was that the loss had caused them to reprioritize their lives and to make major changes in the ways they ran their lives.

One of the most frequent changes people made in their lives was to focus more on the here and now, rather than always focusing on future goals or past failures. The loss of their loved one had made them acutely aware of the shortness of time and the fragility of life. Some people decided to cut back the time they spent on jobs and careers to spend more time with family. Others decided to pursue a new career or education that they had always been putting off for the future.

> I think I'm much more conscious of the life around me, where people are going in their lives. I see a lot of people without much life, and I don't want to do that. I don't want to be lifeless. You have to be really conscious of what you're doing and where you're going. I'm very close to my father. The family has gotten really, really close—my children. I've changed my whole lifestyle, so I've changed how I evaluate people. I think I've changed everything. I take less for granted, appreciate things, people, weather and surroundings. I am more aware. (Victoria, 42, whose mother died of brain cancer)

> One thing I learned is to take each day to deal with whatever you're doing, day by day. For sure, I make it a point here at home, especially with the little ones, to always give a hug—special hug we call it—on a daily basis to reinforce we're not here, no guarantees, tomorrow. The positive from that is not to take each other for granted. The minor things, the coffee cup left on the table, it doesn't matter, it's no big issue. We could be here today and gone tomorrow. With J's death, there isn't anything that can hurt me; no one, nothing can ever hurt me like that. I'm not laughing at fate, but the idiots that we have in this world can't hurt me after watching him disappear, disintegrate in front of me. One of the words to use is "unconditional." You go through life with conditions, boy you're setting yourself up for big disappointments. You have to come from the heart, unconditional. Nothing was going to keep me from him. That gave me the edge to deal with the taboos, what people thought. So I have empowered myself to feel like walking on air sometimes. We went through the whole way together. It was great. (Ginny, 45, who lost her 36-year-old brother to AIDS)

> I probably take a lot shorter term view of what's going on. I think there's a lot more of *now* than there ever was before. I think we all tend to respond

that way to things—you know, we've got plenty of time, and things will take care of themselves. I've said things to people, and asked people to do things that I'd no more done 6 months ago than fly. I came from a family, hell, everybody lived into their nineties. If there's anything I want to do, don't put it off, is the whole thing I'm saying. (Keith, 61, whose 67-year-old wife died of ovarian cancer)

When I saw her die, such an angry and upset person. This cancer does affect the brain. I saw her in this state, and I started my goal to live as completely every day of your life that you have left, and not to fall in the same pitfall of existence that she experienced. In a way, her death did serve to reinforce and help my feeling of nonguilt about that because when you're dead, you're dead, as far as I'm concerned. I don't believe in psychic this and that, or reincarnation. Sometimes I'm up in the woods and stuff, 10,000 feet I just climbed, I feel guilty—I shouldn't feel that good. But I don't do that much anymore. (Joel, 48, whose 78-year-old mother died of pancreatic cancer)

I sit here alone in this big house, four or five empty bedrooms, R's empty bedroom, new kitchen, big yard, everything nice. No one here but me. I could have done with less. You know—less prosperous. Maybe only one car, less things. We could have enjoyed more together. Things we buy aren't important. It's not the same. No one to share. I don't need all this. It means nothing to me. It's not the same. Yes, enjoy life more, every minute in every day. (Raul, 65, whose 64-year-old wife died of brain cancer)

Becoming More Sensitive and Thoughtful

Many people talked about positive changes in their personalities as a result of their loss experience. They may have become more tolerant, more sensitive, more patient, more loving with others. Several people described becoming less controlling and more willing to take life as it comes.

I learned about compassion, I learned about suffering. Suffering leads to compassion. Compassion leads to beauty. It was an opportunity to look at myself and to be noncomplacent. I was always very complacent before. I thought I had it made. I was stagnating. It opened my heart, my mind and my spirit. I wish it had happened another way, but that's the way it happened. (Arnold, 50, whose 70-year-old mother died of breast cancer)

I started thinking, "I've got to find something positive to let go, to get to acceptance. So, ok, I'll work on me. I'll try to do something for my growth. That will be a positive thing that will come out of his death." One of the things that I promised to do was to be more humble, more tolerant. I'm a Type-A, I like efficiency, effectiveness, I get impatient. I would look at individuals, not just that they're ineffective, inefficient, but try to be a little more caring about others who are going through a situation. I went to a funeral of one of D's classmates a few months ago. I didn't know the kid, I didn't know his mother, but I knew what she was going through. I feel my perspective in life is different. I *am* more humble. I cry now about things that I never cried about before. (Laura, 48, whose 28-year-old son died of a brain tumor)

I think I somehow learned by going through 2 years of this experience to be a bit more laid back about things—when you can't control them, to not worry that you can't control them. Up until that time I would try my best to control them, and if I couldn't control them, I would worry like heck because I couldn't. I think now, having gone through it and having come out on the other side, I see it's ok not to worry about it. I see it's ok to do what you can do, and it's ok to forget it when you can't do any more. (Millie, 46, whose 83-year-old father died of cancer)

I'm more pragmatic. There have been life situations that come up, and I don't view them as being as dire or as big a crisis as they normally would have been. I don't take things quite so seriously as I used to. That's spilled over to my interpersonal relationship with my boyfriend. I feel lighter, I feel happier. (Cindy, 48, whose 74-year-old father died of pancreatic cancer)

Throughout this whole thing there developed a softness in me, and a greater sense of my vulnerable side. An inner peacefulness that I have felt. Now I can always recognize (people who have gone through this)—they have a softness to them, a side of life that many people do not see, and then once they see, a lot of them have a real sense of compassion. That's what I felt that I didn't have before—this sensitivity. (Lee, 50, whose 74-year-old father died of cancer)

He taught me to have an appreciation for people who were sick. Before his illness, when I would see someone in a walker or a wheelchair in a restaurant, an older person walking with a cane, I would think, "Oh, come on, get out of my way." Then when he became ill, and we didn't think he was going to leave the hospital, I would see these older people walking with a cane, and think, "How lucky, how wonderful for the family to have that person alive." So he gave me that. He also gave me a stronger sense of life, more compassion for people, an understanding of the pain that people go through when someone has an illness in the family. (Della, 50, whose 74-year-old father died of cancer)

His illness was for me to learn something. I learned patience. I learned compassion. I learned forgiveness. I learned that my priorities were worthless. And I learned that, no matter how bad things can be, there's still love and humor in the world. There were so many lessons for me. My priorities were screwed up. You clean your slate, in other words. You learn your own strengths. (Angel, 60, whose 64-year-old husband died of AIDS)

I learned a lot about love, and empathy. Not so much sympathy, because there was nothing to be sympathetic, but empathy. I can look at people now and have more feeling for their pain, for their feelings. I think I have learned more patience and tolerance for—I see real old people in wheelchairs, people who are having a struggle. I feel more for them than I did before taking care of mother. (Lena, 58, whose 79-year-old mother died of cancer)

People certainly felt they had more to give to other grieving people than they would have before the loss. They may speak of their own awkwardness and discomfort when faced previously with someone who had experienced a loss. Now they say, they understand and wish they had responded differently. Now when they meet someone who is bereaved, they respond easily and differently from before. Indeed, many bereaved people say they know instantly that they are in the presence of someone who has also been bereaved because there is more compassion, awareness, and understanding of everything it means to have a loss among people who have experienced it.

Realizing Personal Strength and Competence

One of the most common responses of the people in our study was that they had discovered strengths and competencies in themselves that they did not realize they had (for similar findings, see Calhoun & Tedeschi, 1989; Lund, Caserta, & Dimond, 1993). Many of the participants in our study had been caregivers to their loved ones before the loved ones died. They described engaging in activities that they would have never believed they could do—providing nursing care to the loved one, being assertive in talking with physicians, battling insurance companies and hospitals for services for their loved ones.

> Watching Richard die was horrible, but even that was—I got something from that, even. Sacrificing, which is how I would characterize the last 3 years of my life when he died, sacrificing much of my own self was frustrating but that was good. I learned a lot from that. I learned so much. I learned how much I can put up with. I learned there's nothing to be feared in life. Even, I could lose this house and live on the street, and I know I could do it. There's nothing I couldn't do. (Nora, 46, whose 46-year-old husband died of AIDS)

> I found personal growth. And perspective—I feel I see a generational flow that I was aware of, but didn't really feel a part of before. And I saw myself acting in a role of competence where I had to pull on all my resources just to get through sometimes. I would have to be directing the medical people about what I wanted to do. A person like me who hates showing anger and can't stand conflict. I would have to stand and demand care from the nursing home, and it was necessary and I did it. So I came away with a feeling of competence and strength, and gratitude. The gratitude not for having to go through it, I would never have asked for it, but I can see how the experience was a real benefit to me. I was forced to grow. (Martha, 46, whose 83-year-old father died of cancer)

People who had not been caregivers also described discovering strength in themselves in how they coped with the loss of their loved one. Some people said that they expected they would fall apart on the death of their loved one, but were pleasantly surprised that they actually coped quite well with the death.

Others described how they had found new, more adaptive ways of coping when confronted with the trauma of their loss.

> There were plenty of positive things. In fact I'm still feeling—I felt a lot of "Gee, I didn't know that I could be this tough. I didn't know." There were all those kind of feelings. But even on a day-to-day basis right now, I feel a lot stronger and a lot more capable of dealing with life in general and the sadness. Life is sad. Life is joyous and life is sad. Instead of getting depressed and overwhelmed by its sadness, I'm able to put it in what for me is its proper perspective. Its helped me put my ego in its proper perspective. (Nora, 46, whose 46-year-old husband died of AIDS)

> I realize now that there were times I thought I couldn't keep going. Now I realize that this was probably one of the most meaningful things I've ever done, or will do. That it had the whole spectrum of life. It made a great impact on my existence by doing it—raising my children, that kind of thing it could be compared to. (Rosa, 59, whose 94-year-old mother died of unknown causes)

> Part of me didn't know that I had the strength for this. If you had asked me 10 years ago, could I have gotten through this and still be sitting and talking, I would have said, "Not on your life!" But it's amazing what you *can* do when you have to. Maybe that's one of the ways I've been able to live with myself because I did all I could. The other thing is, I did repriortize my life to a great degree after my brother's death. I had been a workaholic, not really available to my children; I was very much career-oriented. I started to freelance from the house so I would be more available. (Cara, 45, whose 46-year-old brother died of lung cancer)

As we noted in chapter 2, many women who lost their husbands said that, although they missed their husbands, they had found strength and tremendous personal growth in the freedom they now had to make their own decisions and to live the lifestyles they wished.

> I think that when you lose a loved one, it's a rebirth for yourself. You can't always dwell on the loss of the loved one. You have to look forward to what you are going to do with your life now—who you are as a single person, which is very very disturbing. Many people have been married much longer than I was, and they have to find out who they are. And it's a whole new experience, learning who you are, knowing who you are as a single person. That's one of the hard parts about being a widow or widower. A lot of people don't have time to think of who they are, because they're always attached to someone. And it's exciting. I mean, it's not bad, but it's exciting and it's also a little fearful to have to do that. Every day's a little learning experience for myself, of doing new things and learning new things as a single person. (Joy, 48, whose 49-year-old husband died of colon cancer)

> I found out how strong my children are, and how important they are to my life. I found out a lot about myself, too. I really am stronger than I thought

I was, and I thought I was pretty strong, but I'm stronger even than that. Not having the relationship of a husband, a close relationship like that, is—this sounds terrible, maybe—I find that I can do what I want, without hurting anybody, without asking anybody. I can just make decisions on my own, and take credit or blame for the results; and I'm ready to do that. I enjoy that. And it's not *bad*. That's one of the positives of being where I am. (Interviewer: You make decisions more thoughtfully now.) Yes I do. I have to look at both sides of things. Before I only looked at one side. And I've learned that some of the things I like to do are not frivolous. They are important. Whereas, your husband or your mate or your family might not understand what you want to do, and discount the importance of it—such as friends, and music. (Paula, 56, whose 62-year-old husband died of lung cancer)

Realizing the Importance of Relationships

Losing a loved one shatters assumptions that there will always be time to express your love to family members and friends, to share thoughts, dreams and memories, to do those things you want to do together, to simply be together. The most common regret that people in our study expressed was that they had not said everything they wanted to say to their loved one before he or she died:

I think what bothers me most about the whole thing still is not being able to talk to my father, not knowing whether he knew or didn't know he was dying, or how he felt about it. We didn't tell him what was happening, so I didn't know whether he knew or not. I didn't know. There was that communication lost. I regret that *a lot*. If anything bothers me I keep thinking about that. (Carla, 34, whose 79-year-old father died of cancer)

On the other hand, people frequently said that through their loss they had gained an understanding of the importance of their relationships that was now enriching all their relationships (see also Calhoun & Tedeschi, 1989; Malinak, Hoyt, & Patterson, 1979; Zemore & Shepel, 1989). They valued the people in their lives, and the time they could spend with these people, like they had never valued them before. They made more time for others and tried to be more positive and constructive in their relationships with others. And they were no longer afraid of expressing openly the love they had for their family members and friends.

I learned that when you love someone, the relationship is so important—. It's enhanced my relationship with other people because I realize that time is so important, and you can waste so much effort on small, insignificant events or feelings. I feel that in my present relationship I'm better able to be a real good friend, and I don't take things so personally. I don't feel that someone's got to fill me up. I can fill myself. I feel stronger as a person. I have more confidence in myself. (Karen, 47, whose partner died of cancer)

I hold onto the fact that when we learned he was sick, we got to know our son better than parents ever know their children. We got way past parent–child syndrome, able to show love. Very unusual to get past roles. We totally accepted him, he knew it, and we appreciated his honesty. Our love for him was limitless. He showed us what life was all about. (Al, 54, whose 31-year-old son died of AIDS)

Resolving Family Conflicts

As we discussed in chapter 4, the loss of a loved one can bring family conflicts to the surface and exacerbate them. In some families, however, these conflicts are confronted and resolved, leading individual family members to feel relieved of the burden of the conflicts and closer to other family members than they may ever have been in their lives.

Most of all, he helped to bridge—he came to grips—he—finally encountered with my mom all the problems that we'd had during my growing-up years. And he validated me as a person. And was able to say to my mother that she was wrong. So my dad healed me. And he completed me, my social growth. And yet, I did the same for him. Because I know that I gave him the strength and gave him the ability to see and to finally acknowledge the problems that had gone on for years and years. And once he was able to do that, during this period of talking things out and not bottling all this anger and frustration up, he was able to get stronger. He physically became stronger and emotionally became stronger. And I think, then, this period of his illness we finally had a chance to do a father and daughter relationship and a friend and friend relationship, with his living here. And he was happy—it gave me a great deal of happiness, and he was happy. I feel like we were blessed. (Judith, 33, whose 74-year-old father died of pancreatic cancer)

In some cases, the conflicts may have been with the family member who died. The fact that the death was anticipated for some time before it happened allowed some family members to resolve their conflicts with the dying family member. The surviving family members then often felt a tremendous weight had been lifted from them and that they could go on with their lives after the death occurred.

During the last years of her life my mom stopped drinking, so I came to know her in way that I was unable to when I was growing up. I learned a lot about the reasons why my parents did some of the things they did, felt some of the ways they felt and acted some of the ways they acted. It did not exactly reconcile me to the situation, but it's sort of a balance. I carried around a lot of resentment for my older brother who kind of divorced himself from family proceedings as early as possible. I never appreciated how scared he was at the time. I seem to have gotten a lot of the screwiness out of my system in one real acute, nasty episode of time. (Will, 42, whose 80-year-old mother died of pancreatic cancer)

I was able to experience my mother in a positive way—The stories at her funeral, going through her personal papers. When you're dealing with a frail, elderly person who is so needy, on top of that an alcoholic, it's very scary to be around them, because they keep almost sucking your lifeblood, they keep taking from you. Once they're dead, the threat is gone. You feel safe, and then you can open up. It's safe to … pull in all the good stuff about them. And to forgive, and accept healing. And for me, death had to precede all that. I always wanted to forgive the alcoholism in my family and was disappointed in myself that I couldn't. Where does all the guilt come from? For me the guilt is no more than when my mom was alive. You trade an active guilt for a kind of "I wish I had" guilt hindsight. Back then when she needed love and compassion and understanding, and I was able only to be superficial, that was the best I could do. Then I guess the job of the living after the death is to hire a new board of directors that's in everyone's head—find the tools you need to hire the proper board of directors that are going to support you instead of knock you down. (Nellie, 44, whose 78-year-old mother died of lung cancer)

Losing the Fear of Death

Finally, many participants in our study said that they had always believed they could not face death and had feared the death of loved ones and their own death. But the experience of watching a loved one die and coping with that loss had erased their fear of death. They no longer saw death as frightening or horrible. Instead, many people were intrigued by the mystery of death and more peaceful about their own deaths.

We grow in hard times. I've been more available to joy and loving than before. I'm not afraid of death as I was before. I embrace life more—a powerful reminder to live well. (Attie, 30, whose 30-year-old friend died of AIDS)

Death is a part of life but we don't talk about it, we don't want to think about it. It's sort of like a dirty word or something. I think most of us are so unprepared for dealing with a loved one and our own death. I just think it needs to be more out in the open. We need to talk about it, we need to teach classes about it. It needs to be not such a dirty word because we all act as if it's not going to happen, and it's going to happen to all of us. I think we all spend out time burying our heads in the sand. I think part of the reason it's so terrifying is because we know so little about it. Watching John die, seeing him get closer and closer to death, took a lot of fear away for me of the process because it wasn't so terrible. I mean it *was* terrible, but it wasn't terrible—he knew he was dying, he came to accept it. He did have pain and he also had medication to cope with the pain. It wasn't as horrible as I thought it would be. I thought watching somebody die would be just, you just couldn't bear it. It's less frightening to me now, that's one thing. Another thing is that having lost people close to me, quite a few—my mother, my father, my brother's wife, John, Jim—I've learned that once someone dead they're gone forever. Too late for "I-wish-I-hads." Take advantage of time you have with person alive. You sometimes take those near you for granted. Tell others how much you love and appreciate them. I'm not fearful of death. Live your life to the fullest. (Jenna, 48, whose 45-year-old friend died of AIDS)

WHAT DOES IT MEAN
TO FIND SOMETHING POSITIVE?

Several theorists and researchers have written about the meaning and function of finding something positive following a trauma. Tedeschi and Calhoun (1995) distinguished between theories that view finding something positive as a way of *coping* with the trauma, and theories that view finding something positive as part of a true *transformation* that occurs within individuals in the wake of a trauma.

Taylor (1983, 1989) viewed the search for something positive in a trauma as a cognitive strategy people use to cope with the trauma. Finding something positive helps people to imbue the trauma with meaning. If they can find something positive, they do not feel as victimized or that life is capricious and unpredictable. Instead, by interpreting the event as having provided something positive, people can enhance their self-esteem and their sense of the world as benevolent and controllable. In addition to looking for ways one has grown in a trauma, Taylor argues that people find something positive by imaging worse situations ("my mother could have lingered in pain for years but she only lived a few days"), comparing themselves to less fortunate others ("it's harder on people who lose a spouse at a young age"), and focusing only on those aspects of a situation that were positive ("our family became closer through this loss").

Other theorists, however, have argued that the traumatic events like loss can create true developmental changes in people by confronting them with new situations and issues (Baumeister, 1989; Frankl, 1963; Thompson, 1991; Thompson & Janigian, 1988). Loss can shatter expectations for the self and make life goals unattainable. For example, several of the widows and widowers in our study mentioned their deep disappointment that the many plans they had made with their spouse for retirement would never be realized. Reevaluating one's life and developing a new perspective and set of goals can restore a sense of order and purpose to life. Losing a loved one presents people with new roles and demands. For example, people who lose their parents may now perceive themselves as the "head of the family now" or "the last one left in their generation." Young widowhood may mean being thrust abruptly and involuntarily into single parenthood. This shift in roles and in self-perceptions can lead to major developmental changes. Observing yourself doing things you never thought you could do certainly also can lead to growth and change in self-perceptions.

Growth can be painful, however, so even if loss can lead to true developmental change in people, those people who perceive they have grown in their loss may still suffer many symptoms of distress and problems in adjustment. The next section explores previous studies and our own data to examine the relationship between finding something positive in the loss and adjustment.

FINDING SOMETHING POSITIVE
AND ADJUSTMENT

Several cross-sectional studies find that people who perceive positive life changes in the wake of adversities like loss tend to be better adjusted (that is, they exhibit less negative affect and fewer symptoms of posttraumatic stress disorder) than those unable to find such benefits (for a review, see Affleck & Tennen, 1996). Because these studies were cross-sectional, however, it is not clear whether perceiving positive life changes is a cause of better adjustment or a consequence. And several studies have not found any relationship between perceiving life changes and emotional adjustment (Elder & Clipp, 1989; Fromm, Andrykowski, & Hunt, 1996; Park, Cohen, & Murch, 1996; Tedeschi & Calhoun, 1996).

Taylor's perspective on the function of perceiving positive life changes suggests that seeing something positive in a loss sometimes represents defensiveness or denial. People can portray themselves as good copers by finding something positive and minimizing the impact that the loss has had on them. They may cling to positive illusions—believing that they have changed for the better following the loss when family members and friends them would disagree. One of the few studies to investigate this line of argument compared people who had lost a loved one in a motor vehicle accident to a control group of people who had not lost a loved one (Lehman et al., 1993). These researchers found that those bereaved people who said they had found something positive in their loss did not score higher than the control group on measures of the ability to enjoy life.

Our own study had a major advantage over almost all others that have previously examined the role of perceiving positive life changes in adjustment. Rather than simply being cross-sectional, our study was longitudinal, and could look at the changes in adjustment that occurred over time in people who perceived positive changes and those who did not. For example, it may be that people who perceive themselves as growing from their loss initially are more distressed than people who do not perceive themselves growing—again, growth may be painful. But over time, people who perceive themselves growing may adjust better than those who do not perceive any growth in themselves as a result of the loss.

In our study, people who said they had found something positive in their loss by 6 months following the loss had lower levels of distress at 6, 13 and 18 months postloss than people who had not found something positive in their loss (for detailed analyses, see Davis, Nolen-Hoeksema, & Larson, in press). This was true even when we statistically controlled for how distressed people were shortly after their loss. Thus, people who were able to find something positive in their loss showed better adjustment to their loss than people who were not able to find something positive. The relationship between finding something positive and adjustment increased with time, suggesting that experiencing personal growth may be a long-term process that unfolds over time, affecting adjustment.

Interestingly, no particular way that people found something positive in their loss—none of the specific themes described earlier in this chapter—was more strongly associated with adjustment than another. It seemed that simply finding something positive was the key to better adjustment—regardless of what that positive was. A close examination of previous studies of people following a trauma also suggests that it is not how many positive things people find following a loss that predicts adjustment, but simply whether or not they find anything positive (Davis, Lehman, & Wortman, 1997). Thus, if people can find any way in which they have grown or their perspectives have changed for the better or their relationships have improved, they seem to adjust better to their loss, than if they can find nothing positive at all.

WHO FINDS SOMETHING POSITIVE AND WHO DOES NOT

We might expect that losses that violate the natural order and our most basic assumptions would present survivors with the most difficulty in finding anything positive. Yet, in our study, one of the most surprising results was that parents who lost a child (usually an adult child) were more able than any other family group to find something positive in their loss (Fig. 6.1). Indeed, the parents seemed to be striving to instill some positive meaning into their loss, more than any other family group.

> I learned a lot about myself and my son. We were very close. We always were very close, but the past 3 years have been a real deepening of our understanding of each other. He taught me a lot. He taught everybody around him. And I learned a great deal about other people's compassion. I couldn't get over the nurses. I finally recognized one day to one of them how hard it must be for her, because they all liked Steve so much. Then she started crying and we hugged each other, and she said, "Thank you. Thank you for thinking of me." [I saw] just how much people supported me and my son daily in so many thoughtful ways, and how good people are when they have a chance to show it, and what a terrific person my son was. That's why I talk to his picture, because I want to continue to remember what he taught me. (Penny, 62, whose 32-year-old son died of AIDS)

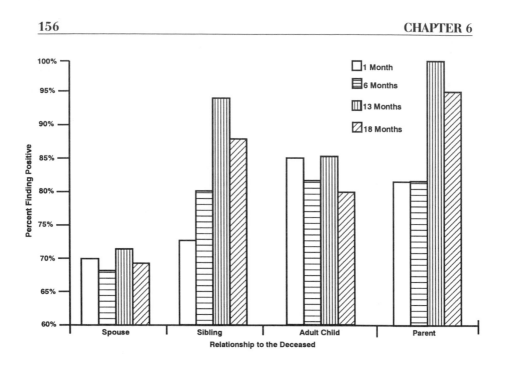

FIG. 6.1. Percent of family members able to find something positive in loss.

I loved him and I know he knew that I loved him. He knew that his mom loved him. He knew that his sister loved him. We got a chance to show him that we loved him and left no doubt in his mind, and that's more than a lot of parents can say. We got way past the "you're my son, you do as I say" mentality. We became really, really close, very good friends. He could talk to us and say anything he wanted to about anything he wanted to, and he knew it. He knew that we loved him no matter what. Most parents aren't able to reach that plateau with their children. It's just like we've lost a son but we've gained an extended family. I think we're very, very fortunate in what we have. I know that we were extremely fortunate in having our son. We didn't have him long, but we had him long enough to really, really love him and to enjoy him. And I don't think you can really ask for a hell of a lot more than that. (Sam, 53, whose 31-year-old son died of AIDS)

Parents who lose a child may need more than any other family group to construct some positive meaning and consequence from their loss to overcome the sense of injustice and confusion they feel over losing their child. It is likely that the parents in our study, all of whom lost a child after an extended illness, would be better able to find something positive than parents who lost a child through violent means, such as homicide, suicide, or a senseless accident.

The family group that was least able to find something positive in their loss was bereaved spouses (see Fig. 6.1):

> I frankly can find no good has come out of death. My situation has improved over what it would have been were she alive ... I wouldn't own a house, I wouldn't have $50,000 in the bank ... honestly, I'd prefer not to have that and to have her alive. (Charles, 62, whose 52-year-old wife died of liver cancer)

> No, nothing positive. It's just very cruel, very hard, very wrong. (Randolph, 65, whose 60-year-old wife died from a brain tumor)

For people who lose their spouse, the changes in their roles are often seen only as negative—they feel alone, isolated, without their lifelong companion and helpmate. It can be very difficult for them to see any positive benefit to these role changes. Many older people who lost their spouses expressed bitter disappointment that their expectations for living the "golden years" with their mate were now vanquished. They may have saved and planned for decades for these years, now only to have lost the one person with whom they wanted to live out these years.

People who had lost their parents or a sibling were especially likely to mention changes in their own self-perceptions and life goals and priorities as a result of their loss (see also Scharlach & Fredriksen, 1993). They said their priorities had changed or that they had decided to make a career change or spend more time with their family. They also often tried to improve their health habits and reestablished religious ties, perhaps because of a greater sense of their own mortality.

> I found many gifts from it. It has shaken me to rethink living—and looking at her life in terms of my life. I'm aware in a different way of life's tentativeness. So I'm trying to be more appreciative and active in my own life. So I'm trying to be more involved with the kids, and their lives. This shaking has provided me with a chance to look at that stuff. (Sallie, 45, who lost her 70-year-old mother to cancer)

Also, a number of bereaved adult children and siblings commented on how family members rallied together and grew closer around the loss, providing something positive:

> We definitely learned a lot about ourselves and about each other within the family circle. There was a rallying of support, and a camaraderie that I think only shows itself, truly shows itself, when something like this occurs. I think you always assume that it's there, but it was tested, and we were pleasantly surprised, very pleased with how each one took their role, and no one was ever left to feel as though they were abandoned. There was a lot of support, a lot of physical and mental support. (Gil, 40, whose mother, 68, died of a brain tumor)

There were no differences between people who lost a loved one to AIDS and those who lost a loved one to another illness in being able to find something positive at 1 month and 6 months after the loss, but by 13 months postloss, differences emerged. People who lost a loved one to AIDS were more likely to say they had found something positive in their loss than those whose loved one had had another illness (90% vs 79% at 13 months, and 93% vs 75% at 18 months).[1] This was somewhat surprising, especially because we had found that people who lost a loved one to AIDS had more difficulty making sense of their loss (see chap. 2). Yet, many people who could not make sense of their loved one's death were able to find something positive, often some aspect of personal growth or growth in their relationships, as a result of loving and caring for a person with AIDS.

One personal change that people who had lost a loved one to AIDS often reported was a change in their attitudes toward homosexuality that occurred as they came to know their loved one and the community of support around him during his illness. Margarita, a 39-year-old Hispanic woman whose brother died of AIDS said,

> I think my mother and I have become more tolerant of homosexuality. I was not a tolerant person. There was always a right and wrong to everything. By experiencing that my own brother was a homosexual—had AIDS—which we never would have approved of, we developed a different perspective. We learned we had to be tolerant and that this was nobody's fault, and that there is nothing to be ashamed of. I wish I had not been so self-righteous when my brother told us he was gay. I wish I had told him that I understood and it was ok.

Micky, 43, whose brother also died of AIDS, said

> I think about death differently. I certainly think about AIDS and homosexuality differently. I didn't make a 180 degree turn, but I certainly learned a lot. I'm not involved in AIDS organizations or anything, but I know a lot more about AIDS than I did before, and I don't have any anxiety about it. I would be a lot better prepared now to talk with other people about it.

One Irish woman, Christine, came to the United States to care for her brother, who was dying of a brain tumor. He was not gay, but he was in an inpatient hospice where AIDS patients were also being cared for. She said

> Another distinct thing that may sound strange to you is my feeling on homosexuality. Perhaps naively on my part, I had only seen the negative in that, whereas at the hospice where some of the others were homosexuals, I suddenly saw them in a different light, and grew to admire them and to see the positive side instead of the negative side, and I think that's wonderful … it is quite a shift. When we were told about the hospice and we were told there were six beds for AIDS patients, and um, how did we

---

[1]Chi-square tests showed differences significant at $p < .10$ at 13 months and at 18 months.

feel about it ... and we said we didn't mind, but really subconsciously I was really worried about it. But it was stupidity, naivete rather, and I feel quite differently about it now.

The coping strategies used by people who were able to find something positive in their loss tended to be adaptive ones. Not surprisingly, they were more likely than people who did not find anything positive to be using reappraisal as a method of coping. That is, they were purposely trying to reappraise their loss in positive terms as a way of coping. In addition, people who found something positive in their loss were more likely than those who did not to be coping by engaging in active problem solving, by seeking social support, and by engaging in expression of their emotions.[2] The fact that seeking something positive was not associated with avoidance or distraction coping suggests that it is not simply a form of defensiveness or denial. Instead, seeking something positive in the loss was part of a package of active coping strategies.

People who sought something positive in their loss tended to be highly optimistic in general.[3] Indeed, we found that being dispositionally optimistic predicted finding something positive in the loss, even after we statistically controlled for people's levels of distress and several other characteristics (Davis, Nolen-Hoeksema, & Larson, in press). It seems that being dispositionally optimistic—believing that things in life generally work out for the best—gives people the worldview to search for positive meaning even in tragedy such as loss (see also Affleck & Tennen, 1996; Park, Cohen, & Murch, 1996; Tedeschi & Calhoun, 1996).

There were several characteristics of the people in our study that were not related to their ability to find something positive. Perhaps surprisingly, people who were religious or spiritual were not better able to find something positive than those who were not religious or spiritual. Some people did say that their loss experience had strengthened their religious or spiritual beliefs:

I experienced very much a growth in my own faith, a deepening awareness of what I had spiritually. (Angela, 44, whose 43-year-old brother died of AIDS)

Others reported, however, that the loss had led them to question severely their religious and spiritual beliefs (see also Schwartzberg & Janoff-Bulman, 1991).

---

[2]Differences between the two groups on reappraisal were significant at $p < .001$ at all four interviews. Differences between the two groups on problem solving and seeking social support were significant at $p < .05$ at all four interviews. Differences between the two groups on emotional expression were significant at $p < .05$ at the 1-, 6-, and 13-month interviews.

[3]Differences between the two groups on dispositional optimism were significant at $p < .001$ at 1-, 6-, and 13-months and at $p < .10$ at 18 months.

You may recall, however, that religious and spiritual people were better able to find meaning or make sense of the loss, however (refer to chap. 2). Religious beliefs apparently give people a context for understanding why their loss occurred, but do not necessarily lead people to grow personally or find other positive things in their loss.

The quality of people's social support also was not related to their ability to find something positive in their loss. We were a bit surprised at this because people often said that what they found positive in their loss was a growth in their relationships with others. Yet, it seems that finding something positive is quite a private, personal process that is neither strongly facilitated nor strongly impeded by the support of others. Instead, finding something positive is connected to one's personal outlook on the world and typical ways of coping with stress.

SUMMARY

Despite the pain of losing a close loved one, many bereaved people are able to find something positive in their loss. They talk about a sense of personal growth and personality change, a realization of personal strengths, a reprioritizing of life goals, a greater appreciation of relationships, and a loss of fear of death. Some theorists have suggested that these represent true developmental changes and others suggest that finding something positive is more simply a cognitive coping strategy meant to regain a sense of control and self-esteem. People who were able to find something positive in their loss in our study showed better adjustment over time than those who did not find something positive. They also used more adaptive coping strategies and were generally more optimistic about life.

So how do we help people find personal growth and other positive life changes in the wake of a loss? Simply providing them with support does not seem to be enough. Chapter 7 discusses interventions that may help people to find personal growth and adjust to their loss.

Voices

Some additional examples are provided of how people said they grew and found positive life changes following their loss. We also provide excerpts from people who said they did not find anything positive in their loss.

> If he had lived I would have been more frustrated, I would have continued working the same job, we would have went for the two new cars and everything like that, and that same negative feeling would have been there. Even though we were doing good with his kids, there was still that longing

or that emptiness, that character of me that I wasn't aware of, that I never acknowledged. And I can do that now. (37-year-old woman whose 36-year-old husband died of cancer)

I can function and live a normal life. Enjoy my own company. I like myself. I've learned that I can make a life for myself. That I can function and that I can be happy. It was a new beginning. Material things lost their meaning or value to me. Those things only had value because it was something that we both built together—jewelry, furniture. I got rid of it all and bought new furniture because it had no more meaning. Something that we had built together and now had no value. I never flew before he died. After, I got on plane and it didn't bother me; that fear disappeared. I don't have a problem with telling people "no" anymore. No more "have to's," no more guilt. (58-year-old woman whose 68-year-old husband died of cancer)

I feel that I've started the last third of my life, and it's different, it isn't something that I was really aware of, but I find that I'm single again. It's a funny feeling after being married so long. Although there were times when he wasn't with me, I was one of a couple. And now I do exactly the same things, but I'm a single person, so my attitude is different. That's one of the things that surprised me very much. I looked at people very differently. I imagined them looking at me differently. That was something that was hard for me to come to grips with. So much in our society is based on pairs, so when you find yourself by yourself, you have to start looking at things completely different. (71-year-old woman whose 82-year-old husband died of cancer)

I think there's something that happens when you lose your last parent, where you finally grow up, you finally are responsible only for your own life. And that can be very freeing. Obviously I've learned the end result of not taking care of yourself. (44-year-old woman whose mother died)

Her death has given me a new awareness of responsibility. I don't have my Mom to ask anymore. It's up to me. You can't help but feel your own immortality when you're around someone that dies. So I'm aware of that, but I don't dwell on it. (52-year-old woman whose 78-year-old mother died of lung cancer)

Sometimes I think maybe I should be more depressed about it, but I don't know. I get a little guilty feeling. It's hard to explain. Like, maybe I really don't deserve the good that's coming out [as a result of husband's death]. I really feel like I should be much more towards the "moderately well" [classification on the coping scale] than towards the "very well" and I wonder, I just wonder. I don't know. I mean, I feel fine. There are [bad] days, but basically they're so few and rare that that's something I'll study and think about. That's why I feel that much more positive than negative has happened through [her husband's death]. A lot of people are still very depressed. There are just so many different facets to it—circumstances, things that happen, things that you don't expect in life. Perhaps if [her new husband] had not come into my life, I would be in the "moderately well." I don't know. I have no way of knowing. I think that's probaby with a lot of people. And I can handle that "moderately well." I don't think I would be in "not at all." That's just not me. (56-year-old woman who lost her 61-year-old husband to prostate cancer)

The only thing positive is that I strenthened my religious feeling with the idea that maybe God did need her; maybe he needed her more than I did. Maybe she's up there saying a prayer for me so I won't end up in Hades for eternity, so maybe it was needed. I think this idea of a person who is a good person in their life attaining their reward, and being in a position to help you—that meant more to me than anything else. I know as well as I know my own name that if there's anything she can do to help me, she will be doing it, wherever she is. I know that. Thirty-eight years with one woman—I know her as well as a man can know a woman. But then she was still a mystery to me, including the day she died. (63-year-old man who lost his 61-year-old wife to cancer)

I know the first few months were really hard. I was in shock. Now it's kind of like I forget that he's dead sometimes. I was finally able to listen to a song that was meaningful to him. My daughter—a week ago she put it on and we just both sang the song together and cried together, but didn't say too much about it. I can still talk about it. It doesn't hurt as much. I just thought, having experienced somebody so close to you dying, I thought I would have a different outlook in life, that I'd be more positive in life and that I would want to enjoy my life more and do more positive things, and I really haven't seen a change. That's kind of a disappointing to me. I thought being so close to somebody and seeing death like that—it really hasn't changed me. (37-year-old woman who lost her 35-year-old brother to AIDS)

I lost my mother and I lost my best friend. It's hard to think of anything positive that's come out of it. It tore apart our whole family. I mean, we're not fighting or anything like that, but we don't have that time like we used to have. We don't have the family time, the family get togethers—it's all gone. She did everything. (30-year-old woman whose 58-year-old mother died from lung cancer)

I know eventually there will be a lot, probably, of positiveness that comes out, but it's still hard now. And what makes me upset with myself is that, I mean I have a concept of life after death, and I just—it's me, it's not him. I just feel I should be coping better. (48-year-old woman who lost her 46-year-old husband to cancer)

I think it's interesting that there's this cliche about having gone through an experience like this, you're tougher or in some way wiser. I haven't found that to be so. I still feel vulnerable and weakened by it, not strengthened and wiser. I very much dislike the exposure that you go through, in the sense that there's so little privacy between people who are curious or loving [and you]—your life is like an open book. I know that's contrary because you need people so much, but I found that disturbing to a degree. You're so much more public property after such an epic event in your life. (44-year-old woman who lost her 57-year-old husband to brain cancer)

7

Interventions

I don't think you can go it alone. I don't think it's healthy. There are so many organizations, friends, therapy, whatever—you can't be a tower of strength, so get help. (Fran, 48, whose friend died of AIDS)

Therapy has helped in terms of the process that you go through when somebody dies. It confirms that you're not crazy. The therapy builds your confidence to handle what you're experiencing. That's important to the extent that family and friends let you down. (Kate, 44, whose husband died of lung cancer)

You have to find somebody that you can really talk to, and just let them listen and listen and not pass judgment. It's been very helpful to me to have somebody that's more or less neutral, but understanding, to talk about this. I certainly got a lot out of those visits with Margaret. She was so understanding, and we just yakked away like everything. I'm not the kind that usually joins support groups, but when hospice offered it, I guess I sensed that I would need somebody to talk to. It has helped a lot. (Pearl, 70, whose husband died of prostate cancer)

The important thing is to have a good relationship with your church, your bishop, your minister, your priest. Because there's times that you need something to carry you over the rough spots that—nothing else can do it. (Lois, 80, whose husband died of cancer)

Pets are wonderful therapy. (Marianne, 79, whose husband died of cancer)

As we discussed in previous chapters, the grief process varies in timing, intensity, and difficulty from one individual to the next. In grief, there is no clear delineation of symptoms. What helps one person cope with grief may not be helpful for another, therefore interventions must be tailored to the bereaved person's circumstances and needs.

Individual counseling, family counseling, and group counseling or peer support groups are most commonly used as attempts to reduce the intensity of the grief response and the negative physical consequences of bereavement. Psychological interventions are designed for the prevention and treatment of pathological grief. But interventions can take many other forms. For example, acquiring a pet, going for a walk, attending church, or having lunch with a sympathetic friend can also be viewed as interventions to the extent that they help alleviate the painful feelings that are part of a normal grief response.

Counseling may be provided by professionals (e.g., psychologists, social workers, clergy), however in many instances, a lay person or peer counselor can provide the needed support and accompany bereaved people as they acknowledge their loss, express their emotions, readjust to their new roles and senses of identity, eventually integrate the loss fully into their life experiences, and begin to reinvest in new pursuits or people. Difficulty coping is not a prerequisite for grief counseling or receiving support. Even people who are coping relatively well with their grief may find counseling beneficial:

> I did start counseling this year, though. I was starting to get real nervous and depressed on the weekends. It wasn't anything specifically, it was just in general. I didn't realize how out of touch I was. Yet I felt it, and did not know it. And everyone will tell you I did really great going through it. I think I did, too. There was this inner feeling that "I am not myself. I'm not sleeping. I don't have anyone to take care of. What is going on?" I finally decided I needed professional help. It was really bad because when I called Dorothy that day for a referral to a counselor, she said, "Oh, no, you're doing so well!" I said, "I know. That's why I need someone to talk to." And I thought I *was* doing well. I just needed someone's perspective, an objective perspective, not someone telling you what you should or should not do. And I found it really helpful. (Anne, 37, whose husband died of cancer)

> I don't feel like I need counseling, I think I'm coping well enough. I just love having a place I can go, just for me, where I can say whatever I want without worrying about how the other person is going to react. Sometimes I cry, sometimes we laugh. Mostly I just talk about whatever is going on that week. (Karen, 48, whose husband died of heart disease)

When a grief counselor detects severe psychopathology, or when grief is delayed, absent, chronic, disenfranchised, or otherwise complicated, the assistance of a trained psychotherapist is needed. A grief counselor must be able to determine, accurately, when a referral for grief therapy is needed (Rando, 1993; Sprang & McNeil, 1995). Not all professionals are effective or comfortable working with grief, even uncomplicated grief. The director of an agency that supports children and families coping with terminal illness and death told us, "It is difficult to find really good referrals for the families that need more help in coping with illness, death, and grief. I know only a few therapists in whom I have enough confidence to give referrals." Professional work with individuals experiencing complicated or pathological grief is not within the scope of this book. Complete information on that subject can be obtained in the current literature on psychotherapeutic techniques.

We know that most people survive bereavement and manage their grief without outside help, so why intervene? One reason is because with so many support resources available, it simply is not necessary to go it alone. Grief counseling may be more necessary today than in times past because of the lack of more traditional family and community support. A second reason is that grief can sometimes mask more severe emotional problems, specifically clinical depression because depression and grief share so many symptom characteristics. Therefore, it is advisable to identify and encourage coping strategies that lead to lower levels of depression and healthy resolution. Finally, intervention following bereavement may actually result in enhancement of a bereaved person's life by encouraging development of new coping strategies, deepening of one's religious or spiritual beliefs, and appreciation of personal relationships and life experiences.

Research on the efficacy of bereavement interventions is inconclusive. Kato and Mann (in press) combined a qualitative review of existing bereavement intervention studies with a quantitative assessment of the studies in order to assess the overall effectiveness of psychological interventions for the bereaved. The results of their meta-analyses revealed only very weak or no effects for interventions for the depression and other psychological symptoms experienced by the bereaved. There was some evidence that interventions were effective for the physical symptoms often experienced by bereaved individuals, although these effects were small and were only obtained from self-report, rather than objective, measures. Kato and Mann suggest that perhaps the experience of bereavement is simply too intense, or too stressful, to be impacted by a psychological intervention, or that psychological interventions can be effective, but that the interventions evaluated in these studies were not powerful enough to relieve symptoms as intense as those felt by bereaved subjects. Interventions may have been too infrequent, or too short in duration or scope, to produce positive effects. In addition, most interventions studied were not based in theory. Effective interventions will most likely be based on theory and, in turn, interventions based on theory provide useful tests of those theories.

Kato and Mann also point out that methodological flaws in the studies reviewed may have prevented existing effects from being detected. Sampling errors, failure to analyze data separately by gender, and lack of control regarding expected versus unanticipated death were some of the methodological difficulties observed that could mask or fail to detect effects. Future bereavement intervention studies need to include larger and more diverse samples, to utilize more intense interventions, control carefully for confounding variables, use more objective measures, and to test theories of bereavement. Until more rigorous research in this area is conducted, Kato and Mann suggest that little can be concluded regarding the effectiveness of psychological interventions for bereaved persons.

The fact that bereavement outcome studies have failed thus far to demonstrate the effectiveness of interventions does not mean that individual, family, or group counseling is not helpful. For individuals who seek out bereavement support services, and for the vast majority of the people who participated in our study, the positives far outweighed the negatives. That bereavement support resources exist widely and are proliferating rapidly is evidence that many bereaved people desire, or require, assistance that is not readily available to them in their social network.

GOALS OF BEREAVEMENT COUNSELING

Whether a person seeks individual, family, or group support, the goals of bereavement counseling include providing information, normalizing and validating the grieving person's feelings and experience, reducing isolation, maximizing social support, and promoting adaptive coping strategies and techniques. Counseling further aims to provide a safe and caring environment in which the bereaved person may give expression to the sometimes intense emotions that are part of mourning, and eventually assimilate the loss and accommodate to a life without the deceased loved one.

There are no rules, recipes, or protocols when it comes to grief counseling. Although some patterns of similarity exist, we know that each person's grief experience is unique. A skilled grief counselor will be prepared to support each person's style of grieving and to utilize interventions that can best meet the needs and circumstances of the grieving individual. As the bereaved person moves through the grieving process, his or her needs will change and so too must the interventions. Remembering that everyone's timing is also different, grief counselors must remain mindful to not impose their own timing or agenda on the grieving person, rather take their cues from the bereaved and allow the mourning process to unfold naturally.

TASKS OF MOURNING

Several researchers and clinicians have outlined reconciliation needs or "tasks of mourning," which provide a helpful framework for both the mourner and anyone invested in helping someone through the grief process (Lindemann,

1944; Parkes & Weiss, 1983; Rando, 1991; Wolfelt, 1988; Worden, 1982). Understanding these "tasks" helps to frame mourning as an active process in which one participates, rather than a passive state in which one exists until it is concluded. For the helper, these tasks of mourning can provide a structure for outlining much of one's helping role.

Worden (1982) described four tasks of mourning: (a) to accept the reality of the loss, (b) to experience the pain and grief, (c) to adjust to an environment in which the deceased is missing, and (d) to withdraw emotional energy and reinvest it in another relationship. Rando (1991) preferred to emphasize the processes involved in grief work, believing that to operationalize mourning in terms of tasks is to focus on outcomes. The six "R" processes of mourning outlined by Rando are: (a) recognize the loss, (b) react to the separation, (c) recollect and reexperience the deceased and the relationship (d) relinquish the old attachments to the deceased and the old assumptive world, (e) readjust to move adaptively into the new world without forgetting the old, and (f) reinvest in new relationships or activities. As Rando points out, these processes are interrelated and tend to build on one another, however any number of them may occur simultaneously. The processes are outlined in a typical order, but the course of mourning is often nonlinear and fluctuating. Thus, the mourner may move back and forth among these processes.

INDIVIDUAL COUNSELING

Individuals may seek one-to-one counseling or therapy during the illness of a loved one, shortly after bereavement, several months or even years after a death occurs. Counseling grieving people is a specialized area of therapy; traditional goals and techniques of psychotherapy are often not appropriate with grieving clients. According to Worden (1982), the goal of grief counseling is the facilitation of a normal or uncomplicated mourning process to its completion. It is usually inappropriate to directly work on any psychopathology that may be present: "This is a time for healing, not uncovering work" (Young, 1984, p. 22). Whereas psychotherapy seeks to uncover defenses and work toward change, bereavement counseling seeks to support an individual as he or she moves through a natural process in response to the death of a loved one, namely grief.

In individual counseling, the bereaved person benefits from the full and undivided attention of the counselor; the time need not be shared with other family or group members. The counselor may focus more directly on the concerns and feelings of the mourner, and offer suggestions and information specific to that person's grief experience. Probably the most important advantage of individual counseling is confidentiality. Here mourners can feel free to say anything about their thoughts and feelings. Perhaps they need to confess wrongs they believe they committed and work through the guilt they may be suffering. They may need to express deep regrets or resentments they are not comfortable expressing to family or friends. Individual counseling can free mourners of the fear that they are overtaxing their support network, or burdening their family. They may need a safe place to discuss suicidal ideation that so often is a component of a normal grief response without fear of creating panic among family or friends. The time-limited nature of counseling sessions helps to provide a structure and container that often allows mourners to feel more deeply, and express more openly, the intensity of grief. For those who must return relatively quickly to demands of work and life, a counseling session may help them to "compartmentalize" their grief; giving it full attention during the counseling hour may help them focus and concentrate on their work.

In the earliest days and weeks following a death, the counselor's primary function is to allow the grieving person to experience the vacillation between numbness and surging painful emotions. Problem-solving coping is usually not appropriate during this time, the focus is almost entirely on emotion-focused coping strategies. More often than not, the counselor's respectful attention, reassurance, and unconditional regard are the primary interventions needed during this time.

As time passes, the counselor continues to provide an open and accepting place where the repetition of grief work is not met with impatience or advice. Because openly expressing grief over time is not sanctioned in our culture, providing a safe place for honest and free expression of the bereaved person's grief is perhaps the most important function a counselor performs. The bereaved person also must begin to return to daily activities, obligations, and complete practical tasks related to the death. Attention to emotion-focused and problem-focused coping is now appropriate, but emotion-focused coping should precede problem solving. For example, it is important to explore fully a new widow's anxiety about handling her own finances before moving into ways to go about solving her financial problems. Even something as routine as learning to balance a checkbook can produce intense feelings of fear, resentment, anxiety, and sadness. Not uncommonly, bereaved individuals may need a counselor's firm encouragement to seek out, and to receive, material support from family, friends, and community to help them with their problems. Unfortunately, at a time when their internal resources are seriously compromised, they may need to educate those around them regarding the kind of assistance they need. With guidance, they can begin to identify what they need, and how to obtain help from appropriate sources. Equally important, they may be assisted in identifying well-intentioned, but unhelpful offers and supported in saying "no."

I feel that the public needs to be educated about what to do, how to help people that are in this situation. People just don't know what to do. They feel like they're intruding or bothering you. Like friends and neighbors—they're sitting in their homes and they want to help, but they don't know what to do. They're capable of really helping but they just say, "Call me if you need me." I didn't even know *what* I needed. But people need basic things. They need dinner on the table every night, lunch, breakfast. Some people who've been through it know what to do—they reach out in a tangible way. (Sue, 32, whose mother died of pancreatic cancer)

The acute pangs of grief eventually occur less frequently, but missing someone can go on forever. Sadness can continue to be experienced as the bereaved person begins to relinquish old habits and identities that are tied to the deceased loved one, and to begin taking steps toward new goals, activities and, perhaps, new relationships. The primary role of the counselor is to support the emergence of a new identity that incorporates the loss and assists the mourner in moving on in her life.

FAMILY GRIEF COUNSELING

In order to help families cope with grief, it is important to appreciate the impact that death and grief have on a family system. Bereavement is a deeply shared family developmental transition, involving a crisis of attachment and a crisis of identity for all family members (Shapiro, 1994). As family members grieve in their own particular ways, they also are affected by and respond to one other's mourning behavior.

Grief may disrupt family stability as the influence of the loved one becomes limited by illness, and then absent as a result of the death. Often, death represents a real crisis in the family, even when the death was anticipated. A family's first priority in managing the crisis of grief is to reestablish the stability and equilibrium necessary to support ongoing family functioning. Reestablishing a stable family system requires adjustments by all family members, in relationship to one another, in ways that accommodate the loss of their loved one. The greater the stress, disruption, or discontinuity created by the death, the greater the need for adjustments by the family members, and the more likely the need for assistance from resources outside the immediate family.

The family grief counselor strives to support the individuals in the family, as well as the family system. Attention must be moving continually back and forth between individual needs and the family's attempts at coping. Within a single family, an older teen may be drawn toward alcohol or drugs, another may withdraw and become noncommunicative. A preteen may become oppositional or engage in delinquent behaviors. A latency-aged child may become exceptionally "good" or perfectionistic, and very young children may become more clinging and dependent. It is not uncommon for one family member to become the focus of increased attention, later another, then later still another.

The same goals of counseling apply to families as to individuals, the form of delivery changes somewhat to accommodate the family system as a whole. The counselor can provide information about the grief process, and how it will be different for each family member according to his or her age, personality, timing, and relationship to the deceased. Normalizing each person's experience helps families to understand one another. The counselor will also validate the differences and similarities among family members, modeling respect and reassuring them that no one way is more correct than another. Anticipating upcoming events that may be difficult, such as holidays or a visit to relatives, can provide an arena for discussing possible coping strategies or alternative approaches to the events. The counselor may ask each family member, in turn, what they think would help them most to get through the difficult time.

It is widely believed that the emotional expression of grief is an important or necessary part of normal bereavement. However, some research and clinical experience have suggested that exploring distressing feelings in family sessions, especially early on, may disrupt the family's attempts to accomplish its first task of adapting to the loss, reorganizing as a family system (Baker, Sedney, & Gross, 1992; Pollock, Egan, Vanderbergh, & Williams, 1975; Silverman & Worden, 1992a; Vollman, Ganzert, Picher, & Williams, 1971; Weiss, 1988; Wortman & Silver, 1989). Moreover, the shared coping with the crisis of family bereavement requires an enormously complex process of mutual awareness and responsiveness (Shapiro, 1994). Therefore, at least initially, the counselor's role is to assist the family members in regaining stability and routine and in helping them to recognize and understand the differences or similarities of their grief, and to provide suggestions for how they can best respond to one another. As with individual counseling, this is not a time for doing deep family work or attempting to impose techniques for structural or systemic change unrelated to the bereavement. Sharing intense emotions may need to wait.

Not surprising, there appears to be a multitude of courses for families coping with grief. Grief often exacerbates preexisting unresolved issues. So, although intervention is not initially aimed at uncovering these issues, they may emerge and the counselor must be prepared to deal with them as they arise and know when a referral to a professional is appropriate. Family bereavement interventions, initially, resemble basic crisis interventions. The first goal is to stabilize the family system and return it to a state of relative equilibrium in the face of extreme, possibly overwhelming, emotion. This phase of reestablishing stability may vary in duration, depending on the family dynamics involved, the level of disruption caused by the death, and the family's willingness to accept assistance and engage in adaptive coping.

Once a sense of routine and stability have been regained, a number of families will continue to take advantage of growth-producing techniques to enhance the family's functioning. Following the initial acute phase of grief and reestablishment of equilibrium, family sessions may allow the family members to share more fully their private experiences of grief with one another. The structure of the counseling session provides safety and focus that might not otherwise occur spontaneously as part of busy family life.

SUPPORT GROUPS

Support groups, like individual counseling, provide normalization, validation and a safe place for the expression of grief. Support groups help to decrease the sense of isolation that many bereaved people feel. Although the group cannot replace the person they miss, it can at least temporarily provide some relief from their longing and loneliness (Tatelbaum, 1990). Group members may learn new coping strategies as they hear about how others have approached the tasks of mourning. Within a group context, grieving people are able to observe others for whom bereavement is more recent or further away than their own. In this way, they can gain a sense of their own movement through their grief process (Rando, 1988). This can be particularly helpful for someone who may be feeling "stuck" in their grief, and can serve as encouragement for someone who is feeling like they will never feel better. Hughes (1995) asserted that, despite the small percentage of bereaved people who seek out a group and the lack of empirical support regarding the effectiveness of grief groups, those who do attend speak with appreciation for the gains they made in emotional under- standing and self-esteem, and usually become confirmed advocates.

> I think an emotional support group would be a very important opportunity. Specifically for women in the middle—you've got your kids, and your husband, and your frail, elderly parents. Those women need support, because the quality of life for the husband, kids, and frail parents depend on that woman. If we could at least keep her feelings acknowledged and validated. (Tara, 44, whose mother died of lung cancer)

> I've been going to the [hospice] support group they have once a week, for all the people who lost their loved ones—over a year now. With some other people, we sit around, you know, and everybody tells their problems. You feel then you're not the only one, that some other people are hurting too. Some come once or twice and they quit, some come back. (Alan, 65, whose wife died of a brain tumor)

> If you have a support group or support people to help you get through it, at least you minimize your pain. The pain, the sadness, the loss will be there. (Carol, 46, whose mother died of cancer)

> Find a support group. I used 12-step. I was really fortunate. During that time in my recovery a lot of people came into my life that had gone through some of these circumstances, lost someone close to them. They lost

somebody due to a terminal disease right while they were in recovery or before they got in recovery. We did a lot of talking together. It helped me get through some of the different stages that I was going through. (Richard, 27, whose father died of renal cancer)

It is preferable, although not essential, that bereavement support groups be facilitated by someone who has expertise in working with bereaved people and is knowledgeable about group dynamics. Facilitated groups have the advantage of a person (or persons) who assumes responsibility for the structure and organization of the group, and who can act as a participant observer to monitor and guide the group process.

A facilitator's first task is to establish a climate of safety and trust among the participants. A feeling of safety must be created early in the course of the group, otherwise the group members will feel reluctant to share their feelings and experiences, or they will stop attending the group. Groups that are not "safe" can cause significant distress and damage to vulnerable grieving members (Galinsky & Schopler, 1977, 1981). A climate of safety is best accomplished by reassuring all members that there are both similarities and differences in their respective grief experiences. It should be clear that the purpose of the group is to provide support during bereavement, and not to work on personality change or emotional disorders as in a psychotherapy group. Group members should be informed, and frequently reminded, about the limits of confidentiality, and that any information shared in the group should be kept in confidence. The facilitator must be watchful for confrontational, coercive, or attacking behavior and skillfully step in when corrections need to be made.

A facilitator must model a caring, respectful attitude toward all group members, and demonstrate an understanding of their individual experiences. When a group member is speaking, the facilitator can model giving them full attention without attempting to comment on, or alter, what they are saying. The facilitator can also demonstrate a genuine desire to understand the person's experience by reflecting back what was said, and asking for clarification.

Not uncommonly, some group members need encouragement to share their feelings and experiences, or they will direct their communication only to the group leader. The facilitator needs to initiate and encourage interaction among participants. Asking a direct question of a participant is one way of encouraging a reluctant person to speak. For example, "Joe, I'm wondering what has been the hardest thing for you this past week?" can help an otherwise quiet group member to speak. Alternatively, asking the group at large, "Has anyone else ever had the kind of thoughts Mary just described?" invites group members to explore the differences and similarities in their experiences.

The facilitator either sets the rules and limits of the group, or guides the group members in doing so. There are no hard and fast rules, different groups may function differently. Many people appreciate when groups start and end on time.

Some groups have an "I pass" rule which simply allows any group participant to choose *not* to speak. Some groups may discourage cross-talk, giving the speaker an opportunity to talk without interruption until they are finished and without fear of comments from others. The facilitator must clearly outline whatever the rules of the group are, and then be watchful and diligent about maintaining them. Also, the facilitator must be skilled at protecting group members from judgment, advice giving, or inappropriate problem solving. Gentle reminders about the purpose and process of the group may be needed from time to time.

The benefits of a group experience are enhanced when a facilitator is skilled in dealing with barriers to communication. Participants need to know that they fit in, that their presence in the group is important, and that what they say will be valued. Barriers to communication often occur in the form of advice giving, asking questions, offering interpretations, sharing similar experiences, and interrupting. The group leader must be aware of when to be assertive and to say, "I want to make sure Fran is finished," or "I see that we're beginning to get into some advice giving when we really need to be just listening to what Jesse is saying."

Problem behaviors are particularly challenging in a bereavement group because the participants can be in acute emotional pain. Common behavior problems include individuals who monopolize group time, are particularly quiet or reluctant, who interrupt, moralize, give advice, or believe their pain is "bigger" than another's. Group members appreciate a facilitator who deals competently with problematic behavior. Flexibility and sensitivity are required because at times it may be appropriate for one person to take more time than another, or for one group member to offer advice. Many such problems can be minimized by carefully screening and referring clearly inappropriate people, paying close attention to the group composition, and avoiding extreme differences among prospective members.

As with one-to-one counseling, group members are acutely sensitive to the genuineness of those who offer help. It is important that a group facilitator be real in the group, while maintaining professional objectivity. This task requires the facilitator to be very skilled at "conscious attention" (see Speeth, 1982; Young, 1984). The facilitator must notice, as impartially as possible, both internally and externally, whatever is happening at a given moment. Attention must be divided and shift constantly between the self and the group members, between focused concentration and panoramic attention. Unlike psychotherapy groups, the bereavement group facilitator should be willing to be directly involved by sharing personal feelings and impressions of what is happening in the group. Sharing personal experience may help group members feel safe, but the focus must be immediately directed back to the group members after any self-disclosure.

At the conclusion of each group meeting, the facilitator should summarize what happened during the course of the meeting. Summarization includes a review of the issues discussed and progress made. It further helps to clarify understanding. It also indicates closure and signals the end of the group meeting. Because bereavement groups so often involve the expression of intense emotions, the facilitator should begin the closing process approximately 10 to 15 minutes before the end of the time allotted by saying something like, "We've shared some intense feelings tonight, and I want to be sure we bring our time together to an appropriate end. Is there anything that anyone wants to say in closing?" Group members then have an opportunity to say anything that feels unfinished, and they are provided a chance to compose themselves and prepare to return to their life activities and responsibilities.

HOSPICE

Perhaps the most significant and all-inclusive intervention for families coping with death and bereavement can be found in hospice. For individuals who are dying, and for the family and friends who care for them, palliative care—the focus of hospice—can make the difference between a "good day living or a bad day dying" (Corr, Nabe, & Corr, 1997, p. 188). Eleven hospice agencies assisted us in recruiting the participants for our study, and we observed that each hospice differed markedly in size and scope. Despite their vast differences, each agency sought to diminish the distress and enhance the experience of those who were coping with terminal illness and loss. Hospice care can be provided in a hospital or inpatient facility, however most hospice services are delivered in the home.

Corr, Nabe, and Corr (1997) delineated 10 aspects of hospice philosophy and principles. First, hospice is not a facility, but a philosophy. It is not the place in which the patient and family receive care, but rather the outlook, attitude, or approach that is central in hospice care. Second, the hospice philosophy affirms life, not death; the emphasis is on quality of life. Third, hospice is a form of palliative care that is mainly concerned with alleviating distressing symptoms when cure is no longer a reasonable expectation. Fourth, hospice provides care to the patient and family unit. Fifth, hospice is holistic care, approaching the dying individual as a whole person and addressing the physical, psychological, social, and spiritual needs and those of the family. Sixth, hospice offers continuing care to the family following bereavement. Seventh, the hospice approach combines professional skills and human presence through an inter-disciplinary team approach that may include doctors, nurses, social workers, psychologists, counselors, clergy, home caregivers, and volunteer aides. Eighth, hospice services are available round the clock, 7 days a week. Ninth, hospice programs support their own staff and volunteers, recognizing that caregivers need to be well supported in order to do this difficult work effectively and with care. Tenth, although originally focused on care for terminally ill patients (specifically cancer patients), the hospice philosophy can be applied to a variety of individuals and their family members who are coping with a life-threatening illness, dying, death, and bereavement.

The interdisciplinary team approach of hospice seeks to provide a variety of interventions. Doctors and nurses can provide medical information and monitor medications and treatment. Social workers can help families access services and resources in the community. Clergy can offer spiritual guidance and counsel. Counselors can assist the families in understanding their experience and encourage healthy coping strategies. Home care workers and volunteer aides provide material support such as cleaning, cooking, or providing respite for family caregivers. For many families, hospitals appear to be cold, impersonal, intrusive places. Having their loved ones home in the last weeks or months of their lives is important to them, and could not be possible without hospice support.

Overwhelmingly, our study participants praised the value of hospice, reflected in the following quotes:

> She didn't want to die in the hospital. When she got real sick, we never took her to the hospital. What for, sticking needles in her? She got her wish. She died at home with all the kids. We couldn't do that for my dad. He had a stroke, had to be in the hospital. He died alone in the middle of the night. They called us in, but he was gone already. So I said, "We're not doing that for mom—machines and all that—no, no. (Megan, whose 99-year old mother died of heart and kidney failure)

> I am a nurse, I thought I'd take care of the situation, that I would be ok. I really learned how much I needed support of people coming in, sending me away to *help* me. You need to have hospice and let other people *do* that. The hospice situation was a very positive experience. My sister had arranged it and I doubted it, but I found I needed them. (Christine, 49, whose father died at 73 of Lou Gehrig's disease)

> We found that they were excellent people. They gave you support. They didn't give you a whole lot of information that was not necessary at the time, but it certainly was a lot more factual and timely than the medical community would give. (Donald, 58, whose mother-in-law died of congestive heart failure)

> The hospice was wonderful. They were lifesavers for our family. (Andrea, 46, whose husband died of melanoma)

> I have such respect for these people, I wish I had a lot of money to give them. I am just in awe of them. I conceivably can see myself doing that. I don't see me doing it for maybe a year or two. But its certainly something I've thought of. I would like to look into it, maybe, in the future. (Diana, 42, whose mother died of bone cancer)

I turned into a nurse for him, the last 2 weeks. I had a lot of help from folks in the local hospice. They sort of guided me through it. That was a real positive experience, too. They were in every day for at least 2 or 3 hours. I'd get out and do shopping, or go for a swim, things I could do for myself. Really incredible people, it's amazing what they did, and how they did it with an incredible spirit. It was amazing. I mean, these people were, they brought a little light with them when they came. It didn't have to be doom and gloom that somebody was dying in this house. They really opened it up a lot. It was nice, I mean *he* really appreciated having them here too. He loved having new faces come in and talk to him. yeah, they were really great. I know I couldn't have done it without them. They were an instance of one system that gave you 24 hours of help. There were a couple days when it was like—you know—they sort of talked me through it. It was great, I can't say enough about them. It happened to me a couple times, I just really didn't want to deal with it any more. The folks from the hospice would say, "It's time for us to come in for 10 hours. Take off. Get out of there. Go on." (Kristina, 39, whose father died of liver cancer)

I think the oncologist probably knew how limited our time was, and didn't want to say anything because he just wanted to keep her spirits up. I can understand that. But it would have been nicer to know realistically what to expect. We could have gotten more out of the time we had. The hospice helped us in that way. Hospice was honest and very helpful in what to expect, keeping in touch. (Kevin, 45, whose wife died of breast cancer)

Instead of getting worse, it gets better with understanding. Especially if you're working with the hospice people, you're getting an influx of information constantly pouring in on you, and anything they don't happen to tell you, you can always call them. So you're always well informed and you're never left out in left field. They claim in the hospital that they don't have enough time to give you personal attention. (Valerie, 65, whose father died of acute leukemia)

I learned how natural, how beautiful death is, thanks to hospice. I had never seen anyone die. Hospice does a great job of preparing people about what to expect and being supportive. (Lisa, 58, whose father died of cancer)

The hospice organizations that participated in the Bereavement Coping Study were interested in learning how their services could be improved, so we asked participants if anything about hospice had been unhelpful. Most participants had nothing negative to say about hospice, but some provided candid criticism. Smaller hospice organizations may be staffed almost entirely by volunteers, and may lack the resources to do long-term or comprehensive follow-up. One study participant had this complaint about the smallest of the hospices:

I guess the one thing about hospices and support groups, they kind of—I don't know if they don't mean to or if they're busy—but they sort of *drop* you about a month after your husband died. I guess, actually, the [hospice]

I had did follow through pretty well, but it's sort of like after they've been dead for a year, then there's no real support out there, unless you join a widows' group. (Marie, 48, whose husband died of brain cancer)

Caregivers of dying persons are in need of accurate information, and often feel frustrated when they feel they have not received it. Although most participants felt more informed by hospice workers than by medical professionals, this observation was offered by one participant:

Our hospice program left me ill prepared, as I was really the caregiver. They came and they had nurses come into our house, so we did it all at home, but they were giving my mother information and leaving me out of it. So things were happening at the end, and this I was really upset about, I was just screaming and kicking after it happened that they didn't tell me these certain things. Yes, it's very important for the patient to understand what's going on, because she was totally on the ball until 2 days before. We had no idea it was going to happen that fast. We thought she had maybe another 3 weeks or something. And they didn't tell me what signs to look for! I can understand that my mother might not want me to know certain things, I can understand that, but the fact that they encouraged her to shield me from things, I mean in a certain way—like they'd close the door and talk. That was good for certain things, but she would tell me only things she wanted me to know. Which is kind of weird because we don't have that kind of relationship, but things got kind of ugly at the end. They just didn't tell me everything. Otherwise they were great! They came when we called them. They were really on the ball. Maybe it was just that nurse. She should have taken me aside and said, "These are the things you need to look for," but she never did. (Jennifer, 24, whose mother died of cancer)

We noted previously that hospice philosophy and principles need not be limited to caring for cancer patients, however progress is still needed in providing hospice services to other situations, such as the death of an infant:

The hospice situation was not [working] ... they only knew how to handle the aged. They didn't know how to handle babies. (Christopher, 28, whose infant son died at 48 days of age)

This young father went on to describe his appreciation for one of the hospice nurses who subsequently developed a training for the hospice about serving children and infants. For this family, the development and implementation of services for families coping with the loss of a small child helped them to find meaning in the loss of their own child.

In chapter 4 we described the ways in which social support can become burdensome. This, too, can occur with hospice workers whose primary function is to provide the needed support:

There were three people mainly involved and then there were some home health caregivers. And what I found was that they all wanted to be a support to me, and it was more of a burden on me to try to use all of them as a support. I had to put up my boundaries, and I did, as to who I could use for support. My expectation was that they were there more for my mother than for me. I think their expectation was they were there just as much for me. Me being who I am, I just don't want to emote with everybody. I also have my own support network. (Cathy, 50, whose mother died of lung cancer).

By far, most complaints about hospice were about wanting more of what hospice offered—more information, more preparation, more support. In this regard, it seems that most of the negative comments we heard about hospice were regarding "errors of omission."

I kept bugging them to be more informative. When I ask a question, I don't want it to be sugar coated. The main thing was natural death, and I didn't know what natural death was. I was not alerted to the fact they did not eat anymore, and I'm in a panic saying I need IVS over here, I want them to be a little more, I don't know, maybe some families want to be in the dark, but for me … I wanted to know more, how to cope, and then I could get very bitchy and very demanding. (Kristen, 45, whose brother died of AIDS)

Hospice is so great. They're spread so thin. If they could've had someone stay with me the next 2 days after his death. His friend left me alone in the apartment. It was kind of rough. I cleaned the apartment the day Andy died, and then sat there. It was rough, really rough. (Diane, 68, whose son died of AIDS)

When the time came to physically remove his body, no one had prepared me for the sorts of emotions I might feel … I really think I would have done better if I'd had some preparation … hospice should have put it on their agenda as things that need to be [discussed]—"Some people have difficulty with this, and is there anything about that process that you'd like to talk about before it happens." They didn't do that and I'm not mad at them, I don't think they failed as a result of that, I just hope in the future that they add it to their agenda. (Rosemary, 57, whose husband died of lung cancer)

Some families complained that they were given information they were not prepared to hear, or that it was delivered too abruptly:

The only thing I wasn't comfortable with, and it happened two times, and that was that the nurses were quite blunt and the doctors were also, pretty much telling Mom "you're dying." It was difficult for me to have them be so blunt. (Brenda, 40, whose mother died of lung cancer)

Brenda goes on to describe how her mother chose not to know the seriousness of her illness, that she did not want to know she was terminal or how long she might have to live, and that the family was willing to go along with the facade. Her remarks remind us not to assume that an individual, or a family, wants all the facts:

My mother never did really get on with her life, she never drove, couldn't go to work, lost her hair, pretty much threw in the towel, but she really didn't think she was dying. Then shortly thereafter the nurses said, "You're dying," and after she left, I went up to the bedroom, and my mother said, "did you know I was dying?" It was hard, trying to protect her, wanting to keep her from dying, keep her from suffering, all this heartache, I think that's what was so horrifying that hospice would come in and say basically, look you're dying. I don't think we wanted to hear it, I don't think we wanted her to hear it. The doctor was pretty blunt, it was almost unfair, he was evaluating her eyesight, and he said, "See what I mean, her eyes don't work." and I thought what about her dignity, she's still with us! It was uncomfortable. Actually under the circumstances I think they do pretty well.

A common complaint from families coping with the last stages of their loved one's life is that they feel invaded by what seems a multitude of well-meaning strangers. Recognizing that assistance is needed, the feeling of privacy being invaded and the sanctuary of home intruded is an added stressor for many:

It seemed like a lot of people converged at once. It was so distressing. (Elaine, 59, whose son died of melanoma).

Organizations, including hospice organizations, weather difficulties and change. The families they serve are also affected. Family members can become extremely attached to a particular hospice worker or volunteer who has come into their life at such a critical time. The absence of that person, whether due to personal emergency, or to organizational policy, can represent an unexpected and unwelcome stressor to the family:

The way it played out there was just so much change in the [hospice agency] at the time when Franklin was the sickest, that was not helpful. The social worker wasn't there because her mother had died. The nurse was grieving, and then the whole constant change they were putting us through, and then taking Derrick away. They told us he was being taken off the case about a week before Franklin died. So we fought to keep him—threatened to sue if he was removed from the case. Derrick stayed with us when Franklin died. (Alexandra, 51, whose husband died of AIDS)

Family members and friends are not the only ones who can unintentionally make a hurtful comment:

If anything, there were too many platitudes. (Jane, 56, whose 99-year-old mother died of multiple causes)

The only thing that happened, and I understand it, I honestly do, this nurse made the remark. We were persuaded that I should have someone come in twice a week in the morning. Well I found out that in those 4 hours you just barely get out of the house … for those 4 hours I was paying this gal $19 an hour. I said something about it not being worth the money, and the nurse said, "you have two cars, you don't need two cars." I know it's because we live in Marin County and have the house paid for. What she didn't realize is that we paid $30,000 for it in the first place. (Jessica, 70, whose husband died of prostate cancer)

Some people really don't want their loved one home, but feel they have no choice:

As far as hospice is concerned, they were very good to me, but their whole theory is they don't want the patient to go into the hospital, and I believe it comes to a point where physically and mentally it's too much on a person to have them be at home. I really don't believe in the hospice aspect because the last week of my mother's death I couldn't move her, and she was awake around the clock and needed attention. (Erica, 48, whose mother died of bladder cancer)

PERSONAL QUALITIES OF A GOOD HELPER

There are many ways in which any caring person can offer supportive interventions for bereaved people. Interventions can be made in formal settings as just described, or informally as in a conversation between coworkers. A social worker providing information about community resources can also reassure and comfort. Assistance that is ongoing and encompasses many dimensions of grief may be provided by a close friend. Sometimes what is needed is brief and specific to a particular issue, perhaps a member of clergy assisting a bereaved person with a spiritual dilemma precipitated by the death. Nurses and doctors treating a bereaved person can attend not only to presenting physical symptoms, but might simply take the time to listen to the story of the death. The more informed and aware any of us can be about grief and what is helpful to bereaved people, the more opportunities we may have to offer help. Even the smallest gesture can mean the world to a person in grief.

Several studies have shown that one of the most important determinants of the effectiveness of any intervention is the quality of the relationship between the counselor and the client. This is true for anyone interacting with the bereaved in a helping capacity. We have mentioned that not all professionals, and certainly not all lay people, are comfortable with or skilled at supporting the bereaved through the mourning process. What characteristics, then, are important for individuals who wish to help grieving persons? Wolfelt (1988) outlined six personal qualities that serve to form the foundation of a supportive relationship with the bereaved person. These personal qualities are not all inclusive, but they are fundamental in creating a safe environment in which a bereaved person may share grief. First, and perhaps the most complex quality, is *empathy*. Empathic responsiveness requires the listener to become involved in the emotional world of the griever while maintaining sufficient personal boundaries. Empathic communication with the mourner strives to fully under-stand the meaning of the experience, and occurs when the helper responds to the emotional level of the mourner in the moment. The second quality is *respect*, which includes fully accepting the mourner's experience, resistance, defenses, and timing with patience and affirmation. Respect is accomplished from a stance that the helping relationship is one of "working together," and is not possible when the helper presumes to know what is best for the mourner to think, feel, and do. The third quality is *warmth and caring*, which is demon-strated through a sense of personal closeness as opposed to professional distance. People in grief are particularly sensitive to who understands and cares, and who does not. They know, primarily through nonverbal behavior, when they are in the presence of a warm and caring person. The fourth quality is *self-awareness*, in interactions with the griever in general life experience. Caregivers need to evaluate constantly how their own experiences and feelings impact the helping relationship, how they are being impacted by their experi-ence of the mourner, and to be open to learning more about what is helpful in each new counseling relationship. The fifth personal quality of effective helpers is *congruence*. Put simply, the helper must "practice what is preached" and model the values and beliefs she embraced for the mourner. The last personal quality is *knowledge* of the information available related to grief and mourning. Full knowledge of research findings and a theoretical understanding of grief assists the helper in assessing the needs of the mourner, and providing the best possible assistance, and knowing when professional intervention is needed.

TASKS FOR HELPERS

Identifying tasks for helpers is a logical extension of the tasks of mourning, and several researchers have done so, based on their theories of grief and mourning (see Corazzini, 1980; Rando, 1984; Wolfelt, 1988; Worden, 1982). Rando (1984) offered a particularly comprehensive outline that she groups into seven broad phases. Rando's outline may be especially useful to people who work extensively with bereaved individuals over the entire course of mourning. Worden's model proposes ten specific tasks that are easily understood and employed by those experienced in working with bereaved people, but also by those who may have less direct or ongoing involvement with the bereaved but still want to offer assistance when and where they can. We turn now to a description of Worden's 10 tasks and suggest specific interventions for each.

1. *Help the Survivor Actualize the Loss.* The mourner needs to come to both an intellectual and emotional understanding and acceptance that the loved one has died and will not be returning. In the initial moments and days following the death, viewing the body, going through the memorial and funeral services,

and visiting the grave can help the person come to realize that the death is real. Later, performing tasks such as cleaning out closets and drawers and giving away clothing and possessions belonging to the deceased will further a sense of reality. A caring support person can offer to accompany the bereaved person to the mortuary or grave site, or to be available when the closets are cleaned. All that is required is an understanding, respectful presence. Empathic listening and gentle questioning will encourage the survivor to recount the circumstances of the death and memories of the deceased.

Wolfelt (1988) pointed out the role that denial plays in protecting the bereaved person from pain that overwhelms the capacity to cope. Acute grief is a process of alternating tendencies, one to deny and push away the pain and the other to confirm the reality of the death. In supporting the bereaved, one must trust that ultimately, rather than immediately, a complete acceptance of the reality of the death will occur.

It is widely accepted that anyone who wishes to support a grieving person must not try to hurry the process, never push, but rather to follow the grieving person's cues. Full realization is accomplished over time, sometimes months or even years.

2. *Help the Survivor Identify and Express Feelings.* People in grief do not always recognize what they are feeling, particularly when the feelings are unpleasant or unfamiliar. They may be confused by what they feel, or unable to fully express their emotions. They may be reluctant to express their feelings, possibly wanting to protect family and friends or believing they are a burden. Cultural taboos may further inhibit the free expression of grief in its many forms. Providing a safe and accepting environment for realizing and expressing emotions is a precious gift to a bereaved person.

One of the most effective ways to help a person understand the experience and to feel understood is to identify and reflect back the feelings that are being expressed. "That really made you angry," or "You're feeling very lonely today," are examples of reflecting feelings. Another approach is to ask open-ended questions (e.g., questions that cannot be answered "yes" or "no") such as, "What times are hardest for you?" or "What is the sadness like for you?" The use of provisional language provides the grieving person an opportunity to explore reactions to loss. For example, saying, "Sometimes people say they occasionally feel anxious or impatient, I wonder if you ever feel that way?" Provisional language minimizes defensiveness, encourages a variety of thoughts and opinions, encourages creative thinking and problem solving, and increases accuracy of communication and understanding.

3. *Help the Survivor Live Without the Deceased.* There are inevitably problems that must be addressed and decisions that must be made. A person in grief will often have difficulty focusing, concentrating, or making decisions. The goal of a helper is not to merely take over, but to gently encourage and

empower. For example, if a widow had formerly left all financial matters to her husband, she may need to learn how to balance a checkbook or manage her financial affairs. A supportive helper can gradually assist her in learning such tasks.

When overwhelmed, a bereaved person might benefit from a stable, calm friend who can help prioritize and identify problems or actions that can wait until later. Breaking tasks down into smaller manageable chunks can also serve to relieve undo stress. Suggesting and encouraging new coping strategies, or old abandoned ones, can likewise be beneficial. Several of our study participants told us that answering our questions about various coping strategies suggested new possibilities that they adopted, or reminded them of previous coping strategies they had abandoned or forgotten but subsequently used again. Acquiring new coping skills helps to alleviate feelings of helplessness and powerlessness in the face of deep loss.

4. *Help the Survivor Emotionally Relocate the Deceased.*   According to Worden (1991b, p. 48) the goal of a helper is to "help survivors find a new place in their life for the lost loved one—a place that will [also] allow the survivor to move forward with life and form new relationships." Each survivor needs to find his or her own way of integrating the deceased loved one into their current life experience.   Creating an annual golf tournament to provide academic scholarships in the name of the deceased was one family's way. Wearing an item of jewelry that belonged to the deceased might be another. Routinely visiting a special place and allowing time to remember might be another. A 13-year-old girl whose mother died took a few moments before she went to sleep each night to "talk with" her mother, briefly recounting the events of the day. Whatever method employed, a supportive person will encourage such activity and remind the mourner that restructuring the relationship with the loved one does not dishonor or betray the loved one, but rather makes it possible to move forward into the future.

5. *Provide Time to Grieve.*   Some people appear to stabilize and regain their equilibrium quickly. Others may take a long time. To be effective in supporting one in grief, a helper must be able to recognize, and be willing to be available when grief resurfaces. Sometimes it is possible to predict such occurrences, as with holidays or anniversary dates, and a bereaved person will be grateful for a phone call or note at such times. In other circumstances, grief may reappear without notice and after quite a long time. Simply knowing that there is an open invitation to call, regardless how long since the death, provides comfort and reassurance.

6. *Interpret "Normal" Behavior.*   Normalizing is an extremely important component of supporting people in grief. Simply asking, "Do you ever feel like you're going crazy," has provided immense relief to many bereaved people who have that experience but feel inhibited from expressing it. The physiological

symptoms that accompany grief can be confusing or frightening. Helping someone in grief to recognize that their shortness of breath and heart palpitations are likely a manifestation of grief and will pass with time provides reassurance and guidance. Advising that visual or sensory hallucinations are common in bereavement can prevent unnecessary distress should they occur.

7. *Allow for Individual Differences.*   This principle is critical for helpers. We have discussed at length the many and various ways that people may experience grief. Often, people in grief look to others to provide information that cannot be given—they want to know how long their pain will last, when will they feel better, will they ever love another person again, how should they "do this?" It can be both frustrating and liberating for a bereaved person to be reassured that their grief experience is uniquely theirs and will unfold over time. They may benefit from being cautioned not to compare their experience with others. And, they may be helped to understand why another family member is not grieving in precisely the same way. Modeling an open, accepting approach to the individuality of a grief experience can assist family members in respecting and honoring each other's differences.

8. *Provide Continuing Support.*   As described before, grief is a process through which one moves, not a state in which one exists. There are times of acute distress in which more focused support and attention may be required. There may also be periods of well being. Typical descriptions of the mourning process over time is that it is like traveling through an emotional terrain with peaks and valleys that become further apart and less extreme in magnitude. Another analogy is that of floating down a river. At times the water is smooth, and sometimes there are rough waters to be endured. The helpers that are valued most are those who remain available and willing, over time, to lend a hand or listen empathically. People who have been helped in this way often say, "She never said or did anything that was so profound. It's just that she was there."

9. *Examine Defenses and Coping Styles.*   Inquiring about and exploring the various coping styles and strategies that a bereaved person uses helps the bereaved become more cognizant of what is useful, what is not useful, what helps and what does not. In becoming more aware, choosing the strategies that are most helpful becomes easier and assists the bereaved person to feel empowered in their own mourning process. A helper may ask, "What helps you get through the day?" or remark, "Taking a walk was a great idea, it seemed to distract you for awhile." Likewise, exploring coping strategies that may not be so helpful can lead to identifying new ones that better serve the person in grief.

10. *Identify Complicated Grief Reactions and Refer.*   It is extremely important that assistance offered to a bereaved person be within the limitations and comfort zone of the individual offering the support. There is a great deal that any caring person can offer a bereaved person, either on an ongoing basis, or in one brief contact. To attempt to offer support that is outside one's expertise

is to do a bereaved person a great disservice. It is a gift, not a failure, to acknowledge one's own limitations and assist the bereaved person in taking advantage of appropriate resources.

Some supporters of the bereaved may assist in only one, or a few, of the ways suggested. For example, a friend might call weekly and initiate lunch dates twice a month to prevent the bereaved from becoming isolated. A family member might be available to hear the griever review and recount the relationship with the deceased, and to offer a welcoming shoulder to cry on. Other supporters (counselors, support group facilitators, clergy, family, and friends) might be actively involved in the entire grief process, and might be called upon to assist in most or all ways described.

OTHER FORMS OF INTERVENTION

Where bereavement is concerned, any activity that reduces pain and enhances functioning can be regarded as a worthwhile intervention. People vary in the amount and kind of techniques that they will embrace. For some, a single intervention is all that is needed, many will incorporate several into their overall coping strategy, and some will try everything presented to them. Following are some suggested interventions that may be employed as part of, or in conjunction with individual or group counseling, or may be the sole intervention adopted by a person in grief.

Bibliotherapy

Bibliotherapy is the use of literature for therapeutic purposes (Rubin, 1978). Only a few decades ago, literature on coping with bereavement was nearly nonexistent. Today, entire sections in bookstores are earmarked for this topic, and it is easy to find quality literature for addressing issues relevant to specific types of loss.

Books can provide some of the same assistance as support groups or counseling. Some people seek out books that provide information about the grief process and practical suggestions for coping with loss (see Rando, 1988). Reading about grief and mourning can provide normalization and validation. Some people find comfort and a reduced sense of isolation from books in which the authors describe their own grief process (e.g., Ericsson, 1992; Lewis, 1961).

> Reading has served me in place of counseling. To me, reading has always been the way I learn best, so it's natural to me. (Marjorie, 46, whose father died of cancer)

But some people do not find books helpful. They may feel distressed over books recommended or given them by well-intentioned friends and family:

> I've read books. People gave me books, poems. I didn't get anything out of those kind of things. It's individual. (Harry, 60, whose wife died of peripheral neuropathy)

Reading, especially immediately after a death, may seem an overwhelming task or may increase the pain of grief. Some people find, weeks or months after the death, assistance or comfort from books that they could not read immediately following the death.

Writing

Many people find writing or journaling to be particularly helpful during periods of mourning. The form of writing is unimportant: some record what they are thinking and feeling, others write poetry and essays about their grief, still others write letters to their deceased loved one describing their grief or saying things they wish they had said while their loved one was still alive. Writing provides a medium for their expression of grief, and helps to concretize their experience. Moreover, keeping a journal provides an individual with the means to observe their progress through the grief.

> I remember making a conscious choice, a month or so after the funeral, that I would not discuss it with my friends—they'd heard it and they didn't need to keep hearing it, although I needed to keep processing it. So that's when I began to write. The word processor got used a lot for a while. What I needed to do was just keep the process going. (Jonelle, 45, whose father died of cancer)

Humor

Not all grief work is serious, heavy, and solemn. Humor is an often overlooked or unrecognized intervention. Families who are supporting a terminally ill loved one often report humorous moments as among their favorite memories. People in grief, either one-to-one or in support groups will commonly modulate the intensity of their emotions through the use of humor. In grief, laughter can be just as prevalent as tears.

> It doesn't all have to be sad. You can have some wonderful, happy times. My father wanted to go fishing, but he was too ill. So my brother bought some live fish and put them in a garbage can in the driveway. He set up camp stools and cold beer, drove our father around the block and then they sat down and fished. Everyone had a good time. For days, my father told everyone how big the fish he caught was. (Patricia, 41, whose father died of lung cancer)

You find the serious things but you also find the fun and the humor in life, too. Humor is probably one of the best parts of it—to laugh again and to find funny things in life to laugh at. (Caroline, 57, whose husband died of prostate cancer)

The one thing that really surprised me was how much laughter there was in the group. One minute we'd be crying, and the next minute we'd all be laughing. I didn't expect the humor and the laughter, but it was wonderful. It was great because it helped keep the evening from becoming too intense. And it was so respectful, you know, not at anyone's expense. It felt so good to laugh with those people who know how much it hurts. (Suzanne, 47, whose husband died of melanoma)

In bereavement, humor often takes on a decidedly gruesome quality, called "gallows humor," which may be offensive to some. In counseling people in grief, a good rule of thumb regarding the use of humor is to always allow the grieving person to initiate the humor, to laugh only after they do, and to never laugh beyond the moment when they stop.

Rituals

Rituals are powerful and often overlooked interventions that can be helpful at any time during the mourning process, and for years to come. *Rituals* are ceremonial acts that include symbolic or metaphoric meaning. According to Kollar (1989), rituals help to create a special kind of reality that transcends daily life and offers an affirmation of the continuing bond to the deceased. The symbolic acts of a ritual, whether simple or elaborate, can provide an intensity of experience that might not otherwise be possible. Most often, a public memorial or funeral service is the only ritual performed after a death. Many bereaved people find, however, that private and personally meaningful rituals are powerful and beneficial weeks, months, or even years after the death. A bereaved person may be encouraged to consider incorporating ritual into their life, but it is important that the ritual be initiated by the bereaved. If pushed or forced, rituals can be harmful and interfere with successful mourning (Cook & Dworkin, 1992).

I play all the music that we shared. I feel such a link with her in that music. (Sherman, 57, whose wife died of lung cancer)

We planted a Japanese Maple in the backyard. We call it dad's tree. On special occasions we can make ornaments to hang on it, or we can just gather around it and sing and tell stories. (Karen, 43, whose husband died of melanoma)

I made a memory book for each of my children and gave it to them on Father's Day. (Shannon, 47, whose husband died of cancer)

We were getting rid of the computer to get a new one. All of Jim's files were in it. It's not like I ever thought I'd read them or need them, it just felt hard to let go of them. So I wrote a letter to Jim, and I saved it into the computer, and my letter went with it. I cried the whole time I wrote it, but it felt like a really healing thing to do. (Mandy, 47, whose husband died of heart failure)

The Internet

Information and support are now available on the internet. This resource may be particularly beneficial to people who are unable to attend a support group or cannot afford counseling. Griefnet (griefnet@griefnet.org) is a nonprofit organization that provides services to lay people, many of whom have experienced dramatic loss, or professionals who work with people in bereavement on a regular basis. Griefnet provides a library of tests and a resource center with links to other nonprofit organizations that are likely to be helpful to people in grief. In addition, subscribers may participate in online support groups. Staffed by volunteers, Griefnet reportedly receives 50,000 visits to their web site per week.

Association for Death Education and Counseling

The Association for Death Education and Counseling (ADEC) in Hartford, CT, is an interdisciplinary organization whose membership includes educators, counselors, medical professionals, clergy, general directors, social workers, philosophers, psychologists, and well-being specialists, writers, and volunteers. ADEC works to promote and share research, theories, and practice in dying, death, and bereavement. The goal of ADEC is to enhance the ability of professionals and lay people to be better able to meet the needs of those with whom they work in death education and grief counseling. Toward that goal, ADEC offers a newsletter, annual conference, and certification program.

The Bereavement Coping Study as an Intervention

When we began recruiting participants for the Stanford Coping Study, we shared the concern of the hospice workers that going into people's homes during such a difficult time would add to the participants' stress and distress. To the contrary, most of our participants spoke of how much they enjoyed the interviews, how helpful it was to think about the questions we asked, and how much they appreciated being able to speak so frankly about their grief and their loved one. A number of people said they discovered new ideas for coping based on the questions we asked, and some said the interviews helped them realize that they needed to get some professional counseling. Moreover, a quarterly Project

Newsletter sent them by the Coping Study staff served to give them a sense of "community," and diminished isolation. Many of our participants viewed the interviews as interventions that contributed to their own coping:

> This, the interview process, has been really good in helping me to deal with it. It's nice to sort of sum up every now and then, really sort of think about how I'm dealing. (Stuart, 39, whose father died of liver cancer)

> This has been like a therapy on its own because I started with this quite a while ago, and the one thing that's been so wonderful for me is that you always seem to come at the right time. And to be able to talk to somebody who is completely objective has always been a help. (Beth, 54, whose mother died of breast cancer)

> It's been good therapy for me. Sometimes talking to strangers is easier, because you're not thinking, "Do they think I'm a crybaby?" You just say it, and get it out, and I think that's therapeutic. (Melissa, 59, whose mother died of old age)

> It's therapy for me to talk to you. The hurt is there whether I talk about it or not. It helps. It's difficult to go to a support group now. (Penelope, 52, whose son died of AIDS)

> The interview has made me see how important it is to have other people around, how aware you are of support groups. Answering the questions made me realize how many people gave me help and support. (Monica, 58, whose mother died of lung cancer)

> It makes me think about him more than I would have. It's good therapy because it is a healing process to think about these things. (Vivian, 37, whose father died of kidney disease)

> Sometimes it does good for you to come here and I can let out my feelings with you because I don't know you personally. You're just questioning me. At the same time, it's helping me understand me, helping me see myself. When I'm answering these questions, I'm really seeing what point in life I'm in right now, and what I have to do in the future. (Julie, 58, whose husband died of cancer)

> Despite my avoidance of the interviews—don't have time, too busy—I was still committed to doing it. Since I didn't do any support groups, and since I did the avoidance and denial of the death, the interview gave me a big panorama of possibilities, how people have responded just because of how the questions were framed. It gave me an idea of the extremes I or other people could have done. It also gave me a framework to see where I fit within the extremes. So instead of it being just an experience mode, it gave me what I call a multidimensional way of responding—that I was able to respond with the head that thinks, the heart that feels and the body that moves; kind of opened up to a broader perspective. So that when I do my normal stuff in my relationships, I'm not cutting myself off from my parents'

death. Kind of gave me more of a grace, a bigness. So, I feel like the interview was a deep learning experience. I feel like it's a growth experience that's worth the time. (Peter, 40, whose mother died of pancreatic cancer)

_____

Voices

At each follow-up interview, we asked our study participants what advice they would give to someone who was about to go through the same experience they did. Their responses reflect the interventions they found to be the most helpful and important in their own mourning processes.

I'd give the same advice that I got. Get into therapy immediately. Don't wait. Or a support group, or a combination of both. It gives you insight that books don't. (Juliet, 43, whose mother died of cancer)

Be there for them. Be a friend. You don't have to continually talk, just be there. (Deborah, 53, whose brother died of AIDS)

What was so helpful for me was that I saw my therapist at least once a week, and it was a time I could just address the terrible stuff that was going on in my life, because you can't be addressing it all the time every day, because you've really got a lot of work to do. But to take time out for yourself, and get the help that *you* need to keep *yourself* going. Because not only does it help you, but also it helps the person you're caring for. It helps you deal with what a terrible things they're going through. (Harriet, 53, whose mother died of pancreatic cancer)

They should seek some kind of help, whether it's a support group. or a friendship group, a religious group, a counselor. I think people need to have someone with them to go through this process. (Stephanie, 46, whose mother died of cancer)

You have to face the truth, accept the facts, so you can go on. (Sam, 35, whose father died of pancreatic cancer)

After the loved one is gone, allow the person who is grieving to talk about it until there is no more talking. Then keep a journal to talk to the person who is lost. Express—get it out. Feelings are like a cut, you have to open it up to air so it can heal. Don't let it fester. (Joseph, 58, whose mother died of congestive heart failure)

We took care of everything he wanted to take care of as far as "I want this kid to have that." He talked to all the children. He really accepted that he might die any second. And then, he went on with living. (Martha, 63, whose husband died of pancreatic cancer)

Find the fine balance between head and heart. (Julian, 40, whose mother died of brain cancer)

Analyze your priorities, come true to yourself and your gut level feelings about the situation, and then make a plan and execute it. There's no time for procrastination. Remind yourself that if death is inevitable, you won't want to look back and say, "If only." (Daniel, 40, whose mother died of brain cancer)

Take one day at a time. Make sure you care for yourself as well as the person who is ill. You need to take a step back and take a perspective, because you can become so overwhelmed. So, just one day at a time and make it through each day. Don't look too far forward, and don't go backward. (Lauren, 52, whose father died of prostate cancer)

It's very beautiful to die at home. Celebrate the living every moment. Don't run from it. (Eileen, 51, whose husband died of a brain tumor)

You have to give yourself a reason to live, and not just exist. I work with senior citizens. I get such smiles and hugs and love. You have to make *your* life be worth living, and only you can do it. Nobody else can do that for you. (Ruth, 54, whose aunt died of colon cancer)

Do all you can to be informed and understand that there is a point where you've done all you can and let go. Nurture yourself as well as the person who is sick, you can't give out from an empty cup. (Rachel, 36, whose father died of lung cancer)

You don't "get over" a loss. No, you just learn to live with it, but you have to also accept the fact that you're changed as a result of it. You're never going to be able to go back to the way you were before it. (Eric, 35, whose mother died of a brain tumor)

Show them true love and be there for them, yet let them have space. Pray a lot. Accept their feelings. (Molly, 33, whose husband died of carcinoma)

Be glad for every day you have together—cherish it. Forgive yourself for not being always perfect. (Janice, 78, whose husband died of lymphoma)

Be nice to yourself. Get a massage. Pamper yourself. As you're taking care of the dying, also take care of yourself. Write it in your notebook: "I'm taking this time off for me. I'm going to this class. I'm going to meet this person." I would actually label it and book it—5 hours for Mom, 1 hour for me. I think it's so, so important. (Paul, 40, whose mother died of pancreatic cancer)

It almost feels arrogant to give advice to people who are going through this. My experience would not be like anybody else's. I almost don't think there is advice to give except that there are things to learn from it, and all you can do is just wait and let the learning happen. No matter who it is and how close you are to them, there's learning to be had, and you won't even have to fight for it. It will come. Just wait. It will come as you go through it, it will come after, it will come a long time after, but there will be something there. It will happen. You can certainly look for it. You use your sense of humor, you can see yourself frowning and using your resources. And if you are introspective maybe you can appreciate it at the time you're going through it, although you feel like you're in a maelstrom. You can at least look out and see: This serves me now, this will serve me later. I almost feel arrogant giving advice, because I think anybody who just copes with it deserves a pat on the back. (Florence, 46, whose husband died of AIDS)

Don't try and take yourself too seriously. That's dangerous to your health. (Jim, 48, whose mother died of pancreatic cancer)

Take all the help you can get from the very beginning. My dad tried to kind of push help off, I think because he didn't want to realize how close it was either. I didn't realize how close it was that she was going to die. That was really hard. That's what people need to do. They need to take help from people. And they need to listen to what the dying person is saying. (Sally, 32, whose mother died of lung cancer)

Just take it a day at a time. Get some help, a support group or something like that, so you don't feel like you're all alone. (Marilyn, 46, whose mother died of breast cancer)

Try to be patient but firm. Tell them you love them. Support their decisions. Give your opinion honestly when asked. Take help when it's offered, ask if it's not. Explore all options and resources and alternatives and don't be afraid to ask. There's so many people who are embarrassed and keep it all in the family. I don't think the kids could have done it, nor could I, without hospice. I'm not too proud. Ask questions. Don't take the doctor's word for law. Question authority. The more knowledge the better—you know where you're starting from. (Carol, 40, whose husband died of a brain tumor)

Seek out the nearest and closest support they could find. Be willing to be open-minded, and if they're not happy with one support group, seek out another. Or seek out a person you can rely on. (Martin, 60, whose stepson died of AIDS)

I just know it's been really helpful to talk to other people who have lost their husbands, and just talk about how things are going for them now. I think hooking up with people is important. (Elizabeth, 48, whose husband died of a brain tumor)

Have faith. When one chapter closes, another begins. (Robert, 67, whose mother died of rectal cancer)

Surround yourself with family and friends. My family and friends have given me a lot of support. Get out amongst people, get out and make new friends. Go to lunch with someone. (George, 62, whose wife died of breast cancer)

To give, and I don't mean sympathy. Give support. (Agnes, 41, whose mother died of cancer)

I would give them positive advice. At least realize that the child can have a quality of life, and is not going to *know* any different anyway. It can have happiness. They can see that their child has a lot of happiness and a lot of love. (Christopher, 28, whose infant son died of congestive heart failure)

Your spirituality, whatever religion you might be, is primary. To me, your relationship with God would be your primary thing. Associate with people. Don't hide yourself away, during the process as well as after because you need support. I happen to thrive on being with people and friends, not everybody is that way. But I still think you need support as you're going through it, whether it be family or friends. People need to feel comfortable that they can come and help you, so you need to encourage that. Hope—because in this day and age not all illness is terminal. They have all kinds of cures. But realistic hope. You have to face the facts and work it out together. (Lisa, 53, whose husband died of pancreatic cancer)

Structure it. Structure this death as you would the birth or the coming of a baby. You of course would have a shower and bottles ready and a nursery set up. You're going to bury a person—start structuring it. We're going to hit a time when you're going to be ambulanced out, so let's clear some furniture. It's ok to recognize the fact that death is coming. Don't act like it's not, because it's structure just like the coming of a birth; that's ok to do. Plan ahead. So when things do hit, it's not as devastating. Call hospice. Do what you have to do. (Maria, 31, whose mother died of cancer)

I just wish people could be more educated when it comes to someone who is gay, and what the lifestyle is all about and how it isn't something that people embrace; it's the way they were born. (Marion, 52, whose son died of AIDS)

The thing that helped me most was a booklet hospice gave me about what to expect during the last days, hours, like when having a baby for the first time. It's important to know what to expect. Makes it easier, no surprises. (Blanche, 51, whose cousin died of AIDS)

Try to get hospice in early. My mom was really stubborn. It took me months to get hospice care into their house, so it really put a huge strain on the family. I had my own uncertainty about what hospice is. I think everyone should know about how fabulous it is, and somehow maybe hospice could do some work to let people know how fabulous they are. (Janelle, 30, whose mother died of cancer)

Our doctor didn't refer us to hospice soon enough, and that was a real problem. It's about doctors being clear about what they can and can't do because there came a point when we needed the doctor every 10 minutes. The doctor is unable to give that kind of service and hospice was able to give it. So before we got the that breaking point, Mom really suffered when we didn't have hospice and the doctor was unable to help us. Doctors need to be clear and to refer to hospice as soon as possible. She had to go to the hospital, and the social worker there said she should be in hospice, and urged the doctor to refer her. Finally he did. (Meredith, 38, whose mother died of pancreatic cancer)

Pace yourself, take breaks, love the process, see it as your job. Laugh and cry a lot. Allow for dreams, care for bodies. Surround yourself with people who bring you comfort. Allow yourself to do whatever you need to do. (Tamara, 36, whose mother died of colon cancer)

Appendix

This appendix presents details of the methods and measures used in the Bereavement Coping Project discussed in this volume.

PARTICIPANTS AND RECRUITING

Altogether, 455 participants were interviewed for the core study that provided most of the data presented in this volume. These participants ranged in age from 20 to 86 years. Seventy-five percent were women and 25% men. Of these, 104 were the wives or female partners of the deceased, 48 were the husbands or male partners, 139 were the daughters, 41 were the sons, 33 were the sisters, 8 were the brothers, 54 were the mothers, 11 were the fathers, and the remaining had other relationships to the patient (e.g., best friend, daughter-in-law, granddaughter). All of the participants who were not the spouse, child, parent, or sibling of the deceased were either the primary caregiver while the deceased was alive or reported having had a close emotional relationship to the deceased.

Eighty-one percent of the participants were White, 4% were African American, 7% were Hispanic, 4% were Asian or Pacific Islander, 1% was Native American and 3% were of mixed or other ethnic groups. Participants' annual family income in 1989 ranged from less than $10,000 to more than $100,000, with a mean and median income of $35,000 to $40,000, typical of the San Francisco Bay Area at the time. Participants' highest level of education ranged from elementary school to a graduate or professional degree; 59% of the participants had at least some college credit, but only 41% had a bachelor's degree and only 14% had a graduate or professional degree.

Fifty-three percent of the participants had been the primary caregivers to the deceased person when he or she was alive; in 26% of the cases the primary caregiver was someone other than the participant; and in 21% of the cases no caregiver had been required. All deceased individuals had resided in their own homes or the homes of the primary caregivers rather than in nursing homes or other institutions before their death. The median number of months they had been seriously ill before dying was 12.5 months. In the main data set, 69% of the deceased individuals had died of some form of cancer, 15% had died of complications due to AIDS, and 16% had died from other diseases.

Participants were recruited through 11 hospices in the Bay Area. Social workers and nurses assigned to the families approached family members to inquire whether they might be interested in being interviewed. Only one family member per patient was recruited for the study. When more than one family member requested to be interviewed, however, we obliged. The analyses presented in this volume were run for all participants and again using only one randomly chosen participant per family. Because the results of the analyses in both cases were nearly identical, the analyses using all family members are presented.

Social workers and nurses were asked to select randomly which family member to approach, with one exception: If there was a male family member who had been close to the patient, social workers and nurses were asked to approach that man first because we expected it would be more difficult to recruit men than women into the study. Of the family members approached about the study, 80% agreed to participate.

Not all of the 455 participants were interviewed at all waves of the study. Reasons for some participants not being interviewed at a given wave included the participant was too busy to be interviewed, he or she did not want to participate in an interview, or he or she moved away and could not be located. Comparisons of people who did participate in all interviews compared to those who did not showed no significant differences on any of the variables measured in this study. Similarly, at any given wave, those who participated in the interview did not differ significantly from those who did not.

A total of 362 family members were interviewed 1 month following the death of their loved one; 360 family members were interviewed 6 months following the loved one's death; 313 were interviewed 13 months following the death; and 280 were interviewed 18 months following the death.

PROCEDURE

We administered all measures in the context of an interview. For each measure, the interviewers read the instructions to the participant (the instructions provided for published measures were adapted slightly to reflect the interview format) then they read each item or question on the measure to the participant. If the answers to the questions required participants to use a Likert scale or to choose from among a group of possible answers, the interviewers presented the participant with a card with the possible answers printed on it and asked the participant to use the card to choose his or her answers. Almost all interviews were conducted in the participants' homes. Occasionally, interviews had to be conducted over the phone because participants had moved too far away (e.g., to Europe) for an in-home interview to be cost-effective. The interviewers were all female, advanced graduate students or professionals in clinical or counseling psychology. The interview took approximately 2 hours. The follow-up interviews were nearly identical to the initial interviews, except that we did not ask for basic demographic data at the follow-up interviews. Each interview a subject participated in was conducted by a different interviewer so that the interviewers' assessments of the participants would be independent of previous assessments.

MEASURES

Depression

The primary measure of depression was the Inventory to Diagnose Depression (IDD; Zimmerman, Coryell, Corenthal, & Wilson, 1986). The IDD presents participants with structured questions that assess all the symptoms of depression recognized in the *Diagnostic and Statistical Manual* (APA, 1986, 1994). Participants' answers to these questions can be summed to create a continuous measure of depression. This continuous measure was used in the analyses reported in this book. The continuous measure of depression from the IDD has been shown to have good reliability (Zimmerman et al., 1986). In this study, the test–retest reliabilities for this scale across the various interviews ranged from .64 to .71.

In addition, the interviewers completed the 17-item Hamilton Rating Scale for Depression (HRSD; Hamilton, 1960) on each subject immediately after the interview. This scale provides an index of participants' current levels of depression. Information on the presence of specific symptoms of depression can be discovered from the participants' responses to the structured questions of the IDD. Interviewers were also instructed to use participants' nonverbal behaviors and information provided spontaneously by participants during the interview. Interviewers were extensively trained in the use of the HRSD. The reliability of their ratings of participants on the HRSD was checked by having the audiotapes of 10% of the interviews rated by interviewers who had not conducted the original interview and comparing these ratings with those of the original interviewers. The intraclass correlation coeeficient between the original ratings and the secondary ratings was .74. This is comparable to the reliaiblities found in other studies of moderately depressed participants and in studies in which one of the raters was not actually present when the subject was being interviewed (see Vallis, Shaw, & McCabe, 1985). The test–retest correlations between HRSD scores across various waves of the study ranged from .50 to .52. The HRSD has been shown to differentiate well between depressed and nondepressed psychiatric control participants (Hedlund & Vieweg, 1979). HRSD scores also correlated significantly with other clinical rating scales for depression and self-report scales of depression (Hedlund & Vieweg, 1979). In this study, the cross-correlations between HRSD and IDD scores at the various interviews ranged from .74 to .77. To simplify the presentation of results, we concentrate on IDD scores, but most of the results are similar when HRSD scores are used as the criterion for depression.

Anxiety

The Spielberger State Anxiety Scale (Spielberger, Gorsuch, & Lushene, 1970) was administered as a measure of state anxiety. This scale includes 20 items that assess the respondents' current levels of anxiety. In this study, the internal consistency (alpha) of this scale was .93 at 1 month and the test–retest correlations across interviews ranged from .54 to .67.

Posttraumatic Stress Symptoms

A measure of posttraumatic stress symptoms was developed for this study. Respondents were asked if they were currently experiencing each of the symptoms of posttraumatic stress disorder listed in the *DSM–III–R* (APA, 1987) "not at all," "somewhat," "moderately so," or "very much so." Scores on these items were summed to create an total posttraumatic stress (PTS) score. PTS scores had an internal consistency of .82 at 1 month and test–retest correlations across waves of the study of .57 to .68.

General Distress

Respondents' scores on the IDD, State Anxiety Scale, and PTS Scale were converted to standardized scores within each interview then summed to create a General Distress score. The coefficient alpha for this general distress measure was .82 at 1 month.

Coping

Two coping scales were administered in this study. The Coping Responses Scale (Moos & Billings, 1982) includes items measuring a wide range of possible coping responses. Twenty-six of the original items from the Coping Responses Scale were deemed appropriate for this study and included in the interview.

Items from the Coping Responses Scale were submitted to a factor analysis to determine factor scales. Six factors emerged. These factors included problem solving (four items, e.g., "I made a plan of action and followed it," test–retest correlations from .49 to .58), avoidance coping (six items, e.g., "I avoided being with people in general." "I tried to reduce tension by drinking more," test–retest correlations from .61 to .72), seeking social support (five items, e.g., "I talked with a friend," test–retest correlations from .53 to .65), reappraisal (four items, e.g., "I tried to remember the positive times with (loved one)", test–retest correlations from .50 to .61), distraction coping (three items, e.g., "I got busy with other things to keep my mind occupied," test–retest correlations from .43 to .62), and emotional expression (two items, e.g., "I let my feelings out somehow," test–retest correlations from .51 to .63). (Alpha coefficients were not computed for these scales because the individual items on a scale represent distinct ways of coping, and people using one of these ways of coping would not necessarily be expected to use all the ways of coping represented on a scale.)

The Response Styles Questionnaire (RSQ; cf. Nolen-Hoeksema & Morrow, 1991) was also administered to assess how participants tend to respond to their own symptoms of negative emotion. Interviewers read the following instructions to participants:

> People think and do many different things when they feel sad, blue, or depressed. I'm going to read a list of possibilities. Turn to the next scale in your book and please tell me if you never, sometimes, often, or always think or do each one when you feel down, sad, or depressed. Please indicated what you generally do, not what you think you should do.

The Ruminative Responses Scale includes 22 items describing responses to depressed mood that are self-focused (e.g., I think "Why do I react this way?"), symptom-focused (e.g., I think about how hard it is to concentrate) and focused on the possible consequences and causes of their mood (e.g., I think "I won't be able to do my job if I don't snap out of this"). In this study, the internal consistency of this scale (Cronbach's alpha) was .90 at 1 month, and the test–retest correlations between various interviews ranged from .65 to .85. Previous studies have reported acceptable convergent and predictive validity for the Ruminative Responses Scale (Butler & Nolen-Hoeksema, 1994; Nolen-Hoeksema & Morrow, 1991).

Optimism–Pessimism

The Life Orientation Test (LOT; Scheier & Carver, 1985) was used to assess participants' optimism–pessimism. The LOT has eight items of the sort "In uncertain times, I usually expect the best." Respondents rate each item from 1 (*strongly agree*) to 5 (*strongly disagree*); scores are summed so that higher scores mean more optimism. The coefficient alpha for the LOT in this sample was .78 at 1 month, and the test–retest correlations across various interviews ranged from .68 to .82. Scheier and Carver (1985) reported that the scale shows strong convergent validity with other conceptually related scales.

Social Support Measures

Social support was assessed with the Social Support and Activities Scale (O'Brien, Wortman, Kessler, & Joseph, 1993). Twenty-three items on this scale assess participants' sense of isolation from others and qualitative aspects of social support, such as others' willingness to listen and to provide emotional and practical support, and conflict with others. We submitted these items to factor analysis, and four factors emerged: emotional support (eight items, e.g., "Do the people in your personal life give you the idea that it is alright to feel what you are feeling?" "Would someone be available to talk to you if you were upset, nervous, or depressed?", $\alpha = .85$, test–retest correlations from .34 to .72), friction (seven items, e.g., "Have the people in your personal life really gotten on your nerves?" "Have you felt tense from arguing or disagreeing with people in your personal life?", $\alpha = .87$, test–retest correlations from .47 to .75), isolation (five items, e.g., "Have you felt isolated from others?" "Have you felt no one really knows you well?", $\alpha = .72$, test–retest correlations from .42 to .72), and practical support (3 items, e.g., "Is there someone you could turn to if you needed to borrow $10, get a ride to the doctor, or needed some other small immediate help?", $\alpha = .69$, test–retest correlations from .36 to .64). Participants answered each question on a scale ranging from 1 to 5, with high scores on emotional and practical support indicating the participant reported more of these positive qualities of social support in his or her life and high scores on friction and isolation indicating that the participant reported more social friction and isolation.

Making Sense

At the end of each interview, respondents were asked, "Do you feel you have been able to make sense of the death?" Respondents answers to this open-ended question were transcribed. Three coders read each response and coded the overall answer as indicating "yes," "no," or "ambiguous/partly." The kappa coefficients of agreement on this coding were .85 and .87. Disagreements were resolved usually by going with the majority (two of three) raters' opinions. In the analyses reported here, only unambiguous responses of "yes" or "no" were used.

Finding Something Positive

At the end of each interview, respondents were also asked, "Sometimes people who lose a loved one find some positive aspect in the experience. For example, some people feel they learn something about themselves or others. Have you found anything positive in this experience?" Respondents answers to this open-ended question were transcribed. Two coders read each response and coded the overall answer as indicating "yes," no," or "ambiguous/partly." The kappa coefficients of agreement on this coding were .90 and .87. Disagreements were resolved usually by going with the majority (two of three) raters' opinions. In the analyses reported here, only unambiguous responses of "yes" or "no" were used.

References

Achenbach, T. M., & Edelbrock, C. (1983). *Manual for the Child Behavior Checklist*. Burlington: University of Vermont.

Affleck, G., & Tennen, H. (1996). Construing benefits from adversity: Adaptational significance and dispositional underpinnings. *Journal of Personality, 64*, 899–922.

American Psychiatric Association. (1987). *Diagnostic and statistical manual of mental disorders* (3rd rev. ed.). Washington, DC: Author.

American Psychiatric Association. (1994). *Diagnostic and statistical manual of mental disorders* (Vol. 4). Washington, DC: Author.

Anderson, R. (1974). Notes of a survivor. In S. B. Troop & W. A. Greene (Eds.), *The patient, death and the family* (pp. 73–82). New York: Scribner.

Anthony, S. (1940). *The child's discovery of death*. London: Kegan Paul.

Atchley, R. C. (1975). Dimensions of widowhood in later life. *The Gerontologist, 15*, 176–178.

Bahr, H. M., & Harvey, C. D. (1979). Correlates of loneliness among widows bereaved in a mining disaster. *Psychological Reports, 44*, 367–385.

Baker, J. E., & Sedney, M. A. (1996). How bereaved children cope with loss: An overview. In C. A. Corr & D. M. Corr (Eds.), *Handbook of childhood death and bereavement* (pp. 109–129). New York: Springer.

Baker, J. E., Sedney, M. A., & Gross, E. (1992). Psychological tasks for bereaved children. *American Journal of Orthopsychiatry, 62*, 105–116.

Balk, D. E. (1981). *Sibling death during adolescence: Self-concept and bereavement reactions*. Unpublished doctoral dissertation, University of Illinois at Urbana-Champaign.

Balk, D. E. (1983). Adolescents' grief reactions and self-concept perceptions following sibling death: A study of 33 teenagers. *Journal of Youth and Adolescence, 6*, 7–27.

Balk, D. E. (1990). The self-concepts of bereaved adolescents: Sibling death and its aftermath. *Journal of Adolescent Research, 5*, 112–132.

Balk, D. E. (1991a). Death and adolescent bereavement: Current research and future directions. *Journal of Adolescent Research, 6*, 7–27.

Balk, D. E. (1991b). Sibling death, adolescent bereavement, and religion. *Death Studies, 15*, 1–20.

Balk, D. E., & Hogan, N. S. (1995). Religion, spirituality, and bereaved adolescents. In D. W. Adams & E. J. Deveau (Eds.), *Beyond the innocence: Helping children and adolescents cope with death and bereavement* (Vol. 3, pp. 61–88). Amityville, NY: Baywood.

Balmer, L. E. (1992). *Adolescent sibling bereavement: Mediating effects of family environment and personality*. Unpublished doctoral dissertation, York University, Toronto, Ontario, Canada.

Barrett, C. J. (1978). Effectiveness of widows' groups in facilitating change. *Journal of Consulting & Clinical Psychology, 46,* 20–31.

Bass, D., Bowman, K., & Noelker, L. (1991). The influence of caregiving and bereavement support on adjusting to an older relative's death. *The Gerontologist, 31,* 32–42.

Baumeister, R. F. (1989) The problem of Life's meaning. In D. M. Buss & N. Cantor (Eds.), *Personality psychology: Recent trends and emerging directions.* (pp. 138–148). New York: Springer-Verlag

Baxter, G., Bennett, L., & Stuart, W. (1987). *Adolescents and death: Bereavement support groups for secondary school students—a practitioner's manual.* (2nd ed.). Etobicoke, Ontario: Canadian Centre for Death Education and Bereavement at Humber College.

Beck, A. T., & Beck, R. W. (1972). Screening depressed patients in family practice. *Postgraduate Medicine, 52,* 81–85.

Becker, D., & Margolin, F. (1967). How surviving parents handled their young children's adaptations to the crisis of loss. *American Journal of Orthopsychiatry, 37,* 753–757.

Bell, J. (1978). Family context therapy: A model for family change. *Journal of Marriage and Family Therapy, 4,* 111–126.

Benfield, D. G., Leib, S. A., & Vollman, J. H. (1978). Grief response of parents to neonatal death and parent participation in deciding care. *Pediatrics, 62,* 171–177.

Berger, A., Badham, P., Kutscher, A. H., Berger, J., Perry, M., & Beloff, J. (Eds.). (1989). *Perspectives on death and dying: Cross-cultural and multi-disciplinary views.* Philadelphia: Charles Press.

Berlinsky, E. B., & Biller, H. B. (1982). *Parental death and psychological development.* Lexington, MA: Heath.

Bernstein, J. E., & Rudman, M. K. (1989). *Books to help children cope with separation and loss* (Vol. 3). New York: Bowker.

Bohannon, J. R. (1990). Grief responses of spouses following the death of a child: A longitudinal study. *Omega: Journal of Death and Dying, 22,* 109–121.

Bonanno, G. A., Keltner, D., Holen, A., & Horowitz, M. J. (1995). When avoiding unpleasant emotions might not be such a bad thing: Verbal-autonomic response dissociation and midlife conjugal bereavement. *Journal of Personality and Social Psychology, 69,* 975–989.

Bornstein, P. E., Clayton, P. J., Halikas, J. A., Maurice, W. L., & Robins, E. (1973). The depression of widowhood after thirteen months. *British Journal of Psychiatry, 122,* 561–566.

Bowlby, J. (1961). Process of mourning. *International Journal of Psychoanalysis, 42,* 317–340.

Bowlby, J. (1969). *Attachment and loss* (Vol. 1, Attachment). New York: Basic Books.

Bowlby, J. (1980). *Loss: Sadness and depression.* New York: Basic Books.

Breckenridge, J. N., Gallagher, D., Thompson, L. W., & Peterson, J. (1986). Characteristic depressive symptoms of bereaved elders. *Journal of Gerontology, 41,* 163–168.

Brown, G. W., Harris, T. O., & Bifulco, A. (1986). Long-term effects of early loss of a parent. In M. Rutter, C. Izard, & P. Read (Eds.), *Depression in young people: Developmental and clinical perscpectives* (pp. 251–296). New York: Guilford Press.

Butler, L. D., & Nolen-Hoeksema, S. (1994). Gender differences in responses to depressed mood in a college sample. *Sex Roles, 30,* 331–346.

Calhoun, L. G., & Allen, B. G. (1991). Social reactions to the survivor of a suicide in the family: A review of the literature. *Omega: Journal of Death and Dying, 23,* 95–107.

Calhoun, L. G., & Tedeschi, R. G. (1989). Positive aspects of critical life problems: Recollections of grief. *Omega: Journal of Death and Dying, 20,* 265–272.

Candy-Gibbs, S. E., Sharp, K. C., & Petrun, C. J. (1985). The effects of age, object, and cultural/religious backround on children's concepts of death. *Omega: Journal of Death and Dying, 15,* 329–346.

Carey, R. G. (1977). The widowed: A year later. *Journal of Counseling Psycholog, 24,* 125–131.

Carroll, R., & Shaefer, S. (1993). Similarities and differences in spouses coping with SIDS. *Omega: Journal of Death and Dying, 28,* 273–284.

Carver, C. S., Scheier, M. F., & Weintraub, J. K. (1989). Assessing coping strategies: A theoretically based approach. *Journal of Personality and Social Psychology, 56,* 267–283.

Centers for Disease Control and Prevention. (1995). *HIV/AIDS surveillance report.* Atlanta: U.S. Department of Health and Human Services.

Clayton, P. J., Halikas, J. A., & Maurice, W. L. (1971). The bereavement of the widowed. *Diseases of the Nervous System, 32,* 597–604.

Clayton, P. J., Kalikas, J. A., Maurice, W. L., & Robins, E. (1973). Anticipatory grief and widowhood. *British Journal of Psychiatry, 122,* 47–51.

Cohen, S., & Wills, T. A. (1985). Stress, social support, and the buffering hypothesis. *Psychological Bulletin, 98,* 310–357.

Coles, R. (1990). *The spiritual life of children.* Boston: Houghton Mifflin.

Constantino, R. B. (1988). Nursing care of widows in grief and mourning through bereavement crisis intervention. *Dissertation Abstracts International, 41*(1-B), 130–131.

Cook, A. S., & Dworkin, D. S. (1992). *Helping the bereaved: Therapeutic interventions for children, adolescents, and adults.* New York: Basic Books.

Corazzini, J. G. (1980). The theory and practice of loss therapy. In B. M. Schoenberg (Ed.), *Bereavement counseling: A multi-disciplinary handbook.* Westport, CT: Greenwood.

Cornwall, J., Nurcombe, B., & Stevens, L. (1977). Family response to loss of a child by Sudden Infant Death Syndrome. *The Medical Journal of Australia, 1,* 565–568.

Corr, C. A. (1991). Should young children attend funerals? What constitutes reliable advice? *Thanatos, 16,* 19–21.

Corr, C. A. (1993). Children's literature on death. In A. Armstrong-Dailey & S. Z. Goltzer (Eds.), *Hospice care for children* (pp. 266–284). New York: Oxford University Press.

Corr, C. A. (1995). Entering into Adolescent Understandings of Death. In E. A. Grollman (Ed.), *Bereaved children and teens: A support guide for parents and professionals (pp. 21–35).* Boston: Beacon Press.

Corr, C. A., & Balk, D. E. (1996). *Handbook of adolescent death and bereavement.* New York: Springer.

Corr, C. A., & the staff of the Dougy Center. (1991). Support for grieving children: The Dougy Center and the hospice philosophy. *American Journal of Hospice and Palliative Care, 8,* 23–27.

Corr, C. A., Nabe, C. M., & Corr, D. M. (1997). *Death and dying, life and living* (2nd ed.). New York: Brooks/Cole.

Coyne, J. C. (1976). Toward an interactional description of depression. *Psychiatry, 39,* 28–40.

Cramer, D. (1993). Living alone, marital status, gender and health. *Journal of Applied and Community Social Psychology, 3,* 1–15.

Crase, D., & Crase, D. (1976). Helping children understand death. *Young Children, 32,* 21–27.

Crenshaw, D. (1991). *Bereavement: Counseling the grieving throughout the life cycle.* New York: Continuum.

Cunningham, L. (1990). *Teen age grief: A training manual for initiating and facilitating grief support groups for teens.* Panorama City, CA: Teen Age Grief.

Davidowitz, M., & Myrick, R. D. (1984). Responding to the bereaved: An analysis of "helping" statements. *Death Education, 8,* 1–10.

Davies, B. (1991). Long-term outcomes of adolescent sibling bereavement. *Journal of Adolescent Research, 6,* 83–96.

Davis, C., Nolen-Hoeksema, S., & Larson, J. (in press). Making sense of loss and benefiting from the experience: Two construals of meaning. *Journal of Personality and Social Psychology.*

Davis, C. G., Lehman, D. R., & Wortman, C. B. (1997). *Finding meaning in loss and trauma: Making sense of the literature.* Unpublished manuscript, University of Michigan.

Davis, C. G., Lehman, D. R., Wortman, C. B., Silver, R. C., & Thompson, S. C. (1995). The undoing of traumatic life events. *Personality & Social Psychology Bulletin, 21,* 109–124.

Defrain, J., Taylor, J., & Ernst, L. (1982). *Coping with sudden infant death.* Lexington, MA: D.C. Heath.

Demi, A. S. (1984). Social adjustment of widows after a sudden death: Suicide and non-suicide survivors compared. *Death Education, 8,* 91–111.

Derry, S. M. (1979). *An empirical investigation of the concept of death in children.* Unpublished doctoral dissertation, The University of Ottawa, Ottawa, Canada.

Deutch, H. (1937). Absence of grief. *Psychoanalytic Quarterly, 6,* 12–22.

Devereux, W. C. (1984). Children's understanding of the physical realities of death.

DiMatteo, M. R., & Hays, R. (1981). Social support in the face of serious illness. In B. H. Gottlieb (Ed.), *Social network and social support in community mental health* . Beverly Hills, CA: Sage.

Dimond, M., Lund, D. A., & Caserta, M. S. (1987). The role of social support in the first two years of bereavement in an elderly sample. *The Gerontologist, 27,* 599–604.

Donnelly, K. F. (1987). *Recovering from the loss of a parent.* New York: Dodd, Mead.

Dunn, R. G., & Morrish-Vidners, D. (1987). The psychological and social experience of suicide survivors. *Omega: Journal of Death and Dying, 18,* 175–215.

Dyregrov, A., & Matthiesen, S. B. (1987). Similarities and differences in others' and fathers' grief following the death of an infant. *Scandinavian Journal of Psychology, 28,* 1–15.

Edelstein, L. N. (1983, April). Maternal bereavement: Coping with the unexpected death of a child. Northwestern University, *Dissertation Abstracts International, 43*(10-B), 3356–3357.

Elder, G. H., & Clipp, E. C. (1989). Combat experience and emotional health: Impairment and resilience in later life. *Journal of Personality: Special Issue: Long-term stability and change in personality, 57,* 311–341.

Elizur, E., & Kauffman, M. (1986). Children's bereavement reactions following death of the father. In R. H. Moos (Ed.), *Coping with life crises: An integrated approach* (pp. 49–58). New York: Norton.

Epstein, S. (1985). The implications of cognitive-experiential self-theory for research in social psychology and personality. *Journal for the Theory of Social Behavior, 15,* 283–310.

Epstein, S. (1993). Bereavement from the perspective of cognitive-experiential self-theory. In M. S. Stroebe, W. Stroebe, & R. O. Hansson (Eds.), *Handbook of bereavement* (pp. 112–128): New York: University Press.

Erickson, S. J. (1995). *Social support as a mediator of emotional well-being in gay male caregivers of loved ones with AIDS.* Unpublished doctoral dissertation, Stanford University.

Ericsson, S. (1992). *Companion through the darkness: Inner dialogues on grief.* New York: HarperCollins.

Faletti, M. V., Gibbs, J. M., Clark, C., Pruchno, R. A., & Berman, E. A. (1989). Longitudinal course of bereavement in older adults. In D. A. Lund (Ed.), *Older bereaved spouses: Research with practical applications* (pp. 37–51). New York: Taylor & Francis/Hemisphere.

Faschingbauer, T. R., Zisook, S., & Devaul, R. (1987). The Texas revised inventory of grief. In S. Zisook (Ed.), *Biopsychosocial aspects of bereavement* (pp. 111–124). Washington, DC: American Psychiatric Press.

Federal Bureau of Investigation (1996). *1995 crime in the United States,* p. 66.

Ferguson, F. (1978). Children's cognitive discovery of death. *Journal of the Association for the Care of Children in Hospitals, 7,* 8–14.

Fish, W. C. (1986). Differences of grief intensity in bereaved parents. In T. A. Rando (Ed.), *Parental loss of a child.* Champaign, IL: Research Press.

Fleming, S. J., & Adolph, R. (1986). Helping bereaved adolescents: Needs and responses. In C. A. Corr & J. N. McNeil (Eds.), *Adolescence and death* (pp. 97–118). New York: Springer.

Florian, V. (1989). Meaning and purpose in life of bereaved parents whose son fell ill during active military service. *Omega: Journal of Death and Dying, 20,* 91–102.

Folkman, S., Chesney, M., Collette, L., Boccellari, A., & Cooke, M. (1996). Postbereavement depressive mood and its prebereavement predictors in HIV+ and HIV- gay men. *Journal of Personality and Social Psychology, 70,* 336–348.

Folkman, S., Chesney, M. A., Cooke, M., Boccellari, A., & Collette, L. (1994). Caregiver burden in HIV-positive and HIV-negative partners of men with AIDS. *Journal of Consulting and Clinical Psychology, 62,* 746–756.

Fox, S. S. (1985). *Good grief: Helping groups of children when a friend dies.* Boston: New England Association.

Fox, S. S. (1988). Helping child deal with death teaches valuable skills. *Psychiatric Times,* 10–11.

Frankl, V. E. (1963). *Man' s search for meaning: An introduction to logotherapy* (3rd ed.). New York: Vintage Books.

Freud, S. (1917/1957). Mourning and melancholia. In J. Strachey (Ed.), *Standard edition of the complete work of Sigmund Freud.* London: Hogarth Press.

Fromm, K., Andrykowski, M. A., & Hunt, J. (1996). Positive and negative psychosocial sequelae of bone marrow transplantation: Implications for quality of life assessment. *Journal of Behavioral Medicine, 19,* 221–240.

Fulton, R., Gottesman, D., & Owen, G. (1982). Loss, social change, and the prospect of mourning. *Death Education, 6,* 137–153.

Furman, E. (Ed.). (1974). *A child's parent dies: Studies in childhood bereavement.* New Haven, CT: Yale University Press.

Furman, R. (1970). The child's reactions to death in the family. In B. R. Schoenberg, A. Carr, D. Peretz, & A. Kutschner (Eds.), *Loss and grief: Psychological management in medical practices* (pp. 70–86). New York: Columbia University Press.

Galinsky, M. J., & Schopler, J. H. (1977). Warning: Groups may be dangerous. *Social Work, 22,* 89–94.

Galinsky, M. J., & Schopler, J. H. (1981). When groups go wrong. *Social Work, 26,* 424–429.

Gallagher, D. E., Thompson, L. W., & Peterson, J. A. (1981). Psychosocial factors affecting adaptation to bereavement in the elderly. *International Journal of Aging and Human Development, 14,* 79–95.

Gilbar, O., & Dugan, A. (1995). Coping with loss: Differences between widows and widowers of deceased cancer patients. *Omega: Journal of Death and Dying, 31,* 207–220.

Glick, I. O., Weiss, R. S., & Parkes, C. M. (1974). *The first year of bereavement.* New York: Wiley.

Gottlieb, B. H. (1986). Social network strategies in prevention. In R. L. Hough (Ed.), *Psychiatric epidemiology and prevention: The possibilities* (pp. 53–64). Los Angeles, CA: UCLA Neuropsychiatric Institute.

Gottlieb, B. H. (1988). Marshaling social support: The state of the art in research and practice. In B. H. Gottlieb (Ed.), *Marshaling social support: Formats, processes, and effects.* Newbury Park, CA: Sage.

Grollman, E. A. (1967). *Explaining death to children.* Boston: Beacon Press.

Guerriero, A. M. (1983). *Adolescent behavior: Impact on physical health, self-concept, depression, death, and anxiety.* Unpublished master's thesis, York University, Toronto, Ontario, Canada.

Hamilton, M. (1960). A rating scale for depression. *Journal of Neurology, Neurosurgery, and Psychiatry, 23,* 56–62.

Hansson, R. O., Carpenter, B. N., & Fairchild, S. K. (1993). Measurement issues in bereavement. In M. S. Stroebe, W. Stroebe, & R. O. Hansson (Eds.), *Handbook of bereavement: Theory, research, and intervention* (pp. 3–18). Cambridge, England: Cambridge University Press.

Harter, S. (1985). Processes underlying the construction, maintenance, and enhancement of the self-concept of children. In J. Suls & A. Greenwald (Eds.), *Psychological perspectives on the self* (pp. 138–181). Hillsdale, NJ: Lawrence Erlbaum Associates.

Hedlund, J., & Vieweg, B. (1979). Hamilton Rating Scale for Depression: A comprehensive review. *Journal of Operational Psychiatry, 10,* 149–162.

Helmrath, T. A., & Steinitz, E. M. (1978). Death of an infant: Parental grieving and the failure of social support. *The Journal of Family Practice, 6,* 785–790.

Hobfoll, S. E., & Freedy, J. R. (1990). The availability and effective use of social support. *Journal of Social & Clinical Psychology: Special Issue: Social support in social and clinical psychology, 9,* 91–103.

Hoffman, S. I., & Strauss, S. (1985). The development of children's concepts of death. *Death Studies, 9,* 469–482.

Hogan, N. S., & DeSantis, L. (1994). Things that help and hinder adolescent sibling bereavement. *Western Journal of Nursing Research, 16,* 132–153.

Hogan, N. S., & Greenfield, D. B. (1991). Adolescent sibling bereavement symptomatology in a large community sample. *Journal of Adolescent Research: Special Issue: Death and adolescent bereavement, 6,* 97–112.

Hopmeyer, E., & Werk, A. (1994). A comparative study of family bereavement groups. *Death Studies, 18,* 243–256.

Horowitz, A. (1985). Sons and daughters as caregivers to older parents: Differences in role performance and consequences. *The Gerontologist, 25*(6), 612–617.

Horowitz, M., Wilner, N., & Alvarez, W. (1979). Impact of events scale: A measure of subjective stress. *Psychosomatic Medicine, 41,* 208–218.

Horowitz, M. J. (1976). *Stress response syndromes.* Northvale, NJ: Aronson.

Horowitz, M. J., Krupnick, J., Kaltreider, N., Wilner, N., Leong, A., & Marmar, C. (1981). Initial psychological response to parent death. *Archives of General Psychiatry, 38,* 316–323.

House, J. S. (1981). *Work, stress, and social support.* Reading, MA: Addison-Wesley.

Hughes, M. (1995). *Bereavement and support: Healing in a group environment.* Washington, DC: Taylor & Francis.

Hunfeld, J. A. M., Mourik, M. M., Passchier, J., & Tibboel, D. (1996). Do couples grieve differently following infant loss? *Psychological Reports, 79,* 407–410.

Ide, B. A., Tobias, C., Kay, M., & de Zapien, J. G. (1992). Pre-bereavement factors related to adjustment among older Anglo and Mexican-American widows. *Clinical Gerontologist, 11,* 75–91.

Jackson, E. N. (1984). The pastoral counselor and the child encountering death. In H. Wass & C. A. Corr (Eds.), *Helping children cope with death: Guidelines and resources* (2nd ed., pp. 33–47). Washington, DC: Hemisphere.

Jacobs, S., Kasl, S. V., Ostfeld, A. M., Berkman, L., & Charpentier, P. (1986). The measurement of grief: Age and sex variation. *British Journal of Medical Psychology, 59,* 305–310.

Jacobs, S., & Ostfeld, A. (1977). An epidemiological review of the mortality of bereavement. *Psychosomatic Medicine, 39,* 344–357.

Janoff-Bulman, R. (1989). Assumptive worlds and the stress of traumatic events: Applications of the schema construct. *Social Cognition, 7,* 113–136.

Janoff-Bulman, R., & Frieze, I. H. (1983). A theoretical perspective for understanding reactions to victimization. *Journal of Social Issues, 39,* 1–17.

Johnson, C. J., & McGee, M. G. (Eds.). (1991). *How different religions view death and the afterlife.* Philadelphia: Charles Press.

Kane, B. (1979). Children's concepts of death. *Journal of Genetic Psychology, 134,* 141–153.

Kaplan, D., Smith, A., Grobstein, R., & Fischman, S. (1973). Family mediation of stress. *Social Work, 18,* 60–69.

Karpas, R. J. (1986). Concept of death and suicidal behavior in children and adolescents. Doctroral Dissertation, Pace University. *Dissertation Abstracts International, 47,* 3136B.

Kastenbaum, R. J. (1991). *Death, society, and human experience* (4th ed.). New York: Merrill.

Kato, P. M., & Mann, T. (in press). A synthesis of psychological interventions for the bereaved. *Clinical Psychology Review.*

Kirkley-Best, E., & Kellner, K. R. (1982). The forgotten grief: A review of the psychology of stillbirth. *American Journal of Orthopsychiatry, 52,* 420–429.

Klass, D., & Marwit, S. J. (1988). Toward a model parental grief. *Omega: Journal of Death and Dying, 19,* 31–50.

Kleinman, A., & Kleinman, J. (1985). Somatization: The interconnections in Chinese society among culture, depressive experiences, and the meanings of pain. In A. Kleinman & B. Good (Eds.), *Culture and depression: Studies in the anthropology and cross-cultural psychiatry of affect and disorder* (pp. 429–490): Berkley: University of California Press.

Klinger, E. (1977). *Meaning and void: Inner experience and the incentives in people's lives.* Minneapolis: University of Minnesota Press.

Kollar, N. R. (1989). Rituals and the disenfranchised griever. In K. J. Doka (Ed.), *Disenfranchised grief: Recognizing hidden sorrow* (pp. 271–284). Lexington, MA: Lexington Books.

Koocher, G. P. (1973). Childhood, death, and cognitive development. *Developmental Psychology, 9,* 369–375.

Krementz, J. (1981). *How it feels when a parent dies.* New York: Knopf.

Kubler-Ross, E. (1969). *On death and dying.* New York: Macmillan.

Kubler-Ross, E. (1983). *On children and death.* New York: Macmillan.

Laerum, E., Johnsen, N., Smith, P., & Larsen, S. (1987). Can myocardial infarction induce positive changes in family relationships? *Family Practice, 4,* 302–305.

Lamers, W. (1965, November). Death, mourning, the funeral, and the child. Presented at the annual meeting of the National Association of Funeral Directors, Chicago, IL.

Lazarus, R. S., & Folkman, S. (1984). *Stress, appraisal, and coping.* New York: Springer.

Leahy, J. M. (1992). A comparison of depression in women bereaved of a spouse, child, or a parent. *Omega: Journal of Death and Dying, 26,* 207-217.

Lee, W. (1987). Children's conceptions of death: A study on age and gender as factors in concept development. Unpublished doctoral dissertation, Harvard University. *Dissertation Abstracts International, 48,* 2119B.

Lehman, D. R., Davis, C. G., DeLongis, A., Wortman, C. B., Bluck, S., Mandel, D. R., & Ellard, J. H. (1993). Positive and negative life changes following bereavement and their relations to adjustment. *Journal of Social and Clinical Psychology, 12,* 90–112.

Lehman, D. R., Ellard, J. H., & Wortman, C. B. (1986). Social support for the bereaved: Recipients' and providers' perspectives on what is helpful. *Journal of Consulting and Clinical Psychology, 54,* 438–446.

Lehman, D. R., Lang, E. L., Wortman, C. B., & Sorenson, S. B. (1989). Long-term effects of sudden bereavement: Maritial and parent-child relationships and children's reactions. *Journal of Family Psychology, 2,* 344–367.

Lehman, D. R., Wortman, C. B., & Williams, A. F. (1987). Long-term effects of losing a spouse or child in a motor vehicle crash. *Journal of Personality & Social Psychology, 52,* 218–231.

Lepore, S. J., Silver, R. C., Wortman, C. B., & Wayment, H. A. (1996). Social constraints, intrusive thoughts, and depressive symptoms among bereaved mothers. *Journal of Personality and Social Psychology, 70,* 271–282.

Lerner, M. J. (1980). *The belief in a just world.* New York: Plenum.

Levav, I., Friedlander, Y., Kark, J., & Peritz, E. (1988). An epidemiologic study of mortality among bereaved parents. *New England Journal of Medicine, 319,* 457–461.

Lewis, C. S. (1961). *A grief observed.* New York: Bantam Books.

Lieberman, M. A. (1989). All family losses are not equal. *Journal of Family Psychology, 2,* 368–372.

Lieberman, M. A., & Videka-Sherman, L. (1986). The impact of self-help groups on the mental health of widows and widowers. *American Journal of Orthopsychiatry, 56,* 435–449.

Lindemann, E. (1994). Symptomatology and management of acute grief. *American Journal of Psychiatry, 151,* 155–160.

Littlefield, C., & Rushton, J. P. (1986). When a child dies: The sociobiology of bereavement. *Journal of Personality and Social Psychology, 4,* 797–802.

Lonetto, R. (1980). *Children's conceptions of death.* New York: Springer.

Lopata, H. (1973). *Widowhood in an American city.* Morrison, NJ: General Learning Press.

Lund, D. A., Caserta, M. S., & Dimond, M. F. (1986). Gender differences through two years of bereavement among the elderly. *The Gerontologist, 26,* 314–320.

Lund, D. A., Caserta, M. S., & Dimond, M. F. (1993). The course of spousal bereavement in later life. In M. S. Stroebe, W. Stroebe, & R. O. Hansson (Eds.), *Handbook of bereavement* (pp. 240–254). New York: University Press.

Lund, D. A., Dimond, M. F., Caserta, M. S., Johnson, R. J., Poulton, J. L., & Connelly, J. R. (1985). Identifying elderly with coping difficulties after two years of bereavement. *Omega: Journal of Death and Dying, 16*, 213–224.

Lundin, T. (1984a). Long-term outcome of bereavement. *British Journal of Psychiatry, 145*, 424–428.

Lundin, T. (1984b). Morbidity following sudden and unexpected bereavement. *British Journal of Psychiatry, 144*, 84–88.

Lyubomirsky, S., & Nolen-Hoeksema, S. (1993). Self-perpetuating properties of dysphoric rumination. *Journal of Personality and Social Psychology, 65*, 339–349.

Lyubomirsky, S., & Nolen-Hoeksema, S. (1995). Effects of self-focused rumination on negative thinking and interpersonal problem solving. *Journal of Personality and Social Psychology, 69*, 176–190.

Maddison, D., & Viola, A. (1967). The health of widows in the year following bereavement. *Journal of Psychosomatic Research, 12*, 297–306.

Maddison, D., & Walker, W. (1967). Factors affecting the outcome of conjugal bereavement. *British Journal of Psychiatry, 113*, 1057–1067.

Malinek, D. P., Hoyt, M. F., & Patterson, V. (1979). Adults' reactions to the death of a parent: A preliminary study. *American Journal of Psychiatry, 136*, 1152–1156.

Mandelbaum, D. G. (1959). Social uses of funeral rites. In H. Feifel (Ed.), *The meaning of death* New York: McGraw-Hill.

Martin, J. L. (1988). Psychological consequences of AIDS-related bereavement among gay men. *Journal of Consulting and Clinical Psychology, 56*, 856–862.

Martin, J. L., & Dean, L. (1993). Bereavement following death from AIDS: Unique problems, reactions, and special needs. In M. S. Stroebe (Ed.), *Handbook of bereavement: Theory, research, and intervention* (pp.–330). New York: Cambridge University Press.

Martinson, I. M., & Campos, R. D. (1991). Adolescent bereavement: Long-term responses to a sibling death from cancer. *Journal of Adolescent Research, 6*, 54–69.

Martinson, I. M., Davies, E. B., & McClowry, S. G. (1987). The long-term effects of sibling death on self-concept. *Journal of Pediatric Nursing, 2*, 227–235.

Martinson, I. M., McClowry, S. G., Davies, B., & Kuhlenkamp, E. J. (1994). Changes over time: A study of family bereavement following childhood cancer. *Journal of Palliative Care, 10*, 19–25.

Masur, C. (1991). Alternative approaches in the treatment of the bereaved child. In J. D. Morgan (Ed.), *Young people and death* (pp. 108–118). Philadelphia: Charles Press.

Masur, C. (1996). Individual treatment of the bereaved child. In C. A. Corr & D. M. Corr (Eds.), *Handbook of childhood death and bereavement* (pp. 305–321). New York: Springer.

Maurer, A. (1966). Maturation of the concept of death. *British Journal of Medicine and Psychology, 39*, 35–41.

McCubbin, H. I., Larson, A., & Olson, D. H. (1987). F-Copes family crises oriented personal evaluation scales. In H. I. McCubbin & A. I. Thompson (Eds.), *Family assessment inventories for research and practice*. Madison: University of Wisconsin Press.

McGloshen, T. H., & O'Bryant, S. L. (1988). The psychological well-being of older, recent widows. *Psychology of Women Quarterly, 12*, 99–116.

McHorney, C., & Mor, V. (1988). Predictors of bereavement depression and its health services consequences. Medical Care, 26, 882–893.

McIntosh, D. N., Silver, R. C., & Wortman, C. B. (1993). Religion's role in adjustment to a negative life event: Coping with the loss of a child. *Journal of Personality and Social Psychology, 65*, 812–821.

Michela, J. L. (1987). Interpersonal and individual impacts of a husband's heart attack. In A. Baum (Ed.), *Handbook of psychology and health: Stress* (Vol. 5, pp. 205–301). Hillsdale, NJ: Lawrence Erlbaum Associates.

Middleton, W., Raphael, B., Martinek, N., & Misso, V. (1993). Counseling and therapy of the bereaved. In M. Stroebe, W. Stroebe, & R. O. Hansson (Eds.), *Handbook of bereavement: Theory, research, and intervention*. New York: Cambridge University Press.

Miles, M. S. (1985). Emotional symptoms and physical health in bereaved parents. *Nursing Research, 34*, 76–81.

Miles, M. S., & Crandall, E. K. B. (1983). The search for meaning and its potential for affecting growth in bereaved parents. *Health Values, 7*, 19–23.

Moos, R. H., & Billings, A. G. (1982). Conceptualization and measuring coping resources and processes. In L. Goldberger & S. Breznitz (Eds.), *Handbook of stress: Theoretical and clinical aspects* (pp. 212–230). New York: Free Press.

Morgan J. P., Jr. (1994). Bereavement in older adults. *Journal of Mental Health Counseling, 16*, 318–326.

Morrow, J., & Nolen-Hoeksema, S. (1990). Effects of responses to depression on the remediation of depressive affect. *Journal of Personality and Social Psychology, 58*, 519–527.

Murphy, S. (1988). Mental distress and recovery in a high-risk bereavement sample three years after untimely death. *Nursing Research, 37*, 30–35.

Nagy, M. (1948). The child's theories concerning death. *Journal of Genetic Psychology, 73*, 3–27.

Nixon, J., & Pearn, J. (1977). Emotional sequelae of parents and sibs following the drowning or near-drowning of a child. *Australian and New Zealand Journal of Psychiatry, 11*, 265–268.

Nolen-Hoeksema, S. (1991). Responses to depression and their effects on the duration of depressive episodes. *Journal of Abnormal Psychology, 100*, 569–582.

Nolen-Hoeksema, S. (1995). Epidemiology and theories of gender differences in unipolar depression. In M. V. Seeman (Ed.), *Gender and Psychopathology* (pp. 63–87). Washington, DC: American Psychiatric Press.

Nolen-Hoeksema, S., & Morrow, J. (1991). A prospective study of depression and posttraumatic stress symptoms after a natural disaster: The 1989 Loma Prieta earthquake. *Journal of Personality and Social Psychology, 61*, 115–121.

Nolen-Hoeksema, S., Morrow, J., & Fredrickson, B. L. (1993). Response styles and the duration of episodes of depressed mood. *Journal of Abnormal Psychology, 102, 20–28*.

Nolen-Hoeksema, S., Parker, L. E., & Larson, J. (1994). Ruminative coping with depressed mood following loss. *Journal of Personality and Social Psychology, 67*, 92–104.

Noppe, L. D., & Noppe, I. C. (1991). Dialectical themes in adolescent conceptions of death. *Journal of Adolescent Research, 6*, 28–42.

Noppe, L. D., & Noppe, I. C. (1996). Ambiguity in adolescent understandings of death. In C. Corr (Ed.), *Handbook of adolescent death and bereavement* (pp. 25–41). New York: Springer.

Norris, F. H., & Murrell, S. A. (1987). Other adult family stress and adaptation before and after bereavement. *Journal of Gerontology, 42*, 606–612.

Norris, F. H., & Murrell, S. A. (1990). Social support, life events, and stress as modifiers of adjustment to bereavement by older adults. *Psychology & Aging, 5*, 429–436.

Nowicki, S., & Strickland, B. R. (1973). A locus control scale for children. *Journal of Consulting Psychology, 40*, 148–154.

O'Brien, K., Wortman, C. B., Kessler, R. C., & Joseph, J. C. (1993). Social relationships of men at risk for AIDS. *Social Science and Medicine, 36, 1161–1167*.

O'Toole, D. (1989). *Growing through grief: A K-12 curriculum to help young people through all kinds of loss.* Burnsville, NC: Compassion Publications.

Olson, D. H., McCubbin, H. I., Barnes, H., Larsen, A., Muxen, M., & Wilson, M. (1983). *Families: What makes them work.* Los Angeles: Sage.

Osterweis, M., Soloman, F., & Green, M. (1984). *Bereavement: Reactions, consequences and care.* Washington, DC: National Academy Press.

Owen, G., Fulton, R., & Markusen, E. (1982). Death at a distance: A study of family survivors. *Omega: Journal of Death and Dying, 13*, 191–225.

Park, C. L., Cohen, L. H., & Murch, R. L. (1996). Assessment and prediction of stress-related growth. *Journal of Personality, 64*, 71–105.

Parkes, C. M. (1964). The effects of bereavement on mental and physical health: A study of the case records of widows. *British Medical Journal, 2*, 274–280.

Parkes, C. M. (1965). Bereavement and mental illness. *British journal of Medical Psychology, 38*, 388–397.

Parkes, C. M. (1971). Psycho-social transitions: A field for study. *Social Science & Medicine, 5*, 101–115.

Parkes, C. M. (1986). The caregiver's griefs. *The Journal of Palliative Care, 1*, 5–7.

Parkes, C. M. (1988). Bereavement as a psychosocial transition: Processes of adaptation to change. *Journal of Social Issues, 44*, 53–65.

Parkes, C. M. (1990). Risk factors in bereavement. Implications for the prevention and treatment of pathologic grief. *Psychiatric Annals, 20*, 308–313.

Parkes, C. M., & Weiss, R. (1983). Recovery from bereavement. New York: Basic Books.

Parkes, C. M. (1993). Bereavement as a psychosocial transition: Processes in adaption to change. In M. Stroebe, W. Stroebe, M., & R. O. Hansson (Eds.), *Handbook of bereavement: Theory, research, and intervention* (pp. 91–101). New York: Cambridge University Press.

Perlman, D., Gerson, A. C., & Spinner, B. (1978). Loneliness among senior citizens: An impirical report. *Essence, 2*, 239–248.

Pollock, G. H. (1987). The mourning-liberation process in health and disease. *Psychiatric Clinics of North America, 10*, 345–354.

Pollock, P., Egan, D., Vanderbergh, R., & Williams, W. (1975). Prevention in mental health: A controlled study. *American Journal of Psychiatry, 132*, 146–149.

Pruchno, R. A., Moss, M. S., Burant, C. J., & Schinfeld, S. (1995). Death of an institutionalized parent: Predictors of bereavement. *Omega: Journal of Death and Dying, 31*, 99–119.

Radloff, L. S. (1977). The CESD-D Scale: A self-report depression scale for research in the general population. *Applied Psychological Measurement, 1*, 385–401.

Rando, T. A. (1984). *Grief, death, and dying: Clinical interventions for caregivers*. Champaign, IL: Research Press.

Rando, T. A. (1986). Parental bereavement: An exception to the general conceptualizations of mourning. In T. A. Rando (Ed.), *Parental loss of a child*. Champaign, IL: Research Press.

Rando, T. A. (1988). *How to go on living when someone you love dies*. New York: Bantam Books.

Rando, T. A. (1993). *Treatment of complicated mourning*. Champaign, IL: Research Press.

Raphael, B. (1983). *The anatomy of bereavement*. New York: Basic Books.

Raphael, B., & Nunn, K. (1988). Counseling the bereaved. *Journal of Social Issues, 44*, 191–206.

Reese, M. (1982). Growing up: The impact of loss and change. In D. Belle (Ed.), *Lives in stress: Women and depression* (pp. 65–88). Beverly Hills, CA: Sage.

Rook, K. S. (1984). Research on social support, loneliness, and social isolation: Toward an integration. *Review of Personality & Social Psychology, 5*, 239–264.

Rosenblatt, P. (1983). *Bitter, bitter tears: Nineteenth century diarists and twentieth century grief theories*. Minneapolis: University of Minnesota Press.

Rosenblatt, P. C., Walsh, R. P., & Jackson, D. A. (1976). Grief and mourning in cross-cultural perspective. New Haven, CT: Yale University Press.

Rossi, A. S., & Rossi, P. H. (1990). *Of human bonding*. New York: Aldine de Gruyter.

Scheier, M. F., & Carver, C. S. (1985). Optimism, coping, and health: Assessment and implications of generalized outcome expectancies. *Health Psychology, 4*, 219–247.

Rubin, R. J. (1978). *Using bibliotherapy*. Phoenix, AZ: Oryx Press.

Rubin, S. S. (1985). The resolution of bereavement: A clinical focus on the relationship to the deceased. *Psychotherapy, 22*, 231–235.

Rubin, S. S. (1993). The death of a child is forever: The life course impact of child loss. In M. S. Stroebe, W. Stroebe, & R. O. Hansson (Eds.), *Handbook of bereavement: Theory, research and intervention* (pp. 285–299). New York: Cambridge University Press.

Ryan, J. A. (1986). *Ethnic, cultural, and religious observances at the time of death and dying*. Boston: The Good Grief Program.

Rynearson, E. K. (1984). Bereavement after homicide: A descriptive study. *American Journal of Psychiatry, 141*, 1452–1454.

Sable, P. (1989). Attachment, anxiety, and loss of a husband. *American Journal of Orthopsychiatry, 59*, 550–556.

Sanders, C. M. (1979). A comparison of adult bereavement in the death of a spouse, child, and parent. *Omega: Journal of Death and Dying, 10*, 303–322.

Sanders, C. M. (1982). Effects of sudden vs. chronic illness death on bereavement outcome. *Omega: Journal of Death and Dying, 13*, 227–241.

Sanders, C. M. (1993). Risk factors in bereavement outcome. In M. S. Stroebe (Ed.), *Handbook of bereavement: Theory, research, and intervention* (pp. 255–267). New York: Cambridge University Press.

Sanders, C. M., Mauger, P. A., & Strong Jr., P. N. (1979). *A manual for the Grief Experience Inventory.* Charlotte, NC: Authors.

Sarason, B. R., Pierce, G. R., Shearin, E. N., & Sarason, I. G., Waltz, J. A. & Poppe, L. (1991). Perceived social support and working models of self and actual others. *Journal of Personality & Social Psychology, 60*, 273–287.

Scharlach, A. E. (1991). Factors associated with filial grief following the death of an elderly parent. *American Journal of Orthopsychiatry, 61*, 307–313.

Scharlach, A. E., & Fredriksen, K. (1993). Reaction to the death of a parent during midlife. *Omega: Journal of Death and Dying, 27*, 307–319.

Scheier, M. F., & Carver, C. S. (1985). Optimism, coping, and health: Assessment and implications of generalized outcome expectancies. *Health Psychology, 4*, 219–247.

Schwartzberg, S. S. (1992). Struggling for meaning: How HIV-positive gay men make sense of AIDS. *Professional Psychology: Research & Practice, 24*, 483–490.

Schwartzberg, S. S., & Janoff-Bulman, R. (1991). Grief and the search for meaning: Exploring the assumptive worlds of bereaved college students. *Journal of Social and Clinical Psychology, 10*, 270–288.

Schwarzer, C. (1992). Bereavement, received social support, and anxiety in the elderly: A longitudinal analysis. *Anxiety Research, 4*, 287–298.

Shanfield, S. (1983). Predicting bereavement outcome: Marital factors. *Family Systems Medicine, 1*, 40–46.

Shanfield, B., & Swain, B. J. (1984). Death of adult children in traffic accidents. *Journal of Nervous and Mental Disease, 172*, 533–538.

Shapiro, R. J. (1994). *Grief as a family process: A developmental approach to clinical practice.* New York: Guilford.

Shontz, F. C. (1975). *The psychological aspects of physical illness and disability.* New York: Macmillian.

Siegel, J. M., & Kuykendall, D. H. (1990). Loss, widowhood, and psychological distress among the elderly. *Journal of Consulting and Clinical Psychology, 58*, 519–524.

Silver, R. L., & Wortman, C. B. (1980). Coping with undesireable life events. In J. Garber & M. E. P. Seligman (Eds.), *Human Helplessness: Theory and applications* (pp. 279–375). New York: Academic Press.

Silverman, P. R. (1972). Widowhood and preventive intervention. *The Family Coordinator, 21*, 95–102.

Silverman, P. R. (1986). *Widow-to-widow.* New York: Springer.

Silverman, P. R., Nickman, S., & Worden, J. W. (1992). Detachment revisited: The child's reconstruction of a dead parent. *American Journal of Orthopsychiatry, 62*, 494–503.

Silverman, P. R., & Worden, J. W. (1991). Remembering a parent's funeral. *The Director*, 34–42.

Silverman, P. R., & Worden, J. W. (1992a). Children's reactions in the early months after the death of a parent. *American Journal of Orthopsychiatry, 62*, 93–104.

Silverman, P. R., & Worden, J. W. (1992b). Children's understanding of funeral ritual. *Omega: Journal of Death and Dying, 24*, 319–331.

Silverman, P. R., & Worden, J. W. (1993). Children's reactions to the death of a parent. In M. S. Stroebe, W. Stroebe, & R. O. Hansson (Eds.), *Handbook of bereavement: Theory, research, and intervention* (pp. 300–316). New York: Cambridge University Press.

Silverman, S. M., & Silverman, P. R. (1979). Parent–child communication in widowed families. *American Journal of Psychotherapy, 33*, 428–441.

Smilansky, S. (1987). *On death: Helping children understand and cope.* New York: Peter Lang.

Smith, A. C., & Borgers, S. B. (1988). Parental grief response to perinatal death. *Omega: Journal of Death and Dying, 19*, 203.

Sowell, R. L., Bramlett, M. H., Gueldner, S. H., Gritzmacher, D., & Martin, G. (1991). The lived experience of survival and bereavement following the death of a lover from AIDS. *Image, 23,* 89–94.

Speece, M. W., & Brent, S. B. (1992). The aquisition of a mature understanding of three components of the concept of death. *Death Studies, 16,* 211–229.

Speece, M. W., & Brent, S. B. (1993). "Adult" conceptualizations of irreversibility: Implications for the development of the concept of death. *Death Studies, 17,* 203–224.

Speece, M. W., & Brent, S. B. (1996). The development of children's understanding of death. In C. A. Corr & D. M. Corr (Eds.), *Handbook of childhood death and bereavement.* New York: Springer.

Speeth, K. (1982). On psychotherapeutic attention. *Journal of Transpersonal Psychology, 14,* 141–160.

Spielberger, C. D., Gorsuch, R. L., & Lushene, R. E. (1970). *The state-trait anxiety inventory (STAI) form X.* Palo Alto, CA: Consulting Psychologists Press.

Sprang, G., & McNeil, J. (1995). *The many faces of bereavement: The nature and treatment of natural, traumatic, and stigmatized grief.* New York: Brunner/Mazel.

Stambrook, M., & Parker, K. C. (1987). The development of the concept of death in childhood: A review of the literature. *Merrill Palmer Quarterly, 33,* 133–157.

Stroebe, M., & Schut, H. A. W. (in press). The dual process model of coping with bereavement: Rationale and description. *Death Studies.*

Stroebe, M., & Stroebe, W. (1983). Who suffers more? Sex differences in health risks of the widowed. *Psychological Bulletin, 93,* 297–301.

Stroebe, M., & Stroebe, W. (1991). Does " grief work" work? *Journal of Consulting and Clinical Psychology, 59,* 479–482.

Stroebe, M., & Stroebe, W. (1993). Determinants of adjustment to bereavement in younger widows and widowers. In M. Stroebe, W. Stroebe, & R. O. Hansson (Eds.), *Handbook of bereavement: Theory, research, and intervention* (pp. 208–226). New York: Cambridge University Press.

Stroebe, M., Stroebe, W., & Hansson, R. O. (Eds.), (1993). *Handbook of bereavement: Theory, research, and intervention.* New York: Cambridge University Press.

Stroebe, M., Stroebe, W., & Schut, H. (1997). *Sex differences in adjustment to bereavement: An empirical and theoretical review.* Unpublished manuscript, University of Utrecht, The Netherlands.

Stroebe, M., Gergen, M. M., Gergen, K. J., & Stroebe, W. (1992). Broken hearts or broken bonds. *American Psychologist, 47,* 1205–1212.

Stroebe, M. S., & Stroebe, W. (1989). Who participates in bereavement research? A review and empirical study. *Omega: Journal of Death and Dying, 20,* 1–29.

Stroebe, W., Stroebe, M., & Abakoumkin, G. (1996). *Does differential social support cause sex differences in bereavement outcome?* Unpublished manuscript, University of Utrecht, The Netherlands.

Stroebe, W., Stroebe, M., Abakoumkin, G., & Schut, H. (1996). The role of loneliness and social support in adjustment to loss: A test of attachment versus stress theory. *Journal of Personality and Social Psychology, 70,* 1241–1249.

Stroebe, W., & Stroebe, M. S. (1987). *Bereavement and health: The psychological and physical consequences of partner loss.* Cambridge, England: Cambridge University Press.

Swain, H. L. (1979). Childhood views of death. *Death Education, 2,* 341–358.

Tatelbaum, J. (1980). *The courage to grieve.* New York: Lippincott & Crowell,

Taylor, S. E. (1983). Adjustment to threatening events: A theory of adaptation. *American Psychologist, 38,* 1161–1173.

Taylor, S. E. (1989). *Positive illusions: Creative self-deception and the healthy mind.* New York: Basic Books.

Tedeschi, R. G., & Calhoun, L. G. (1996). *Trauma & transformation: Growing in the aftermath of suffering.* Thousand Oaks, CA: Sage.

Thoits, P. A. (1982). Life stress, social support, and psychological vulnerability: Epidemiological considerations. *Journal of Community Psychology, 10,* 341–362.

Thompson, L. W., Gallagher, D., Cover, H., Gilewski, M., & Peterson, J. (1989). Effects of bereavement on symptoms of psychopathology in older men and women. In D. A. Lund (Ed.), *Older bereaved spouses: Research with practical applications* (pp. 17–24). New York: Taylor & Francis/Hemisphere.

Thompson, S. C., & Janigian, A. S. (1988). Life schemes: A framework for understanding the search for meaning. *Journal of Social & Clinical Psychology, 7,* 260–280.

Umberson, D. (1992). Relationships between adult children and their parents: Psychological consequences for both generations. *Journal of Marriage and the Family, 54,* 664–674.

Umberson, D., & Chen, M. D. (1994). Effects of a parent's death on adult children: Relationship salience and reaction to loss. *American Sociological Review, 59,* 152–168.

Umberson, D., Wortman, C., & Kessler, R. C. (1992). Widowhood and depression: Explaining long-term gender differences in vulnerability. *Journal of Health and Social Behavior, 33,* 10–24.

Vachon, M. L., Lyall, W. A., Rogers, J., Freedman-Letofsky, K. & Freeman, S. J. (1980). A controlled study of self-help intervention for widows. *American Journal of Psychiatry, 137,* 1380–1384.

Vachon, M. L. S., Rogers, J., Lyall, W. A. L., Lancee, W. J., Sheldon, A. R., & Freeman, S. J. J. (1982). Predictors and correlates of adaptation to conjugal bereavement. *American Journal of Psychiatry, 139,* 998–1002.

Vachon, M. L. S., & Stylianos, S. K. (1988). The role of social support in bereavement. *Journal of Social Issues, 44,* 175–190.

Vallis, T. M., Shaw, B. F., & McCabe, S. B. (1988). The relationship between therapist competency in cognitive therapy and general therapy skill. *Journal of Cognitive Psychotherapy, 2,* 237–249.

van der Wal, J. (1989-90). The aftermath of suicide: A review of empirical evidence. *Omega: Journal of Death and Dying, 20,* 149–171.

Van Zandt, S., Mou, R., & Abbott, R. (1989). Mental and physical health of rural bereaved and nonbereaved elders: A longitudinal study. In D. A. Lund (Ed.), *Older bereaved spouses: Research with practical applications* (pp. 25–35). New York: Hemisphere.

Videka-Sherman, L. (1982). Coping with the death of a child. *American Journal of Orthopsychiatry, 52,* 688–698.

Videka-Sherman, L., & Lieberman, M. (1985). The effects of self-help and psychotherapy intervention on child loss: The limits of recovery. *American Journal of Orthopsychiatry, 55,* 70–82.

de Vries, B., Dalla Lana, R. D., & Falck, V. T. (1994). Parental bereavement over the life course: A theoretical intersection and empirical review. *Omega: Journal of Death and Dying, 29,* 47–69.

de Vries, B., Davis, C. G., Wortman, C. B., & Lehman, D. A. (1997). Long-term psychological and somatic consequences of later life parental bereavement. *Omega: Journal of Death and Dying, 35,* 97–117.

Walker, K. N., MacBride, A., & Vachon, M. L. (1977). Social support networks and the crisis of bereavement. *Social Science & Medicine, 11,* 35–41.

Walsh, F., & McGoldrick, M. (Eds.). (1991). *Living beyond loss: Death in the family.* New York: Norton.

Wass, H., Dinklage, R., Gordon, S. L., Russo, G., Sparks, C. W., & Tatum, J. (1983). Use of play for assessing children's death concepts: A re-examination. *Psychological Reports, 53,* 799–803.

Wass, H., & Stillon, J. (1988). Dying in the lives of children. In H. Wass, F. Berardo, & R. Neimeyer (Eds.), *Dying: facing the facts* (pp. 201–228). Washington, DC: Hemisphere.

Webb, N. B. (Ed.). (1993). *Helping bereaved children: A handbook for practitioners.* New York: Guilford Press.

Weiss, R. (1988). Loss and recovery. *Journal of Social Issues, 44,* 37–52.

Weiss, R. S. (1987). Principles underlying a manual for parents whose children were killed by a drunk driver. *American Journal of Orthopsychiatry, 57,* 431–440.

Weller, E. B., Weller, R. A., Fristad, M. A., Cain, S. E., & Bowes, J. M. (1988). Should children attend their parent's funeral? *Journal of the Academy of Child and Adolescent Psychiatry, 27,* 559–562.

Whitney, S. (1991). *Waving goodbye: An activities manual for children in grief.* Portland, OR: The Dougy Center.

Wikan, U. (1991). *Managing turbulent hearts.* Chicago: University of Chicago Press.

Williams, D. R., Takeuchi, D. T., & Adair, R. K. (1992). Marital status and psychiatric disorders among Blacks and Whites. *Journal of Health and Social Behavior, 33,* 140–157.

Windholz, M., Marmar, C., & Horowitz, M. (1985). A review of the research on conjugal bereavement: Impact on health and efficacy of intervention. *Comprehensive Psychiatry, 26,* 433–477.

Wolfelt, A. (1983). *Helping children cope with grief.* Muncie, IN: Accelerated Development.

Wolfelt, A. (1988). *Death and grief: A guide for clergy.* New York: Accelerated Development.

Worden, J. W. (1982). *Grief counseling and grief therapy: A handbook for the mental health practitioner.* New York: Springer.

Worden, J. W. (1991a). *Bereaved children.* Keynote presentation at the Thirteenth Annual Conference of the Association for Death Education and Counseling, Duluth, MN.

Worden, J. W. (1991b). *Grief counseling and grief therapy: A handbook for the mental health practitioner* (2nd ed.). New York: Springer.

Wortman, C., & Silver, R. (1987). Coping with irrevocable loss. In G. R. VandenBos & B. K. Bryant (Eds.), *Psychology in action* (pp. 189–235). Washington, DC: American Psychological Association.

Wortman, C., & Silver, R. (1989). The myths of coping with loss. *Journal of Consulting and Clinical Psychology, 57,* 349–357.

Wortman, C. B., Silver, R. C., & Kessler, R. C. (1993). The meaning of loss and adjustment to bereavement. In M. S. Stroebe, W. Stroebe, & R. O. Hansson (Eds.), *Handbook of bereavement: Theory, research, and intervention* (pp. 349–366). Cambridge, England: Cambridge University Press.

Yalom, I. D. (1980). *Existential psychotherapy.* New York: Basic Books.

Yalom, I. D. (1985). *The theory and practice of group psychotherapy* (3rd ed.). New York: Basic Books.

Yalom, I. D. (1989). *Love's executioner and other tales of psychotherapy.* New York: Basic Books.

Yamamoto, J., Okonoji, K., Iwasaki, T., & Yoshimura, S. (1969). Mourning in Japan. *American Journal of Psychiatry, 126,* 74–182.

Young, V. (1984). *Working with the dying and grieving.* Davis, CA: International Dialogue Press.

Zemore, R., & Shepel, L. F. (1989). Effects of cancer and mastectomy on emotional support and adjustment. *Social Science and Medicine, 28,* 19–27.

Zimmerman, M., Coryell, W., Corenthal, C., & Wilson, S. (1986). A self-report scale to diagnose major depressive disorder. *Archives of General Psychiatry, 43,* 1076–1081.

Zisook, S., & Shuchter, S. R. (1986). First four years of widowhood. *Psychiatric Annals, 16,* 288.

Zisook, S., Shuchter, S. R., & Lyons, L. E. (1987). Predictors of psychological reactions during the early stages of widowhood. *Psychiatric Clinics of North America, 10,* 355–368.

Author Index

A

Abakoumkin, G., 93, 96
Abbott, R., 15
Achenbach, T. M., 111
Adolph, R., 121
Affleck, G., 154, 159
Alvarez, W., 9
Anderson, R., 112
Andrykowski, M. A., 154
Anthony, S., 118
APA, 7, 8, 197, 198
Atchley, R. C., 49

B

Bahr, H. M., 75
Baker, F., 144
Baker, J. E., 110, 112, 125, 127, 170
Balk, D. E., 113, 122, 133
Balmer, L. E., 113, 114
Barrett, C. J., 104
Bass, D. M., 96
Baumeister, R. F., 153
Baxter, G., 135
Beck, A. T., 9, 110
Beck, R. W., 9
Becker, D., 110
Bell, J., 114
Bem, D. J., 153
Benfield, D. G., 90

Bennett, L., 135
Berardo, F. M., 93
Berger, A., 126
Berlinskey, E. B., 110
Berman, E. A., 15
Bernstein, J. E., 133
Bifulco, A., 111
Biller, H. B.,110, 111
Billings, A. G., 62, 198
Boccellari, A., 15, 49, 65
Bock, E. W., 93
Bohannon, J. R., 36, 72
Bonanno, G. A., 65
Borgers, S. B., 36, 73
Bornstein, P. E., 6, 15, 40, 48, 75
Bowes, J. M., 132
Bowlby, J., 3, 11, 12, 13, 14, 15, 16, 18, 34, 44, 64
Bramlett, M. H., 95
Breckenridge, J. N., 48
Brent, S. B., 114, 115, 116, 117
Brown, G. W., 111
Burant, C. J., 45
Butler, L. D., 199

C

Cain, S. E., 132
Calhoun, L. G., 47, 144, 148, 150, 153, 154, 159

Subject Index